AVENG

HEAVY METAL

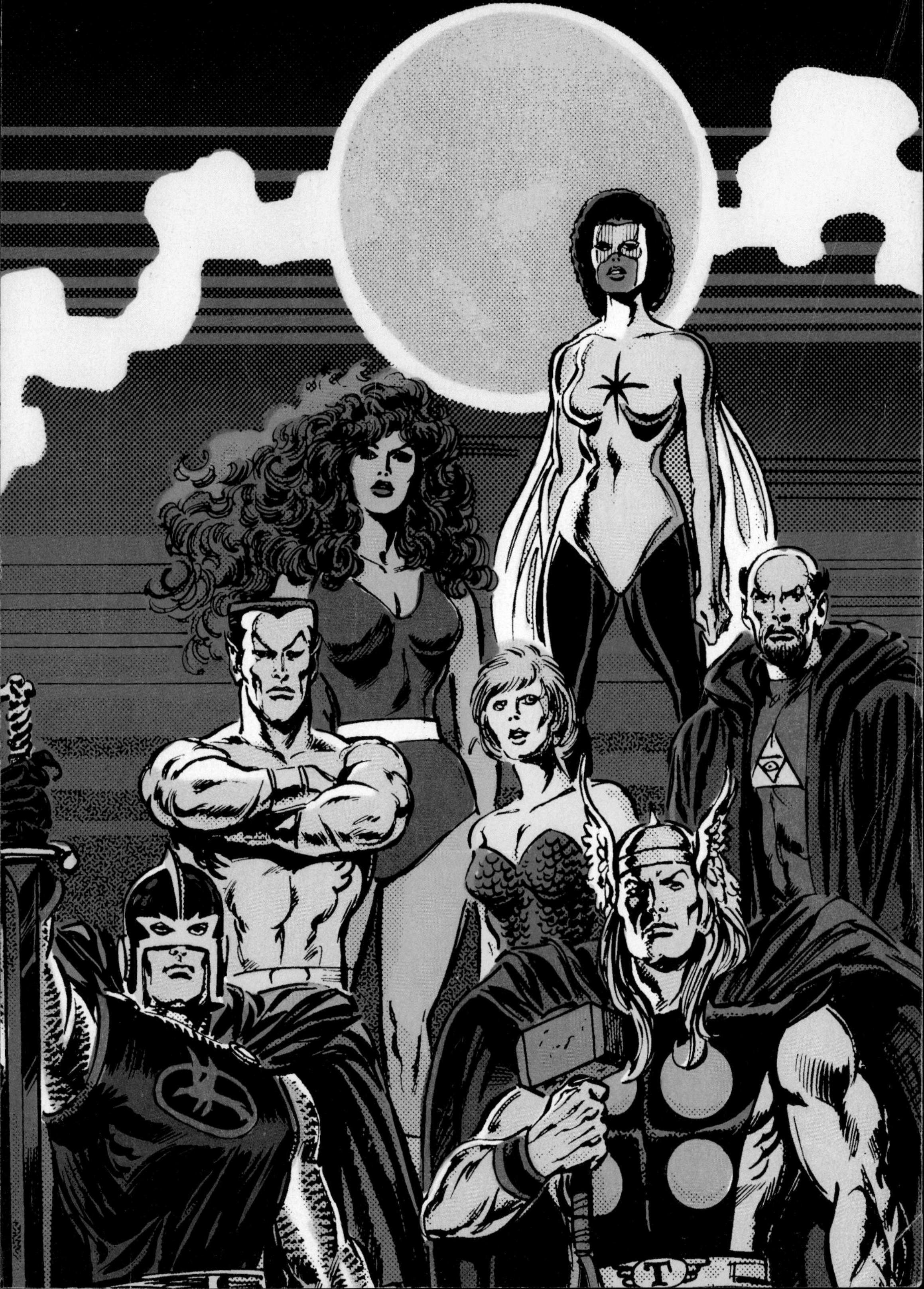

AVENGERS

WRITERS
ROGER STERN, RALPH MACCHIO & WALTER SIMONSON WITH MARK GRUENWALD

BREAKDOWNS
JOHN BUSCEMA

FINISHES
TOM PALMER

COLORISTS
CHRISTIE SCHEELE & PAUL BECTON

LETTERER
BILL OAKLEY

ASSISTANT EDITOR
GREGORY WRIGHT

EDITOR
MARK GRUENWALD

FRONT COVER ARTISTS
JOHN BUSCEMA, TOM PALMER & VERONICA GANDINI

BACK COVER ARTISTS
JOHN BUSCEMA, TOM PALMER & TOM SMITH

AVENGERS: HEAVY METAL. Contains material originally published in magazine form as AVENGERS #286-293. First printing 2013. ISBN# 978-0-7851-8452-2. Published by MARVEL WORLDWIDE, INC., a subsidiary of MARVEL ENTERTAINMENT, LLC. OFFICE OF PUBLICATION: 135 West 50th Street, New York, NY 10020. Copyright © 1987, 1988 and 2013 Marvel Characters, Inc. All rights reserved. All characters featured in this issue and the distinctive names and likenesses thereof, and all related indicia are trademarks of Marvel Characters, Inc. No similarity between any of the names, characters, persons, and/or institutions in this magazine with those of any living or dead person or institution is intended, and any such similarity which may exist is purely coincidental. **Printed in the U.S.A.** ALAN FINE, EVP - Office of the President, Marvel Worldwide, Inc. and EVP & CMO Marvel Characters B.V.; DAN BUCKLEY, Publisher & President - Print, Animation & Digital Divisions; JOE QUESADA, Chief Creative Officer; TOM BREVOORT, SVP of Publishing; DAVID BOGART, SVP of Operations & Procurement, Publishing; C.B. CEBULSKI, SVP of Creator & Content Development; DAVID GABRIEL, SVP of Print & Digital Publishing Sales; JIM O'KEEFE, VP of Operations & Logistics; DAN CARR, Executive Director of Publishing Technology; SUSAN CRESPI, Editorial Operations Manager; ALEX MORALES, Publishing Operations Manager; STAN LEE, Chairman Emeritus. For information regarding advertising in Marvel Comics or on Marvel.com, please contact Niza Disla, Director of Marvel Partnerships, at ndisla@marvel.com. For Marvel subscription inquiries, please call 800-217-9158. **Manufactured between 5/31/2013 and 7/8/2013 by R.R. DONNELLEY, INC., SALEM, VA, USA.**

10 9 8 7 6 5 4 3 2 1

COLLECTION EDITOR
MARK D. BEAZLEY

ASSISTANT EDITORS
NELSON RIBEIRO & ALEX STARBUCK

EDITOR, SPECIAL PROJECTS
JENNIFER GRÜNWALD

SENIOR EDITOR, SPECIAL PROJECTS
JEFF YOUNGQUIST

RESEARCH & LAYOUT
JEPH YORK

PRODUCTION
COLORTEK & JOE FRONTIRRE

SVP OF PRINT & DIGITAL PUBLISHING SALES
DAVID GABRIEL

EDITOR IN CHIEF
AXEL ALONSO

CHIEF CREATIVE OFFICER
JOE QUESADA

PUBLISHER
DAN BUCKLEY

EXECUTIVE PRODUCER
ALAN FINE

HEAVY METAL

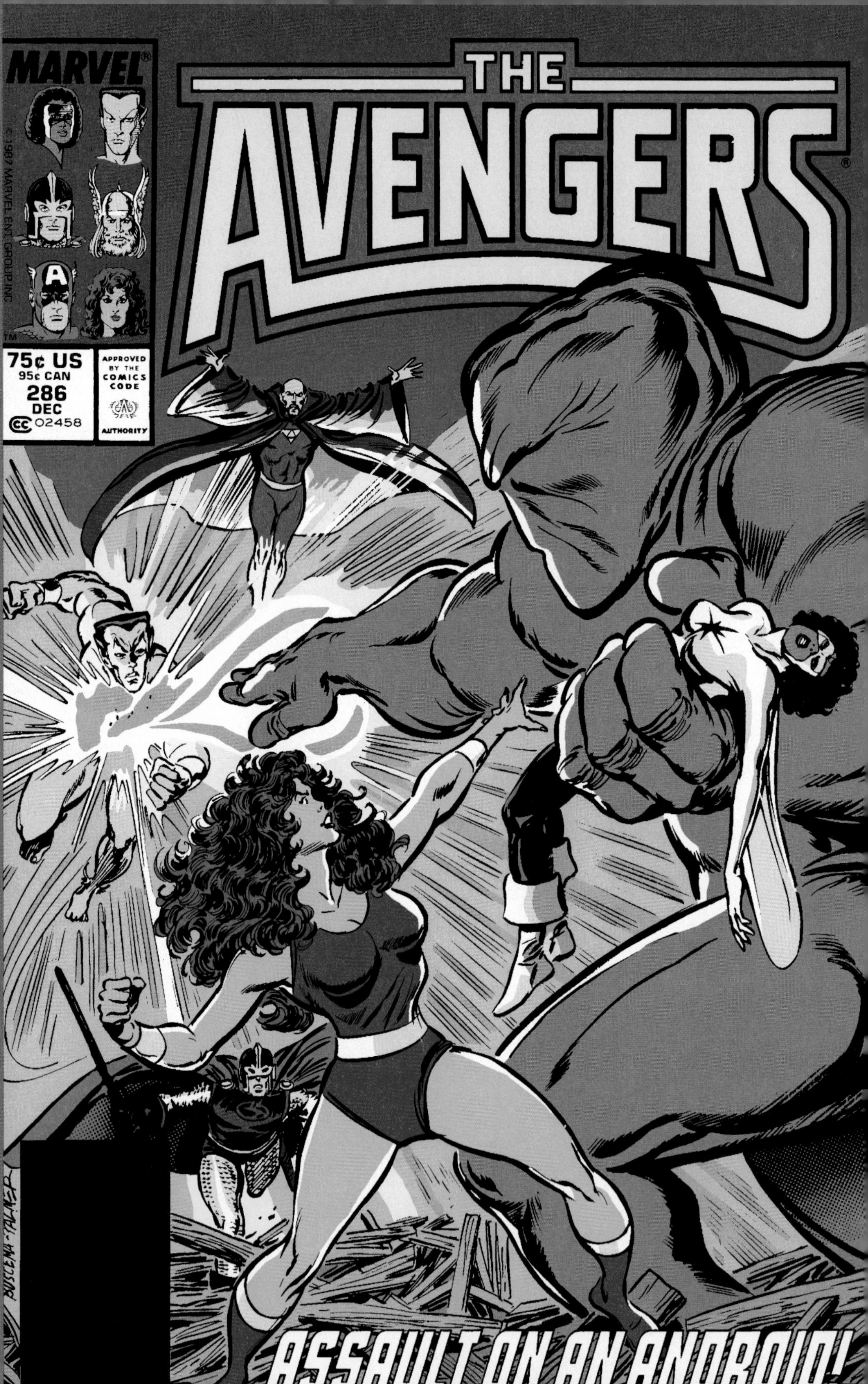
MARVEL
THE AVENGERS
© 1987 MARVEL ENT. GROUP INC.
75¢ US
95¢ CAN
286
DEC
02458
APPROVED BY THE COMICS CODE AUTHORITY
BUSCEMA/PALMER
ASSAULT ON AN ANDROID!

WITHIN THIS UNASSUMING SCIENTIFIC *RESEARCH LAB* IN MANHATTAN, THE WORKS OF A BRILLIANT MIND ARE EXAMINED.

LESSER INTELLECTS PROBE, ANALYZE AND WONDER AT THE *SHEER GENIUS* OF THE BRAIN WHICH CONCEIVED THE NUMEROUS *OBJECTS* BEFORE THEM.

BUT SCIENTIFIC INQUIRY CLAIMS ITS *VICTIMS*.

TODD MARTIN IS NOW ONE.

HIS *MIND* IS NO LONGER HIS OWN... HIS *BODY'S* VERY *MOVEMENT* CONTROLLED BY SOMEONE ELSE FAR, FAR AWAY.

UGH!

SPSSSSS!

MANY MILES DISTANT, SOMEONE SMILES AS HE PULLS THE MENTAL STRINGS THAT MAKE TODD MARTIN HIS *PUPPET*.

HE CAN ALMOST FEEL THE COMFORTABLE FIT OF THE COSTUME--THOUGH *ANOTHER MAN* NOW WEARS IT.

HE CAN ALMOST FEEL THE MANY SMALL *FACIAL CUTS* TAKEN BY THIS HUMAN PAWN AS IT BEGINS ITS LONG JOURNEY...

SKRASH!

...A JOURNEY THAT WILL SOON TAKE HIM INTO THE PRESENCE OF THE AWESOME *FIXER!*

ELSEWHERE, IN THE COMMUNICATIONS CENTER OF THE MIGHTY AVENGERS, ANOTHER GREAT INTELLECT PUTS HIS PLANS INTO MOTION.

DOCTOR ANTHONY DRUID APPEARS IN REPOSE, YET HIS ASTRAL IMAGE IS AWAKE AND ALERT AS HE PREPARES TO SEND IT FORTH FOR THE PURPOSE OF OBSERVATION.

THOSE HE WOULD OBSERVE ARE ALSO MEMBERS OF EARTH'S MIGHTIEST FIGHTING TEAM. WHILE THEIR PHYSICAL MOVEMENTS ARE EASILY MONITORED ON THE SCREENS AROUND HIM, IT IS THEIR INNERMOST THOUGHTS AND DESIRES THAT CONCERN DOCTOR DRUID.

THESE THINGS HE CAN ONLY LEARN THROUGH ASTRAL EAVESDROPPING. NONE WILL KNOW THEY ARE BEING OBSERVED... AND NONE -- SAVE ANTHONY DRUID -- WILL KNOW WHY THEY ARE WATCHED ...FOR NOW.

ROGER STERN • RALPH MACCHIO
PLOT   SCRIPT
JOHN BUSCEMA • TOM PALMER
BREAKDOWNS   FINISHES
BILL OAKLEY • CHRISTIE SCHEELE
LETTERER   COLORIST
MARK GRUENWALD • TOM DEFALCO
EDITOR   EDITOR IN CHIEF

THE FIX IS ON!

NO!

THIS IS NOT WHAT I WANT TO HEAR!

WHOOM!

UMM, C-CALM DOWN, NAMOR! AS YOUR LAWYER, IT'S MY JOB TO KEEP YOU POSTED ON THE LATEST DEVELOPMENTS ON THE CASE.

BELIEVE ME, I DIDN'T COME ALL THE WAY TO THE AVENGERS' HEADQUARTERS ON HYDROBASE TO ANGER YOU.

PLEASE LISTEN, NAMOR.

SPEAK THEN, MR. COSTELLO.

THESE ARE LAWSUITS PENDING AGAINST YOU FOR THE PROPERTY DAMAGE YOU CAUSED WHEN YOUR SUBSEA ARMIES MARCHED AGAINST THE SURFACE WORLD-- THEY HAVE TO BE ADDRESSED.

NOW THAT YOU'VE JOINED A VERY HIGH-PROFILE TEAM LIKE THE AVENGERS, YOU'VE GOT TO CLEAR THESE MATTERS UP, OR YOU WILL DRAG THE AVENGERS' REPUTATION DOWN!

MY HUSBAND, THIS IS SOMETHING WE WILL FACE TOGETHER.

CAN YOU NOT SEE WHAT THIS DOES TO ME, MARRINA?

I AM A PRINCE OF ATLANTEAN BLOOD. I ONCE CLAIMED A THRONE BENEATH THE SEA... AND NOW I AM REDUCED TO DEFENDING MYSELF AGAINST PETTY COMMONERS' TRIFLES!

WHAT CAN I DO FOR YOU, MY LOVE? TELL ME AND IT SHALL BE DONE.

NAMOR, PLEASE DON'T STALK OFF LIKE THIS! I NEED YOUR SIGNATURE ON VARIOUS DOCUMENTS! I HAVE TO PROVIDE YOU LEGAL COUNSEL ON--

"LEGAL COUNSEL"-- BAH! YOU DON'T KNOW THE MEANING OF THE WORDS, MR. COSTELLO.

AS AN ADVISER, YOU RATE DISTANTLY BEHIND MY LORD VASHTI OF THE ATLANTEAN COURT. WOULD THAT HE WERE HERE NOW!

MARRINA, PLEASE SPEAK WITH YOUR HUSBAND. IF HE DOESN'T SETTLE THESE MATTERS, HE'LL NEVER KNOW PEACE IN THE SURFACE WORLD.

I WILL DO WHAT I CAN. NAMOR IS A *STUBBORN* MAN--THOUGH I'M SURE IN HIS HEART HE KNOWS YOU'RE *RIGHT.* I WILL RETURN WITH HIM.

MOMENTS LATER...

OH, NAMOR, DON'T *BROOD* SO. WE HAVE SUCH A *LIFE* AHEAD OF US--SO MUCH FULFILLMENT AND LOVE TO COME.

BUT THIS, MY WIFE, *THIS* COULD DELAY OUR WEDDED BLISS FOR SOME TIME.

IF I SHOULD GO BACK.

BUT THAT IS AN AFFAIR OF THE *SURFACE.* HERE, BENEATH THE WAVES WITH YOU IN MY ARMS-- *ALL THINGS* SEEM POSSIBLE.

OF *COURSE* THEY DO, NAMOR.

MY POOR NÁIVE MARRINA. ONCE BEFORE, BY MY OWN CHOOSING, DID I SIT ACCUSED IN THE *HUMANS'* COURT.* AND ON THAT DAY--

--I COULD NOT CONTAIN MY *RAGE.* COULD I PROCEED WITH SUCH A *TRAVESTY* AGAIN?

* WAY BACK IN *DAREDEVIL* #7.

ELSEWHERE ON HYDROBASE, THE EYES OF DOCTOR DRUID WANDER TO THE FIGURE OF DANE WHITMAN-- THE *BLACK KNIGHT*...

WELL, IT SEEMS AS IF A LOT OF THE EQUIPMENT WE SALVAGED FROM THE *MANSION* AFTER THE *MASTERS OF EVIL'S* ATTACK * IS IN EXCELLENT CONDITION.

SCORE ONE FOR THE *GOOD GUYS.*

JUST TOO BAD *I* COULDN'T HAVE SCORED WITH A CERTAIN EX-LEADER OF THE AVENGERS... JANET VAN DYNE...THE *WASP.*

IT'S MY *OWN FAULT* I NEVER GOT ANYWHERE. EVERY TIME I HAD A CHANCE, I LET IT SLIP THROUGH MY FINGERS!

*ISSUE #273-277.

8

AND NOW, ONE FINAL VIEW FOR DRUID... TO EAVESDROP UPON *CAPTAIN MARVEL* SUPERVISING THE RECONSTRUCTION OF *AVENGERS* FACILITIES IN ITS NEW LOCALE AT THE CENTER OF HYDROBASE...

IT'LL FIT JUST *FINE* HERE.

SOUNDS GREAT, RUSS.

NOW THERE ARE STILL A FEW *ITEMS* WE SHOULD DI--

DI--

DI--

DROPPED YOUR *PIPE* THERE, RUSS. AND YOUR *CHIN*.

WHAT'S THE *MATTER*? NEVER SEEN A SEVEN FOOT *SHE-HULK* CARRYING AN I-BEAM BEFORE?

NOW WHAT SHOULD I *DO* WITH THIS THING?

J-JUST PUT IT OVER *THERE*, PLEASE.

OH, SHE-HULK, GLAD YOU'RE HERE. I'VE SOME ERRANDS TO RUN ON THE MAINLAND AND I NEED YOU TO SUPERVISE THINGS HERE.

MADE IN THE SHADE, C.M.! *I'LL* PUT THESE BOYS TO WORK!

CATCH YOU LATER, PEOPLE!

THAT'S WEIRD LOOKIN'. WHATEVER HAPPENED TO PHONEBOOTHS AND "UP UP AND AWAY"?

WENT OUT OF STYLE TWENTY YEARS AGO.

Y'KNOW, HE DOES HAVE A POINT. I WONDER WHAT IT'S LIKE...

...BEING ABLE TO TRANSFORM INTO ANY *WAVELENGTH* ON THE ELECTRO-MAGNETIC SPECTRUM? DO YOU *THINK*-- OR *FEEL* WHAT'S HAPPENING?

BRRR. CREEPY.

SECONDS LATER, IN THE OFFICE OF F.B.I. AGENT *DEREK FREEMAN* IN WASHINGTON, D.C. ...

YEOW! LADY, YOU HAVE ONE *HECK* OF A WAY OF MAKING AN ENTRANCE! IT'S A GOOD THING I LIKE YOU OR--

SORRY FOR DROPPING IN UNANNOUNCED, DEREK, BUT I NEED SOME *IN-FORMATION.* IT'S ABOUT *CAPTAIN AMERICA.*

"A FEW WEEKS AGO, I CAME ACROSS A COUPLE OF *YOUR BOYS* WHO RAN INTO THE AVENGERS MANSION'S SECURITY WHILE SNOOPING AROUND LOOKING FOR CAP. YOU MUST KNOW ABOUT *THEM.*

"A FEW DAYS LATER, CAP CALLED AND TOLD ME THAT THE GOVERNMENT WAS PRESSURING HIM TO WORK DIRECTLY FOR THEM. AND RIGHT AFTER THAT, HE LEFT ME A MESSAGE HE WAS TAKING AN INDEFINITE *LEAVE OF ABSENCE!**

*FOR THE REASON WHY, SEE *CAPTAIN AMERICA* #329-332.

CAPTAIN, THE AVENGERS DON'T HAVE OFFICIAL *SECURITY CLEARANCE* ANYMORE ... NOT SINCE THE *VISION* MESSED WITH THE PENTA-GON'S COMPUTERS.*

BUT MAYBE I'LL SEE IF I CAN COME UP WITH A LITTLE SOMETHING ... JUST FOR *YOU.*

YOU'RE A *DOLL,* DEREK.

*AVENGERS #254.

OKAY, WHATEVER'S GOING ON WITH CAP IS *WAY* ABOVE MY HEAD, SO NO INFO. THOSE TWO AGENTS WERE ON SPECIAL ASSIGNMENT TO ANOTHER AGENCY. BEYOND THAT-- *RED TAPE'S* GOT ME BLOCKED.

GREAT. I'M *CHAIRWOMAN* OF THE AVENGERS AND I CAN'T EVEN GET A LINE ON ONE OF MY OWN *PEOPLE.*

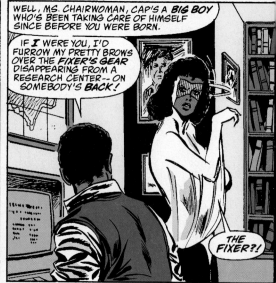

WELL, MS. CHAIRWOMAN, CAP'S A *BIG BOY* WHO'S BEEN TAKING CARE OF HIMSELF SINCE BEFORE YOU WERE BORN.

IF *I* WERE YOU, I'D FURROW MY *PRETTY BROWS* OVER THE *FIXER'S GEAR* DISAPPEARING FROM A RESEARCH CENTER-- ON SOMEBODY'S *BACK!*

THE *FIXER?!*

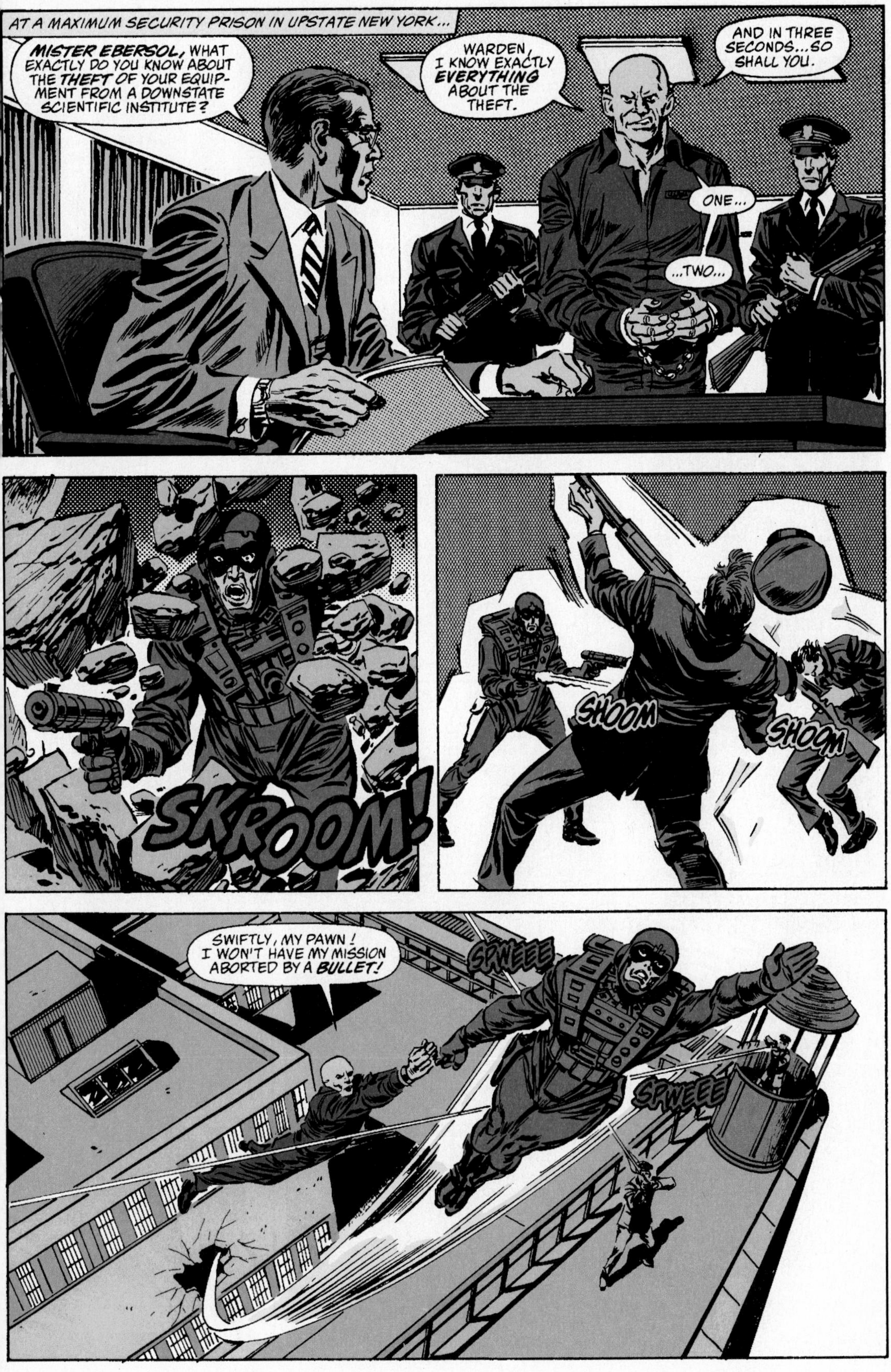
AT A MAXIMUM SECURITY PRISON IN UPSTATE NEW YORK...
MISTER EBERSOL, WHAT EXACTLY DO YOU KNOW ABOUT THE THEFT OF YOUR EQUIPMENT FROM A DOWNSTATE SCIENTIFIC INSTITUTE?
WARDEN, I KNOW EXACTLY EVERYTHING ABOUT THE THEFT.
AND IN THREE SECONDS...SO SHALL YOU.
ONE...
...TWO...
SKROOM!
SHOOM
SHOOM
SWIFTLY, MY PAWN! I WON'T HAVE MY MISSION ABORTED BY A BULLET!
SPWEEE
SPWEEE

AN HOUR LATER, TODD MARTIN AWAKENS IN THE LAIR OF THE FIXER...

NHHHHH...

...WHAT HAPPENED...? WHERE *AM* I?

THAT'S OF NO CONSEQUENCE. YOU'VE SERVED YOUR *PURPOSE* TO ME. NOW THE ONLY PROBLEM IS THE MANNER OF YOUR *DISPOSAL.*

NOW JUST A STINKIN' *MINUTE!* I WANT SOME *ANSWERS,* MISTER!

AND I WANT THEM NOW!

THIS IS WHAT YOU'LL GET-- *NOW!*

≶MFFFPPPFF≶

IN THE MOVIES, THE VILLAIN MAKES A LONG-WINDED *SPEECH* DETAILING HIS *DIABOLICAL PLAN* TO THE HERO BEFORE HIS *ULTIMATE* DEFEAT.

WELL, MR. MARTIN, THIS IS NO MOVIE...

NO!

...AND *YOU* ARE NO HERO.

GOODBYE.

THUS, THE FIRST STEP IN MY MASTER PLAN HAS BEEN COMPLETED.

MY TIME OF IMPRISON-MENT WAS FRUITFUL. MONTHS SPENT PLANNING, CONCOCTING, *SCHEMING* FOR THE MOMENT OF TRIUMPH OVER MY HUMAN ENEMIES.

AND SO MUCH OF WHAT I'VE WORKED FOR IS ON THIS TINY *DATA CARTRIDGE.*

KLIK!

THERE! WHAT I *STILL* NEED--WHAT I *MUST* HAVE-- PINPOINTED ON THE MAP.

SO, *SATISFYING* TO SEE ONE'S GRAND DESIGN TAKING SHAPE--THE ITCH OF *GREAT AMBITION* ABOUT TO BE *SCRATCHED.*

AND SOON I WILL HAVE *MORE* TOOLS TO COMPLETE MY PLANS. *MANY* MORE TOOLS.

ONE, IN FACT, IS VERY *CLOSE* AT HAND.

SHORTLY, BACK ON HYDROBASE, A SIREN SOUNDS...

WOW! YA'D THINK THAT BIG BROAD JUST HEARD THE LUNCH WHISTLE THE WAY SHE PERKED UP!

BWWWEEEEEEEE

IT'S THE PRIORITY ALERT SIGNAL. THIS WILL HAVE TO WAIT.

EEEEEE

DESPITE MY LEGAL PROBLEMS -- I AM AN AVENGER, MARRINA. DUTY BOUND TO GO WHEN CALLED.

AND I'LL BE AT YOUR SIDE, NAMOR.

AND, MOMENTS LATER, AT A SMALL AIRSTRIP...

CONTAIN YOURSELF, DANE! YOU SHALL LEARN SOON. NOW, PLEASE, ALL OF YOU, BOARD THE QUINJET!

DOCTOR DRUID! YOU SUMMONED US?! WHY?

NO, MARRINA. THIS IS AN AVENGERS ASSIGNMENT. YOU MUST REMAIN HERE. THERE MAY BE DANGER.

BUT, NAMOR--

--I AM NOT SOME ATLANTEAN NOBLEWOMAN TO BE WAITED ON AND PAMPERED. I AM AN ADVENTURER... A FORMER MEMBER OF ALPHA FLIGHT! WHEREVER YOU ARE, THAT'S WHERE I WISH TO BE!

VERY WELL, IMPETUOUS ONE. BUT UNTIL SUCH TIME AS YOU ARE DEEMED AN AVENGER, YOU SHALL REMAIN OUT OF ACTION!

VOOM

OKAY, DOC, **I** LOVE A MYSTERY, TOO, BUT SUPPOSE YOU FILL US ALL IN.

I'M NOT AT **LIBERTY** TO SAY. YOU'LL HAVE TO WAIT UNTIL **CAPTAIN MARVEL** ARRIVES TO--

ARRIVED, DOCTOR. NOW WHY HAVE **YOU** MOBILIZED THE TEAM?

WELL, I ASSUMED-- QUITE NATURALLY-- THAT **YOU** WOULD **WANT** US MOBILIZED AS SOON AS POSSIBLE, SINCE **SOMETHING** HAS COME UP.

AND YOU THOUGHT IT PROPER TO ALERT THE **OTHER** MEMBERS **BEFORE** THE CHAIRWOMAN. HMM.

YOU'RE **UP** TO SOMETHING, DOCTOR DRUID. I DON'T KNOW WHAT IT IS, BUT I DON'T THINK I **LIKE** IT.

NOW, AS TO THE **NATURE** OF THE SUMMONS...

"... WE HAVE RECEIVED AN **URGENT CALL** ON OUR DIRECT LINE FROM A CERTAIN PARTY IN **OHIO**.

"I AM CERTAIN YOU'LL AGREE THE PORTENTS OF THE CALL IS IMPORTANT ENOUGH TO WARRANT THE AVENGERS' PRESENCE."

WHEW! THE **TRUCK'S** STILL THERE. BOY, I HOPE **CAPTAIN AMERICA** GETS HERE **SOON**!

IF THE TRUCK LEAVES BEFORE HE GETS HERE, THERE WON'T BE ANY PROOF THAT--

HUH?

BOBBY HUTCHINSON?

Y-YOU'RE-- CAPTAIN MAR-VEL?! BUT I WAS EXPECTING--

I KNOW. BUT CAPTAIN AMERICA IS... UNAVAILABLE RIGHT NOW, SO I HOPE THE AVENGERS WILL DO. THE NUMBER HE GAVE YOU TO CALL WAS ONE OF OUR PRIORITY LINES.

ACCORDING TO CAP'S REPORT, YOU HAVE AN ANDROID IN A BARN NEAR HERE.

*SEE CAP #311 FOR DETAILS.

UH-HUH. RIGHT ACROSS THAT FIELD. CAP SAID IT'D BE OKAY 'LONG AS NO ONE DISTURBED IT.

WELL, A MAN IN A FUNNY-LOOKIN' COS-TUME DROVE UP IN A TRUCK AND WENT INSIDE THE BARN THIS MORNING.

IT MIGHT BE NOTHIN', BUT CAP SAID TO CALL IF I EVER SAW ANY-THING WEIRD GOING ON IN THAT BARN.

OKAY, SON. YOU WAIT HERE. I'LL--

BUK-WHOOOM

DUCK, BOBBY! DUCK!

WHOAAAA!

WHEN THE BLAST SUBSIDES AND THE SMOKE CLEARS...

I HAVE "FIXED" YOUR PROGRAMMING, MY AWESOME *ANDROID.* YOU NO LONGER SERVE THE *THINKER--* HENCEFORTH, YOU ARE *MY* ALLY!

BUT THEN--!

THE *FIXER!* SO YOU'RE RESPONSIBLE FOR THIS!

EH?

VVSSSS!

DON'T THINK I'VE FORGOTTEN WHAT HAVOC YOU WREAKED AS ONE OF THE *MASTERS OF EVIL!*

YAAIIIIIII!

VA'SHOOOM!

BWAKT!

SHLUMP!

17

THIS MUST BE THE *THING IN THE BARN* CAP REPORTED.

IT'S AN *ANDROID* DESIGNED BY THE *MAD THINKER* AND PROGRAMMED FOR COMBAT. IT HAS SOME STRANGE *SKIN TISSUE* THAT ALLOWS IT TO *MIMIC* ANY LIVING BEING IT ESTABLISHES *CONTACT* WITH.

IT'S SUPPOSED TO HAVE GIVEN THE ENTIRE *FANTASTIC FOUR* A HARD TIME!

I'D BETTER AVOID USING MY ENERGY POWERS AGAINST IT, UNLESS I WANT IT TO DUPLICATE THEM!

ALL RIGHT, BIG FELLOW, TAKE IT EASY. NO-BODY'S LOOKING FOR A *FIGHT.* YOU'VE NOTHING TO FEAR FROM *ME.*

A SWIFT MICRO-COMPUTER BANK SCAN OF THE CREATURE BEFORE IT IS UNDERTAKEN...

BUT BEFORE THE ANDROID'S ARTIFICIAL BRAIN CAN REACH A DECISION...

SPOK!

...A *GAS BOMB* INEXPLIC-ABLY SHOOTS FROM THE *BATTLE HARNESS* OF THE STILL UNCONSCIOUS *FIXER.*

GAS! I MUST CHANGE TO ENERGY BEFORE -- OOHHHHHH...

BWOOOF!

WHO CAN SAY WHAT TRANSPIRES IN THE ARTIFICIAL *BRAIN* BEHIND THAT NEARLY FEATURELESS *FACE?*

IT HAS NO *EYES* TO BLAZE WITH ANGER OR SOFTEN WITH COMPASSION.

NO *LIPS* TO SNARL OR SMILE...BETRAY ANY *EMOTION.*

THE INERT FORM IS LIFTED.

IS IT TO BE ANALYZED FURTHER--OR *CRUSHED?*

THE SOUND OF AN APPROACHING *QUINJET* MOMENTARILY DIVERTS THE ANDROID'S ATTENTION.

UNHAND HER, FACELESS ONE--

--OR FACE THE WRATH OF THE TRUE *SUB-MARINER!*

THE AVENGING *SON!*

BWUNT!

CAPTAIN MARVEL KNEW OF THE CREATURE'S POWERS OF *MIMICRY.* WHAT SHE DID *NOT* KNOW WAS THAT THE ANDROID COULD DUPLICATE *HER* POWERS BY SIMPLE CONTACT WITH HER UNCONSCIOUS PHYSICAL FORM!

BWAAASH!

AND, EVEN AS SHE FIRED A CONCUSSIVE BLAST OF ENERGIZED PARTICLES AT THE *FIXER...*

...NOW DOES THE IMITATIVE ANDROID DO *LIKEWISE* TO THE FLYING FIGURE OF *PRINCE NAMOR--!*

NAMOR!

SORRY TO SEE NAMOR TAKEN DOWN. I LIKE HIS STYLE.

TOO BAD HE AND MISS BUG-EYES GOT HITCHED. IT MIGHT'VE BEEN *FUN* TO SWIM IN HIS WAKE SOME-TIME!

THOOMP!

OOPS! KEEP COOL, JENNIFER! ANY *CLOSER* AND SUBBY'S LIABLE TO HAVE *COMPANY!*

SPWEEMM!

SPWEEEM!

SPWEEM!

ALL RIGHT, YOU OVERGROWN SACK OF *SLUDGE*--*THIS* ONE'S FOR CAPTAIN MARVEL!

BOK!

WOK!

AND *THAT'S* FOR THE SUB-MARINER!

BNUNK!

AND *THIS* IS 'CAUSE YOU'RE STILL STANDING!

WHAT--? THE *VAN'S* MOVING OFF DOWN THE ROAD. SOMEBODY'S GETTING--

AW--UGH!

BLAPP!

YOU'RE HURT! YOUR SKIN IS STILL *HOT* FROM THAT BLAST!

AND THE WAY YOU FELL TO THE GROUND, I THOUGHT--

I'VE SUFFERED FAR *WORSE* AND LIVED TO SPEAK OF IT. WHAT CONCERNS ME NOW IS WHY YOU ARE OUT HERE. DID I NOT SAY--

NAMOR, I WANT TO *SHOW* YOU I'M *NOT* SOME HELPLESS FEMALE WHO MUST BE FOREVER LEFT BEHIND!

I MAY NOT BE AN *AVENGER*, MY HUSBAND, BUT THERE IS *MUCH* I CAN DO!

MARRINA!

BLACK KNIGHT-- *MOVE IN!* I'VE CAUGHT THE ANDROID'S ATTENTION!

CAPTAIN MARVEL'S *RESCUE* IS OUR TOP PRIORITY.

YOU'RE THE DOCTOR.

MY ENCHANTED BLADE CAN CUT THROUGH *ANY* SUBSTANCE--

SWITHK!

--AND I'M SURE AN *ANDROID'S* HIDE IS NO EXCEPTION!

DID IT! AND IT'S DROPPED HER!

¿UUMMPH!?

WHEW! I WONDER WHERE *DEAD WEIGHT* IS ON THE ELECTRO-MAGNETIC SPECTRUM?

THE PSEUDO-ORGANIC SKIN OF THE ANDROID ALREADY BEGINS TO **CLEANSE** AND **CLOSE** ITS WOUND.

AND NOW, THROUGH A CRANIAL **OPENING** WHICH THE LESS INFORMED MIGHT DUB A "**MOUTH**"...

...WINDS OF ALMOST 200 MILES PER HOUR ISSUE FORTH TO **SCATTER** THE REMAINING AVENGERS LIKE **LEAVES!**

WHHOOOOSSHH

AND ALMOST A **MILE** FROM THE SCENE OF CARNAGE, A HURTLING SEMI--

--RECEIVES AN UNEXPECTED **HITCHER!**

THE ONLY WAY TO CONVINCE NAMOR OF MY **WORTHINESS** IS TO PROVE IT ON THE **BATTLEFIELD!**

HER LANDING IS SOFT. PERHAPS THE VEHICLE'S DRIVER HAS NOT **NOTICED** HIS NEW PASSENGER.

AND PERHAPS HE HAS.

OHHHH!

THE CREATURE HAS **TURNED** FROM US-- CEASED ITS ASSAULT.

AND A **GOOD** THING, TOO, OR WE WOULD'VE BEEN BLOWN TO **MILWAUKEE** BY NOW!

THE WASP WOULD **NEVER** HAVE LET US ALL GO TRAIPSING INTO BATTLE WITHOUT A **PLAN.**

BUT OUR **NEW** CHAIR-WOMAN DID--AND WE'RE ON OUR **BUTTS** FOR IT!

IT SEEMS AS IF THE STILL FIGURE OF THE **FIXER** HAS PIQUED ITS CURIOSITY. BUT THE CREATURE'S STILL-HEALING WOUND IS **SLOWING IT** A BIT.

NEARBY, A GROGGY **CAPTAIN MARVEL** ASSESSES THE SITUATION...

NAMOR-- WE NEED THE FIXER **ALIVE!** SWOOP IN AND **GRAB HIM** BEFORE THE ANDROID SHAMBLES OVER!

AS YOU WISH, SO IT IS DONE!

SWOOM!

UH- **OH!** LOOKS LIKE TALL AND UGLY STILL WANTS A **PIECE** OF US!

STAY BACK, BOYS! I **OWE** THIS TURKEY FOR A **SNEAK SHOT** BEFORE!

COME **ON**, CAPTAIN MARVEL. WHAT'S OUR **PLAN?**

THAT WAS A **COOL** BREEZE, BOXTOP... WANNA TRY **AGAIN?**

SHE-HULK, I HAVE MENTALLY LOCATED A STRANGE *NERVE GANGLIA* UNDER THE RIGHT ARMPIT.

WHILE THE ANDROID'S NERVOUS SYSTEM IS ALREADY ENGAGED IN REPAIRING ITSELF...

...A SUDDEN *THRUST* THERE MIGHT CAUSE AN *ELECTRICAL SPASM,* "SHORT-CIRCUITING" THE CONSTRUCT, SO TO SPEAK.

WHUNK!

IT'S WORTH A *TRY,* DOC!

OOF! SOMEBODY GET THIS GUY OFF ME BEFORE PEOPLE START TO *TALK!*

THANKS, NAMOR. YOU CAN HAVE THIS DANCE.

MMM—MMMM! LOOK AT THOSE *SHOULDERS!* ONLY GUY WITH A BETTER SET IS WYATT. *

*WYATT WINGFOOT -- SHE-HULK'S STEADY, AND AN OLD BUDDY OF THE F.F.'S HUMAN TORCH.

WHILE WE'VE GOT A BREATHER, I'M GOING TO TAKE THIS *HARNESS* OFF. WE DON'T NEED ANY MORE *GADGETS* POPPING OFF THIS THING.

ALLOW ME TO *HELP YOU UP,* CAPTAIN MARVEL. IT WON'T BE GOOD FOR THE TEAM'S *MORALE* IF YOU'RE NOT SEEN ON YOUR *FEET.*

UHH, THANK YOU, DOCTOR. BUT I'M QUITE *CAPABLE* OF GETTING UP *UNAIDED.*

AND YOU *KNOW* IT, BLAST YOU!

DOC, I COULD'VE POUNDED AT THAT LUG UNTIL *DOOMSDAY* WITHOUT MAKING A *DENT.*

BUT *YOU* CAME TO THE RESCUE LIKE NOBODY ELSE COULD. HERE'S ONE ON *ME.*

SMEK!

THESE SORT OF *EMOTIONAL DISPLAYS* WILL NOT BE TOLERATED, SHE-HULK! THIS IS A *FIGHTING TEAM--*

--NOT A *LONELY HEARTS CLUB!* WE SHOULD BEHAVE AS *WARRIORS,* NOT HIGH SCHOOL CHILDREN!

ANYONE EVER TELL YOU YOU'RE *CUTE* WHEN YOU'RE MAD?

NICE GOING, SHE-HULK. BETTER THAN *I* COULD DO.

WE MAY HAVE TAKEN SOME *LUMPS,* BUT THESE PEOPLE ARE LEARNING TO RESPOND AS A TEAM-- EVEN *WITHOUT* MY DIRECT LEADERSHIP.

I'VE GOT A *LONG WAY TO GO* IN FULFILLING MY RESPONSIBILITIES AS CHAIRWOMAN. BUT I'M FINDING *MY WAY.*

I DON'T WANT TO SPOIL ANYONE'S FUN, BUT THE *FIXER* OVER HERE...

...WELL, HE *ISN'T* THE FIXER! SOMEBODY FIXED *US!*

OHHH...

WH-WHERE *AM* I? HOW DID I GET HERE? WHAT'S GOING *ON?*

THAT'S WHAT *WE'D* LIKE TO KNOW.

WAIT-- IN ALL THE CONFUSION, I'D FORGOTTEN ABOUT *MARRINA!* SHE RAN OFF INTO THE *WOODS* BEFORE.

AND HASN'T RETURNED.

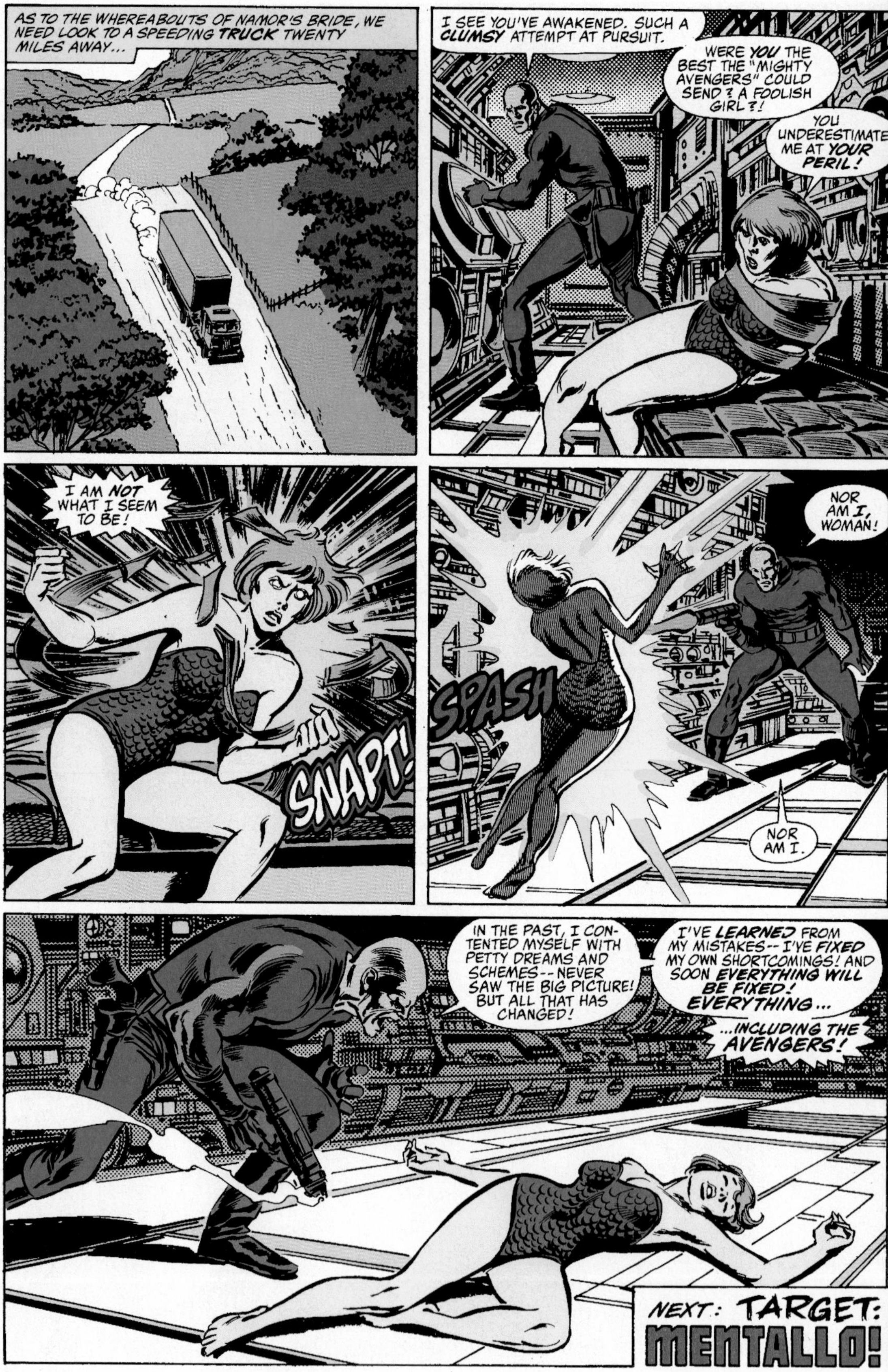

AS TO THE WHEREABOUTS OF NAMOR'S BRIDE, WE NEED LOOK TO A SPEEDING TRUCK TWENTY MILES AWAY...
I SEE YOU'VE AWAKENED. SUCH A CLUMSY ATTEMPT AT PURSUIT.
WERE YOU THE BEST THE "MIGHTY AVENGERS" COULD SEND? A FOOLISH GIRL?!
YOU UNDERESTIMATE ME AT YOUR PERIL!
I AM NOT WHAT I SEEM TO BE!
SNAPT!
SPASH
NOR AM I, WOMAN!
NOR AM I.
IN THE PAST, I CONTENTED MYSELF WITH PETTY DREAMS AND SCHEMES-- NEVER SAW THE BIG PICTURE! BUT ALL THAT HAS CHANGED!
I'VE LEARNED FROM MY MISTAKES-- I'VE FIXED MY OWN SHORTCOMINGS! AND SOON EVERYTHING WILL BE FIXED! EVERYTHING...
...INCLUDING THE AVENGERS!
NEXT: TARGET: MENTALLO!

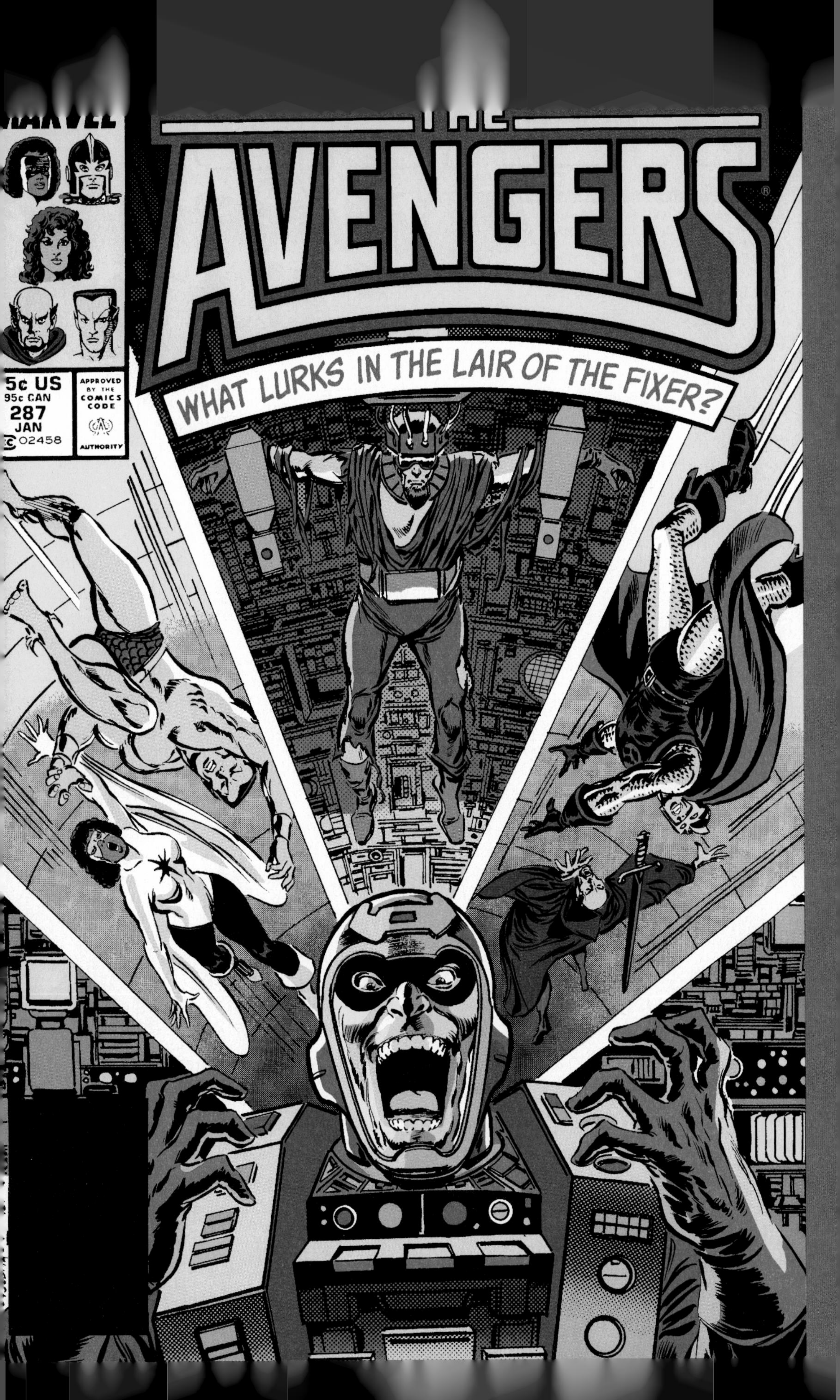
MARVEL
THE AVENGERS
WHAT LURKS IN THE LAIR OF THE FIXER?
95¢ CAN
287
JAN
02458
APPROVED BY THE COMICS CODE AUTHORITY

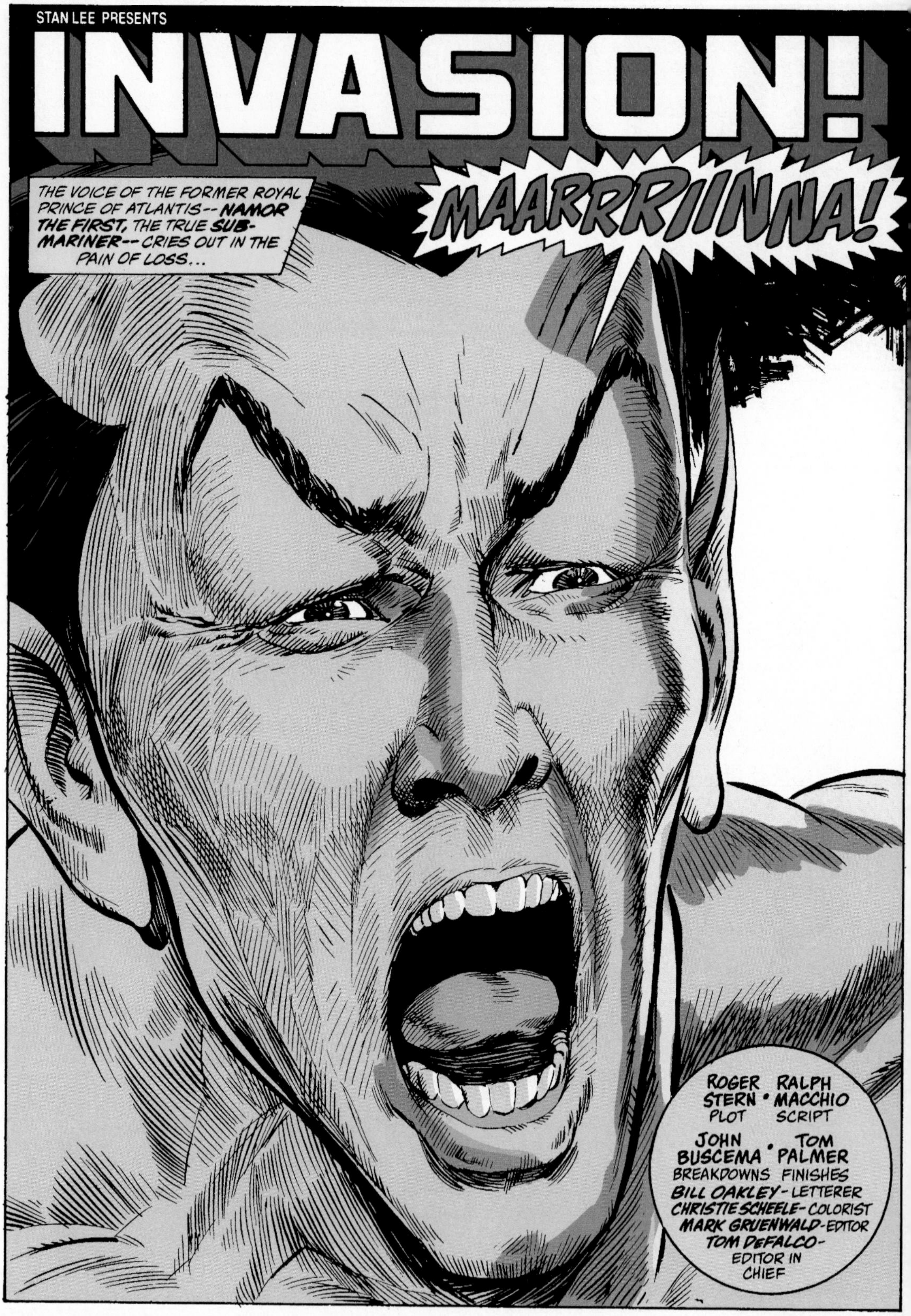

STAN LEE PRESENTS
INVASION!
THE VOICE OF THE FORMER ROYAL PRINCE OF ATLANTIS--NAMOR THE FIRST, THE TRUE SUB-MARINER--CRIES OUT IN THE PAIN OF LOSS...
MAARRRRIINNA!
ROGER STERN • PLOT
RALPH MACCHIO • SCRIPT
JOHN BUSCEMA • BREAKDOWNS
TOM PALMER • FINISHES
BILL OAKLEY-LETTERER
CHRISTIE SCHEELE-COLORIST
MARK GRUENWALD-EDITOR
TOM DEFALCO-EDITOR IN CHIEF

NO ANSWER! WHERE CAN SHE BE? WHEN WE AVENGERS CAME TO OHIO TO ANSWER THE SUMMONS OF A YOUNG BOY, SHE ACCOMPANIED US.

ONCE HERE, I FORBADE HER INVOLVEMENT AS WE FOUGHT AND DEFEATED A RAMPAGING ANDROID!

AND DURING THE MELEE, MY WIFE, MARRINA, DISAPPEARED INTO THE WOODS.*

*IT'S ALL IN LAST ISSUE, PEOPLE.

HOLD, YOUNGSTERS! HAS EITHER OF YOU SEEN A YELLOWISH, SCALY-SKINNED WOMAN IN THE WOODS?

N-NO, SIR!

WHO WAS THAT?

UMMM... THEY MUST BE SHOOTIN' THAT NEW STAR TREK TV SHOW AROUND HERE. YEAH! THAT'S IT.

SEVERAL MILES DISTANT, A SPEEDING SEMI HEADS OVER AN OLD COUNTRY ROAD--

--AND CASUALLY DISCARDS AN UNWANTED PASSENGER...

SHRIIKK!

MOMENTS OF SILENCE, AND THEN...

RROOOOOOMM!

BOY, THESE CROSS-COUNTRY RUNS ARE A *SNOOZE.*

JUST MILE AFTER MILE OF ROAD AND MORE ROAD. JUST ONCE, I WISH I'D HAVE SOMETHING TO TELL THE *WIFE.* JUST *ONCE.*

OHHH...

A...A W-WOMAN?

A WOMAN?!

THAMP!

WHAT? THE SOUND OF *CRUSHING METAL* JUST OVER THE HILL!

COULD IT BE--?

KRENCH

30

ALTHOUGH NOT A TRUE ATLANTEAN, SHE IS IN MANY WAYS LIKE HER WATER-BORN *HUSBAND*...SPAWNED WITH STRENGTH TO WITHSTAND THE CRUSHING PRESSURE OF THE OCEAN'S DEPTHS...

HER POWER IS MORE THAN *EQUAL* TO THE TASK AT HAND.

YOW!

MARRINA!

ARE YOU ALL RIGHT?

ARE YOU HURT?

I SHALL BE FINE, MY HUSBAND. BUT YOUR *CONCERN* IS TOUCHING.

WHAT OCCURRED?

AFTER LEAVING YOU, I FOLLOWED THE *FIXER'S TRUCK* AND WAS CAPTURED. HE USED A *STUN GUN* ON ME-- AND THEN MUST HAVE DROPPED ME FROM THE VAN.

AND *THAT* IS THE FIEND RESPONSIBLE! DISGUISED, OF COURSE!

NOW YOU SHALL KNOW *VENGEANCE,* FIXER! THE VENGEANCE OF *NAMOR THE FIRST*--

NAMOR --DON'T!

THIS *ISN'T* THE FIXER! I WAS LYING IN THE *ROAD* WHEN THIS MAN'S TRUCK BORE DOWN ON ME!

IF HE HADN'T REACTED AS *QUICKLY* TO SLOW THE TRUCK--

I SEE. MY APOLOGIES. I WAS *MISTAKEN.*

≈WHEW!≈

ELSEWHERE, THE SPEEDING SEMI CONTINUES ITS JOURNEY...

...WITH AN EERIE INHUMAN DRIVER AT THE WHEEL.

SOON, THE VEHICLE MAKES ITS WAY INTO A SUBURBAN INDUSTRIAL PARK.

AND INTO A CERTAIN MACHINERY-FILLED WAREHOUSE.

MY INSTRUMENTS TELL ME THERE IS SOMEONE ELSE HERE.

AND IF IT IS NOT THE PARTY I EXPECT-- MY RESPONSE SHALL BE SWIFT-- AND LETHAL!

SEVERAL MILES FROM THE OMINOUS FIXER, THE AVENGERS CONFER WITH STATE POLICE AT THE SCENE OF THEIR RECENT BATTLE WITH THE FIXER-CONTROLLED ANDROID...

...YES. THE AVENGERS WILL HANDLE THE REFINANCING AND REBUILDING OF THE BARN -- AND ALL OTHER DAMAGES INCURRED.

MA'AM, WE'RE JUST NOT USED TO FILING REPORTS ABOUT SUPER HERO FIGHTS WITH GIANT ANDROIDS. IT'S GOING TO READ LIKE A DRIVE-IN MOVIE SCRIPT.

YOU SEEM PERPLEXED, OFFICER. ISN'T THAT SATISFACTORY?

I CAN'T BELIEVE I CAUSED ALL THIS WITH JUST A PHONE CALL!

HIS PULSE IS STEADY. HE WILL BE FINE.

HMMPH. AND THIS IS THE MAN YOU BELIEVED WAS "THE FIXER" UNTIL YOU FOUND OUT HE WAS MERELY UNDER THAT CHARACTER'S MENTAL INFLUENCE. I SEE.

THE INSTRUMENTS READ A COMBINATION OF BOTH ORGANIC AND MECHANICAL LIFE. GO FIGURE, SHE-HULK.

I'M NOT GONNA BE ABLE TO FORGET THIS FOR A LONNNNG TIME.

SO WHAT'S GODZILLA MADE OF, MISTER BLACK KNIGHT?

GUESS THIS THING'S CREATOR WASN'T CALLED THE MAD THINKER FOR NOTHING.

WOULD YOU EXCUSE US FOR A MOMENT, OFFICER? I WISH TO SPEAK PRIVATELY WITH OUR GROUP'S LEADER.

WHY, OF COURSE, SIR. WE'RE JUST ABOUT DONE HERE, ANYWAY.

THANK YOU.

CAPTAIN MARVEL, YOU'RE HOLDING UP REMARKABLY WELL FOR SOMEONE WHO ONLY A HALF HOUR AGO HAD HER LUNGS FILLED WITH NERVE GAS.

THANK YOU FOR YOUR CONCERN, DOCTOR DRUID.

PERHAPS IF YOU SAT D--

I WILL BE FINE, DOCTOR. PLEASE.

AND TO ALLEVIATE YOUR *WORRY*, I'LL TRANSFORM INTO ANOTHER ENERGY STATE SO YOU'LL SEE MY POWER'S INTACT.

JUST...

...GIVE ME...

...A MOMENT.

PLEASE, MY DEAR WOMAN. YOU *CANNOT* DO IT. STILL TOO WEAK.

PRAY, TAKE MY ADVICE-- SIT DOWN AND *I* SHALL SEE TO THE ANDROID'S DISPOSITION.

UHH, DOCTOR-- I THINK WE'RE GOING TO GET A *REAL CHANCE* TO SEE TO HIS "DISPOSITION" --BECAUSE HE'S *WAKING UP!*

LOOK ALIVE, AVENGERS!

THANK HEAVEN FOR *CAPTAIN AMERICA* --WHEREVER HE IS*-- TEACHING ME THOSE ACROBATIC TRICKS!

*CAP'S WHEREABOUTS ARE A MYSTERY TO HIS FELLOW AVENGERS.

I'LL DRAW A BEAD ON HIM!

THE BULLETS! THEY'RE JUST *BOUNCING OFF!*

P'KOW! P'KOW!

I KNOCKED THIS CLOWN OUT ONCE BEFORE BY HITTING SOME *NERVE GANGLIA* UNDER ITS ARM!

BOOMP

BUT THAT ONLY WORKED BECAUSE THE THING WAS *INJURED*--

I DOUBT I'LL--WELL, I'LL BE! IT MUST NOT HAVE FULLY REPAIRED ITSELF!

NICE *MOVES*, JENNIFER. REAL NICE.

OKAY, BOYS, PILE OUT! IT ISN'T *EVERY* DAY OUR NECK OF THE WOODS GETS A VISIT BY THE *AVENGERS!* YAAAHHOOOO!

THIS IS BIIIIIG NEWS!

RUDY, PLEASE! WE ALL KNOW YOU'RE BUCKIN' FOR A JOB AT NBC IN NEW YORK-- BUT CALM DOWN.

CALM DOWN?! YOU'RE IN THE *WRONG BIZ*, BARNEY!

ALL RIGHT, TALL, GREEN AND BEAUTIFUL-- GIMME THE OLD *IVORIES!* SMILE, SWEETIE!

AH-- THINK MAYBE WE COULD PROP THAT GOON UP AND YOU COULD *BELT* 'IM ONE AGAIN-- JUST FOR THE *CAMERAS?* IT'D BE SEEN *ALL* OVER THE STATE! C'MON!

IF YOU DON'T GET OFF MY *CASE*, SQUIRT-- SOMETHING *ELSE* IS GONNA BE SEEN ALL OVER THE STATE!

YOUR *HIDE!*

≶GULP!≷

NAMOR! AND *MARRINA!*

I FOUND HER, DANE WHITMAN-- ALIVE AND REASON-ABLY UNHARMED!

FANTASTIC! WHAT ABOUT THE *FIXER?*

REGRETTABLY, THE FIXER *GOT AWAY.* MARRINA WAS UNABLE TO HALT HIS TRUCK. HE COULD HAVE LEFT THE *STATE* BY NOW.

AS LONG AS *YOU'RE* BOTH UNINJURED-- WE'LL FIND HIM.

PRINCE NAMOR ... IS IT TRUE THAT YOU'RE THE RULER OF THE *MYTHICAL* LAND OF *ATLANTIS* ...UHH, UNDER THE SEA?

MYTHICAL? NO MORE MYTHICAL THAN THE FABLED ARROGANCE AND IGNORANCE OF *NEWSMEN.*

BUT THAT DOESN'T ANSWER--

INDEED, IT DOES.

AND AS THE SUB-MARINER'S GLARE FREEZES ONE OVER-ANXIOUS REPORTER IN HIS TRACKS, IN A FAR AWAY DINER, ANOTHER MAN—*DAN SMALLWOOD*—IS FROZEN BY THE SIGHT OF NAMOR'S WIFE.

MARRINA! IT CAN'T BE!

TH-THAT'S MY *CHILDHOOD SWEETHEART* ON TV! WHAT'S *HAPPENED* TO HER?

I—I NEVER THOUGHT I'D *SEE* HER AGAIN. SHE'S AN *AVENGER* NOW?

IS IT MY *APPROACH*, CATHY?

NAH. IT'S YOUR *TAKE-OFFS* AND *LANDINGS*, RANDY.

AND IN THE INNER SANCTUM OF THE FIXER'S HIDEOUT, NAMOR'S INTERVIEW IS WATCHED BY ANOTHER PAIR OF EYES...

MENTALLO!

DRAWING A *GUN* ON A TRUSTED OLD FRIEND? AND ONE WHOM *YOU* ASKED TO JOIN YOU IN ONE OF OUR *OLD HAUNTS*?

SPARE ME YOUR DRY WIT.

I NOTICE YOU'VE "FIXED" A MIND-SCAN PROOF HELMET TO BLOCK MY MENTAL PROBES. THERE WAS LITTLE NEED FOR SUCH A COUNTER.

WHAT SECRETS SHOULD THERE BE BETWEEN TWO OLD FRIENDS. BESIDES, IT HARDLY TAKES A MIND-READER TO KNOW THAT YOU WANT TO RENEW OUR PARTNERSHIP. HAVE YOU FORGOTTEN WHAT WE TWO *ALMOST* ACCOMPLISHED YEARS AGO—THE TOPPLING OF *SHIELD** ITSELF?

*SUPREME HEADQUARTERS INTERNATIONAL ESPIONAGE LAW ENFORCEMENT DIVISION.

WITH YOUR POWER TO *FIX* ANYTHING—COBBLE *ANY OBJECT* INTO A *WEAPON*...

...AND MY INVINCIBLE ABILITY TO *READ MINDS* AND *PROJECT THOUGHTS*, HOW COULD *ANYONE* STAND AGAINST US?

OUR *FIRST TASK* SHOULD BE--

--WHAT ARE YOU *DOING?* FIXER!

UGH!

WHUK!

WHAT IS THE *MEANING* OF THIS? NOT EVEN THE *FIXER* MAY TREAT MENTALLO WITH SUCH *IMPUNITY!* WHEN I FREE MYSELF--

YOU'LL *NOT* FREE YOURSELF. THERE IS SOMETHING I *DEMAND* OF YOU.

YOU DEMAND?!

FIXER--MY GOD, MAN-- WHAT ARE YOU *DOING?* WHAT HAS COME *OVER* YOU? WHAT HAVE YOU *BECOME* SINCE LAST WE JOINED FORCES?

WHAT HAVE I BE- COME? DO YOU *REALLY* WANT TO KNOW, MENTALLO?

HERE--PROBE MY MIND AND TELL ME WHAT YOU *SEE!* *TELL ME!*

AND EVEN AS MENTALLO SCREAMS IN HORROR, AT A REGIONAL AIRFIELD OUTSIDE DAYTON...

WELL, AVENGERS, WITH A BIT OF HELP FROM THE NATIONAL GUARD, OL' *SILENT SAM* THERE IS READY TO MAKE A SWIFT FLIGHT TO--

--OUR NEW HEADQUARTERS AT *HYDROBASE ISLAND.*

104

I BELIEVE WE SHOULD LAUNCH A SEARCH FOR THE FIXER *IMMEDIATELY*. HE MUST *PAY* FOR WHAT HE TRIED TO DO TO MARRINA.

EASY, NAMOR.

LOOK, I'D LIKE NOTHING BETTER. BUT WE *MUST* DELIVER THE ANDROID TO SAFETY.

WE CAN'T RISK ITS *AWAKENING* AGAIN.

LET THE ARMY GUARD THE CREATURE! *THE FIXER MUST BE FOUND!*

HEY, SUBBY-- *COOL IT!* C.M. GIVES THE ORDERS HERE, AND BESIDES, THE FIXER'S A *LIGHTWEIGHT.*

I DON'T KNOW, JEN. THAT GUY'S GIVEN US A LOT OF GRIEF THIS FAR-- WHO *KNOWS* WHAT HE'S *REALLY* UP TO.

YEAH, BUT--

SUDDENLY...

UHH-- RECEIVING A *MENTAL IMAGE* -- I SHALL TRY...TO MAKE IT...*VISUAL* FOR...YOU!

HELP ME! BEING TORTURED!

TORTURED BY THE FIXER! HELLLLPP!

IT'S *MENTALLO,* THE FIXER'S TELEPATHIC PARTNER!

DO YOU *STILL* CONSIDER THE FIXER A "*LIGHTWEIGHT,*" SHE-HULK?

OKAY, DOC.

I IMPLORE YOU--

VERY WELL.

STILL FEEL *WEAK,* BUT I'M LEADER OF THE AVENGERS, RIGHT? BETTER ASSERT MYSELF.

LET'S HEAD FOR THE QUINJET, TEAM. ALL OF YOU *EXCEPT* MARRINA.

BUT, I--

NO *BUTS* THIS TIME! *YOU* RETURN TO HYDROBASE WITH THE ANDROID. SIGNAL US IF IT REVIVES AGAIN.

SOON...

YES, SHE-HULK, I AM STILL RECEIVING A *MENTAL SIGNAL* --MUCH *FAINTER* NOW-- FROM MENTALLO. WE MUST *HURRY.*

STRANGELY ENOUGH, THE SIGNAL IS COMING FROM INSIDE THAT *WAREHOUSE.*

THAT'S PRETTY ROUTINE. WHERE *ELSE* DO SUPER-VILLAINS KEEP THEIR HEADQUARTERS?

FROM THE ROOF OF THE INNOCUOUS-LOOKING STRUCTURE, *ANTI-AIR-CRAFT GUNS* APPEAR AND OPEN FIRE!

THAKA-THAK!

SPAK!

WE'RE HIT! I'M PUTTING US IN A *POWER DIVE,* DOC! I'LL TRY TO CRASHLAND BE-TWEEN THE BUILDINGS!

HERE GOES!

SKROOOM!

SPASH!

39

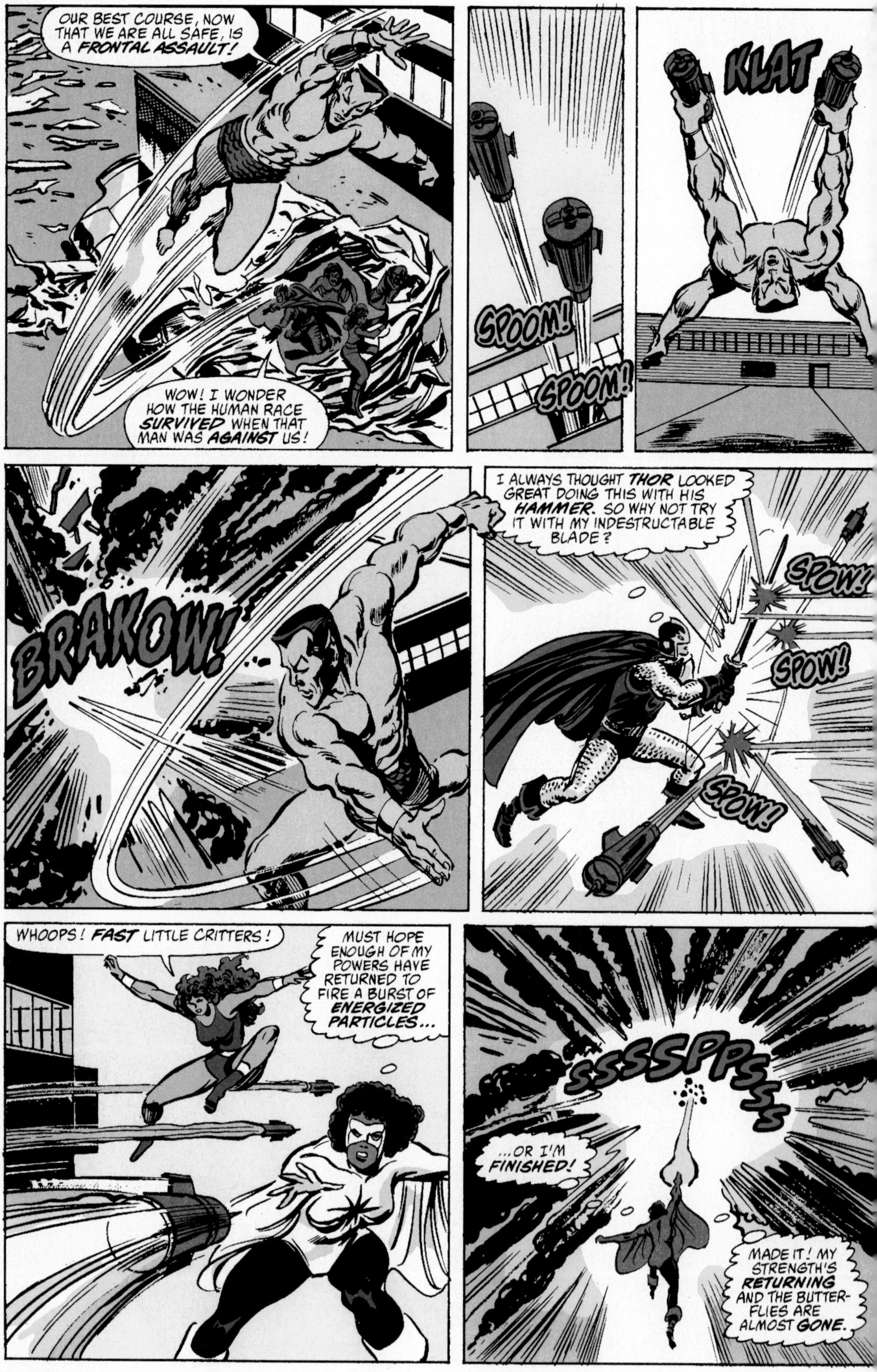
OUR BEST COURSE, NOW THAT WE ARE ALL SAFE, IS A FRONTAL ASSAULT!
WOW! I WONDER HOW THE HUMAN RACE SURVIVED WHEN THAT MAN WAS AGAINST US!
SPOOM!
SPOOM!
KLAT
BRAKOW!
I ALWAYS THOUGHT THOR LOOKED GREAT DOING THIS WITH HIS HAMMER. SO WHY NOT TRY IT WITH MY INDESTRUCTABLE BLADE?
SPOW!
SPOW!
SPOW!
WHOOPS! FAST LITTLE CRITTERS!
MUST HOPE ENOUGH OF MY POWERS HAVE RETURNED TO FIRE A BURST OF ENERGIZED PARTICLES...
SSSSPPSSS
...OR I'M FINISHED!
MADE IT! MY STRENGTH'S RETURNING AND THE BUTTER-FLIES ARE ALMOST GONE.

ENOUGH *GAMES*, FIXER! NAMOR HAS HAD HIS *FILL* THIS DAY!

SHOW YOURSELF!

SUDDENLY, AS IF WITH A LIFE OF THEIR OWN, THICK *ELECTRICAL CABLES* SNAKE AROUND THE STARTLED SUB-MARINER...

THOUSANDS OF VOLTS COURSE THROUGH THE *REGAL FIGURE*...

AARRRR!

SCRRRSSS

BUT THE ENRAGED SEA-PRINCE GRASPS THE MURDER-OUSLY *HOT CABLES* AND INCREDIBLY *REDIRECTS* THE SPEWING ELECTRICITY BACK AT ITS *SOURCE*!

ZZZAAAASSH

SUBBY-- YOU *OKAY?* LOOKED LIKE--

I WILL SURVIVE, SHE-HULK. NAMOR *EVER* HAS.

THEN, WITHOUT WARNING--!

UHHHH!

WHOOOOSSH

41

HELPLESSLY, THE AVENGERS ARE SUCKED BACK--

--INTO TWO LONG PNEUMATIC TUBES...WHIRLING LIKE *LEAVES* CAUGHT IN A VIOLENT STORM.

UMPH-- JUST MANAGED A *HAND-HOLD* SO I COULD GRAB YOU, DOC. BUT DANE'S SLIPPING *PAST*-- CAN'T--

SKRRANCH!

DON'T WORRY ABOUT *ME!*

BLAST-- TURBINE BLADES! I'LL BE CHEWED UP--

--UNLESS I WHIP MY *SWORD* AT THEM AND HOPE IT CATCHES!

WHHRRRR!

EBONY BLADE-- I *LOVE* YOU! THANK HEAVEN NONE OF THE OTHERS WENT THROUGH HERE *FIRST!*

KKRREEESHH!

DANE-- WE HEARD THE *SOUND*-- DIDN'T KNOW WHAT HAPPENED.

LIKE THE MAN SAID... I WILL *SURVIVE*, SHE-HULK. BUT WHAT ABOUT NAMOR AND CAPTAIN MARVEL WHO WERE PULLED INTO A *SEPA-RATE* TUNNEL?

NAMOR-- LET ME GO-- THE WEIGHT OF US BOTH-- TOO MUCH! SAVE YOURSELF!

STILL HAVEN'T GOT THE STRENGTH NECESSARY TO CHANGE INTO ANOTHER ENERGY FORM!

NO! WE BOTH SURVIVE-- OR PERISH!

MY WEAKNESS COULD COST US OUR LIVES!

NOT IF THE SUB-MARINER HAS ANYTHING TO SAY ABOUT IT...

B-TANG!

WWRRRRRNNNCHH!

YOU'VE DONE IT! WE'RE OUT!

LET US HOPE THAT THE OTHERS WERE SO FORTUNATE.

BEHIND ME! WE KNOW NOT WHAT DANGERS LURK AHEAD IN THIS DARKENED CORRIDOR! I SHALL FACE THEM FIRST!

WAIT! I'M THE LEADER OF THE AVENGERS, AND IT'S TIME I BEGAN ACTING IN THAT CAPACITY! THIS IS WHERE MY POWER MAY AID US.

MUST CONCENTRATE-- CALL ON ALL MY ENERGY RESERVES ...

...WILL MYSELF TO BECOME LIGHT. I-MUST-BECOME-LIGHT!

43

I-I'VE **DONE** IT! I'M RISING--AND MY FORM SHOULD ILLUMINATE THE CORRIDOR. DON'T WORRY, NAMOR--I'LL KEEP **PACE** WITH YOU.

SUCH A VERY BRAVE YOUNG WOMAN--NOT YET **UP** TO THE TASK SHE UNDERTAKES...

...BUT UNWILLING TO USE **WEAKNESS** AS AN EXCUSE. IN TRUTH, SHE POSSESSES THE QUALITIES OF **LEADER-SHIP**, THOUGH SHE HAS DOUBT.

BUT THEN--!

OOOHH--C-CAN'T STAY **ALOFT**! MUST C-COME DOWN... NAMOR.

AND AS THE SUB-MARINER REACTS TO HIS WEAKENED COMRADE...

BA-WHOOM

NICE TO SEE EVERY-ONE **MADE IT**! NOW THE GANG'S ALL HERE!

LISTEN TO ME, DRUID-- EVERY **SECOND** WE'RE HERE THE DANGER GREATENS! NOW AS LEADER OF THIS GROUP, I **INSIST** YOU TAKE US DIRECTLY TO **MENTALLO**!

UH--YES...OF COURSE! CONTINUE IN THIS DIRECTION.

FRANTIC MOMENTS LATER...

LOOKS LIKE THE DOC WAS RIGHT ON THE MONEY!

BRUUUNNCH!

I GUESS THAT'S **OUR MAN** IN THE CORNER!

GENTLY WITH HIM. THE **MENTAL STRAIN** HE HAS UNDERGONE HAS BEEN ENORMOUS.

YOU **GOT** IT, DOCTOR.

NOW, MENTALLO, NOW THAT YOU ARE COMFORTABLY POSITIONED-- TELL US WHERE THE FIXER IS!

DON'T KNOW ...CAN ONLY TELL YOU...HE **FORCED** ME TO SEND...THE MENTAL SUMMONS. **FORCED-- ME**...

YOU CAN'T-- **CAN'T** KNOW WHAT HIS MIND IS LIKE! IT WAS **NOT** THE FIXER-- I-- I KNEW! THE CEREBRAL FEEDBACK-- **UNIMAGINABLE!**

HIS MIND-- HUGE-- ALIEN!

ALIEN!

AND FOR ONCE, NONE OF THE AVENGERS HAS A WORD TO SAY.

NHHHH...

SEVERAL HOURS LATER, AT HYDROBASE ISLAND OFF THE EASTERN COAST OF THE U.S., THE DEEPENING MYSTERY IS EXPLORED BY THE PERPLEXED ASSEMBLERS...

INTERESTING. *CAPTAIN MARVEL'S* BEEN STANDING ON THE SIDELINES AND *DRUID'S* BEEN RUNNING THE SHOW SINCE WE GOT BACK TO HYDROBASE.

EASILY NOW. WE DO NOT WISH TO *DISTURB* THIS ORGANIC CONSTRUCT MORE THAN IS NECESSARY. ALLOW THE BELT TO MOVE *SLOWLY.*

THE *CONTRIVANCES* OF SURFACEMEN! WILL I NEVER BECOME USED TO THEIR ALL-CONSUMING *TECHNOLOGY*--AND THE *ZEAL* WITH WHICH THEY EMBRACE IT?

ODD...THIS *CONTAINMENT TUBE* ...IT SEEMS TO HAVE BEEN--

AVENGERS-- QUICKLY-- OVER HERE! THIS CONTAINMENT TUBE HAS RECENTLY BEEN *TAMPERED* WITH!

KEEP YOUR *TOGA* ON, DOCTOR. I'LL CHECK OUT THE *CONTROL PANEL* DOWN HERE AND WE'LL SEE WHAT'S WHAT!

WAITAMINUTE! YOU'RE *RIGHT!*

WELL, DON'T JUST *STAND* THERE, DANISH-- OPEN THE SUCKER UP!

CAUTIOUSLY, DANE. WE'VE HAD *ONE TOO MANY* SURPRISES TODAY!

KL'IK

HERE GOES!

PPTTSSSSS

GOOD LORD-- THE *FIXER* !

MOMENTS LATER, AFTER THE LATEST MYSTERY MAN HAS BEEN EXAMINED BY DOCTOR DRUID...

I HAVE USED EVERY MONITORING DEVICE AVAILABLE TO US, AND CROSS-CHECKED HIS EVERY STATISTIC BY COMPUTER WITH *SHIELD* FILES ON THE FIXER.

THERE IS NO DOUBT-- *THAT* MAN IS THE FIXER!

CAN WE QUESTION HIM?

HE IS HEAVILY *SEDATED* NOW. SOME TIME MUST PASS.

YOU MEAN *MORE* TIME MUST PASS! I WEARY OF THESE PUZZLES, ENIGMAS, AND FALSE IDENTITIES! WE HAVE BEEN MADE *FOOLS* OF AT OUR EVERY TURN !

AND THE SUB-MARINER PLAYS FOOL TO NO MAN! *NO MAN!* I *DEMAND* ANSWERS IMMEDIATELY!

AND WE'LL GET THOSE ANSWERS-- WITHOUT *BICKERING!* NOW... THE BODY THAT WAS ORIGINALLY IN THAT CONTAINMENT CAPSULE WAS THAT OF--

--THE *ADAPTOID!*

"ACCORDING TO THE SHIELD FILES I'VE READ ON HIM, THIS IS AN ANDROID CONSTRUCT CREATED BY *AIM* * WITH THE POWER TO DUPLICATE THE ABILITIES AND APPEARANCE OF ANY BEING PASSING WITHIN *TEN FEET* OF IT.

"YEARS AGO, ITS FIRST INTENDED VICTIM WAS *CAPTAIN AMERICA*-- WHO EVENTUALLY HALTED IT.

* *AIM*-- *ADVANCED IDEA MECHANICS*... A GROUP OF RENEGADE SCIENTISTS DEDICATED TO WORLD TAKEOVER.

"THE ADAPTOID RETURNED ON SEVERAL OCCASIONS TO BATTLE THE *AVENGERS* THEMSELVES AS--

--THE SUPER-*ADAPTOID!*

"ITS ABILITIES TO DUPLICATE EXTEND BEYOND A *SINGLE* BEING. IT IS CAPABLE OF COPYING THE POWERS OF UP TO *EIGHT* SUPERHUMANS AT ONCE.

"AND ALTHOUGH IT SEEMED *UNSTOPPABLE*, ABLE TO REALIZE ITS CREATORS' DREAMS OF *WORLD DOMINATION*, IT WAS REPEATEDLY *DEFEATED.*

"AFTER ITS LAST DEFEAT, THE ANDROID WAS BROUGHT TO AVENGERS MANSION AND PLACED IN STASIS IN A CONTAINMENT TUBE.

"IT MUST HAVE BEEN SET FREE WHEN THE *MASTERS OF EVIL* RANSACKED THE MANSION.* IT ASSUMED THE IDENTITY AND ABILITIES OF THE *FIXER*-- AND SWITCHED PLACES WITH HIM.

"TO DEFEAT AND RECAPTURE THIS CREATURE MAY BE OUR *SUPREME TEST*, AVENGERS. FOR, WE FACE A *MALIGN INTELLIGENCE* CAPABLE OF IMITATING *ALL* OF OUR POWERS *AT ONCE...*

* *AVENGERS #273-277.*

AT THAT MOMENT, IN THE BOROUGH OF QUEENS, NEW YORK...

...A FAMILIAR FIGURE PEERS THROUGH A DIRTY WINDOWPANE...

...UNTIL--!

SSSWWWPP

WHO *ARE* YOU AND WHAT DO YOU *WANT* HERE? SPEAK QUICKLY!

EASY *NOW,* MY FRIEND. I HAVE COME IN SEARCH OF--*YOU!* YOU SEE, WE HAVE MUCH IN COMMON. *MUCH.* AND I REQUIRE YOUR ASSISTANCE.

IF YOU *HELP* ME, I SHALL RETURN TO YOU THAT WHICH YOU *DESIRE MOST* IN ALL THE WORLD-- YOUR *LOST LOVE!*

YOUR WORDS INTRIGUE ME. CONTINUE. YOU HAVE GAINED THE ATTENTION OF--

--MACHINE MAN!

NEXT〉 HEAVY METAL!

49

THE AVENGERS

MARVEL

© 1987 MARVEL ENT. GROUP INC.

75¢ US
95¢ CAN
288
FEB
CC 02458

APPROVED
BY THE
COMICS
CODE
AUTHORITY

"WHEN WAKES **THE SENTRY SINISTER!**"

STAN LEE PRESENTS:

HEAVY METAL!

OVER THE TEXAS PANHANDLE THEY SOAR...

...MACHINE MAN, A SOPHISTICATED ROBOT-- SOLE SURVIVOR OF A DEAD GOVERNMENT PROJECT TO BUILD A MOBILE WEAPONS SYSTEM POSSESSING INDEPENDENT THOUGHT...

...AND THE SUPER-ADAPTOID --AN ANDROID CONSTRUCT, PRODUCT OF A.I.M.*, A RENEGADE GROUP OF SCIEN- TISTS,WHO HAS THE POWER TO IMITATE THE APPEARANCE AND ABILITIES OF ANY BEING.

I HAVE FLOWN WITH YOU ALL THE WAY FROM NEW YORK, ADAPTOID, AND YOU STILL HAVE NOT EXPLAINED TO ME THE NATURE OF OUR MISSION. IS OUR GOAL IN SIGHT YET?

PATIENCE, MACHINE MAN. I HAVE SOUGHT YOU OUT FOR AN ENTERPRISE THAT WILL BENEFIT US BOTH. AND YES, OUR GOAL IS NEARBY.

*ADVANCED IDEA MECHANICS.

| RALPH MACCHIO SCRIPT | JOHN BUSCEMA BREAKDOWNS | TOM PALMER FINISHER | BILL OAKLEY LETTERER | MAX SCHEELE COLORIST | MARK GRUENWALD EDITOR | TOM DeFALCO EDITOR IN CHIEF |

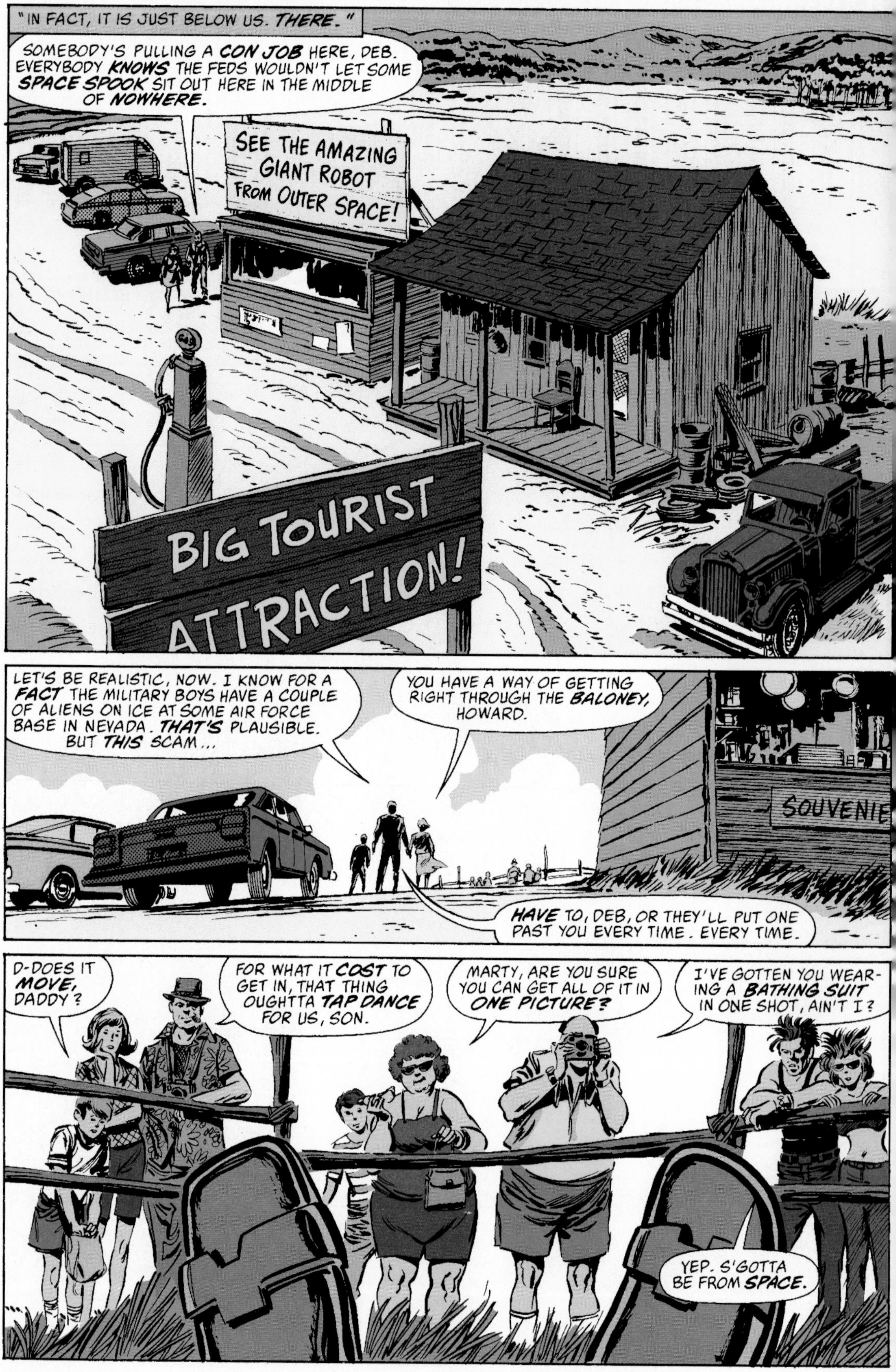
"IN FACT, IT IS JUST BELOW US. THERE."
SOMEBODY'S PULLING A CON JOB HERE, DEB. EVERYBODY KNOWS THE FEDS WOULDN'T LET SOME SPACE SPOOK SIT OUT HERE IN THE MIDDLE OF NOWHERE.
SEE THE AMAZING GIANT ROBOT FROM OUTER SPACE!
BIG TOURIST ATTRACTION!
LET'S BE REALISTIC, NOW. I KNOW FOR A FACT THE MILITARY BOYS HAVE A COUPLE OF ALIENS ON ICE AT SOME AIR FORCE BASE IN NEVADA. THAT'S PLAUSIBLE. BUT THIS SCAM...
YOU HAVE A WAY OF GETTING RIGHT THROUGH THE BALONEY, HOWARD.
SOUVENIE
HAVE TO, DEB, OR THEY'LL PUT ONE PAST YOU EVERY TIME. EVERY TIME.
D-DOES IT MOVE, DADDY?
FOR WHAT IT COST TO GET IN, THAT THING OUGHTTA TAP DANCE FOR US, SON.
MARTY, ARE YOU SURE YOU CAN GET ALL OF IT IN ONE PICTURE?
I'VE GOTTEN YOU WEARING A BATHING SUIT IN ONE SHOT, AIN'T I?
YEP. S'GOTTA BE FROM SPACE.

"WHO IS THAT ROBOT, ADAPTOID? IT LOOKS ALIEN."

"INDEED IT IS, MACHINE MAN. IT WAS CREATED BY THE ALIEN RACE CALLED THE KREE. KNOWN TO ITS MASTERS AS SENTRY 459, THE AUTOMATON'S FUNCTION IS TO STAND GUARD OVER PLANETS OF IMPORTANCE TO THE KREE IN THEIR ABSENCE.

"THIS SENTRY, LEFT ON EARTH MILLENNIA AGO BY A KREE SCIENTIFIC EXPEDITION, WAS AWAKENED FROM ITS PERIOD OF INACTIVITY BY ARCHAEOLOGICAL INTRUDERS SEVERAL YEARS AGO.

I WONDER IF THIS GUY'S BUDDIES ARE EVER GONNA COME BACK FOR IT?

NAH. THIS PILE'A JUNK IS PROB'LY LONG FERGOT BY THE CLOWNS THAT MADE IT.

"DEFEATED BY THE FANTASTIC FOUR, IT WAS LATER REACTIVATED AND DEFEATED AGAIN... THIS TIME BY AN EARTH-BASED KREE SOLDIER. RECENTLY IT BATTLED THAT SOLDIER AGAIN AND WAS ABANDONED NEARBY. *

* "THAT SOLDIER" BEING THE LATE CAPTAIN MAR-VELL (NO RELATION TO THE AVENGER OF THE SAME NAME). SEE CAPTAIN MARVEL #49.

YES. EXACTLY AS I PICTURE IT.

HIS BUDDIES FERGOT, HUH?

IT'S, UH-- A TRICK. UH-- JOKE. UHH...

TELL THEM!

BUT, DAD-- IT'S JUST GETTIN' GOOD!

BUTTON IT, STEVEN!

53

IF THIS IS A PRODUCT OF *ALIEN TECHNOLOGY,* ADAPTOID, HOW DO YOU PROPOSE TO RE-ATTACH ITS HEAD?

HAVE I NOT TOLD YOU, MACHINE MAN? BEFORE CONTACTING YOU, I ABSORBED THE VAST MECHANICAL TALENTS OF A PETTY CRIMINAL CALLED *THE FIXER...*

...AS WELL AS THE MENTAL POWERS OF A CRIMINAL TELEPATH NAMED *MENTALLO.* WITH SUCH ABILITIES AT MY DISPOSAL, EVEN THE REPAIRING OF THIS *SENTRY* IS NOT BEYOND ME.

SSSSSSS

SONNUVAGUN!

HOLD ON THUR, YUH DADBURNED WEASELS! YER A'MESSIN' WITH MUH *MEAL TICKET!*

OOOKKAAAYY! YUH AIN'T LISTENIN'! SO AH'M GONNA PUT SO MUCH *LEAD* INTA YA THEY'RE GONNA NEED A *CRANE* TUH GIT YUH *HIDE* OUTTA HEAH!

SPFOON!

THERE! THAT'LL *TEACH* YUH TUH BE MESSIN' WITH ANOTHER FELLER'S *GOODS!* NO COURT'A LAW IN THE STATE'LL--

--'LL... HEY, WHAT IN THUNDER-ATION'S A GOIN' ON HEAH? AH HIT YUH *POINT BLANK* ON THE NOGGIN! AM AH *SEEIN'* THINGS!?

AH AIN'T'A HAD NO HOOCH IN A FAIR DAY! C'MON, ACT NATCHERAL-LIKE AND *FALL OVER,* FELLER.

THERE. THE FINAL *MICRO-PROCESSOR* IS IN PLACE.

NOW, SENTRY, *ARISE.* ARISE AND JOIN THE ONES WHO WILL TAKE YOU TO A GLORIOUS *DESTINY!*

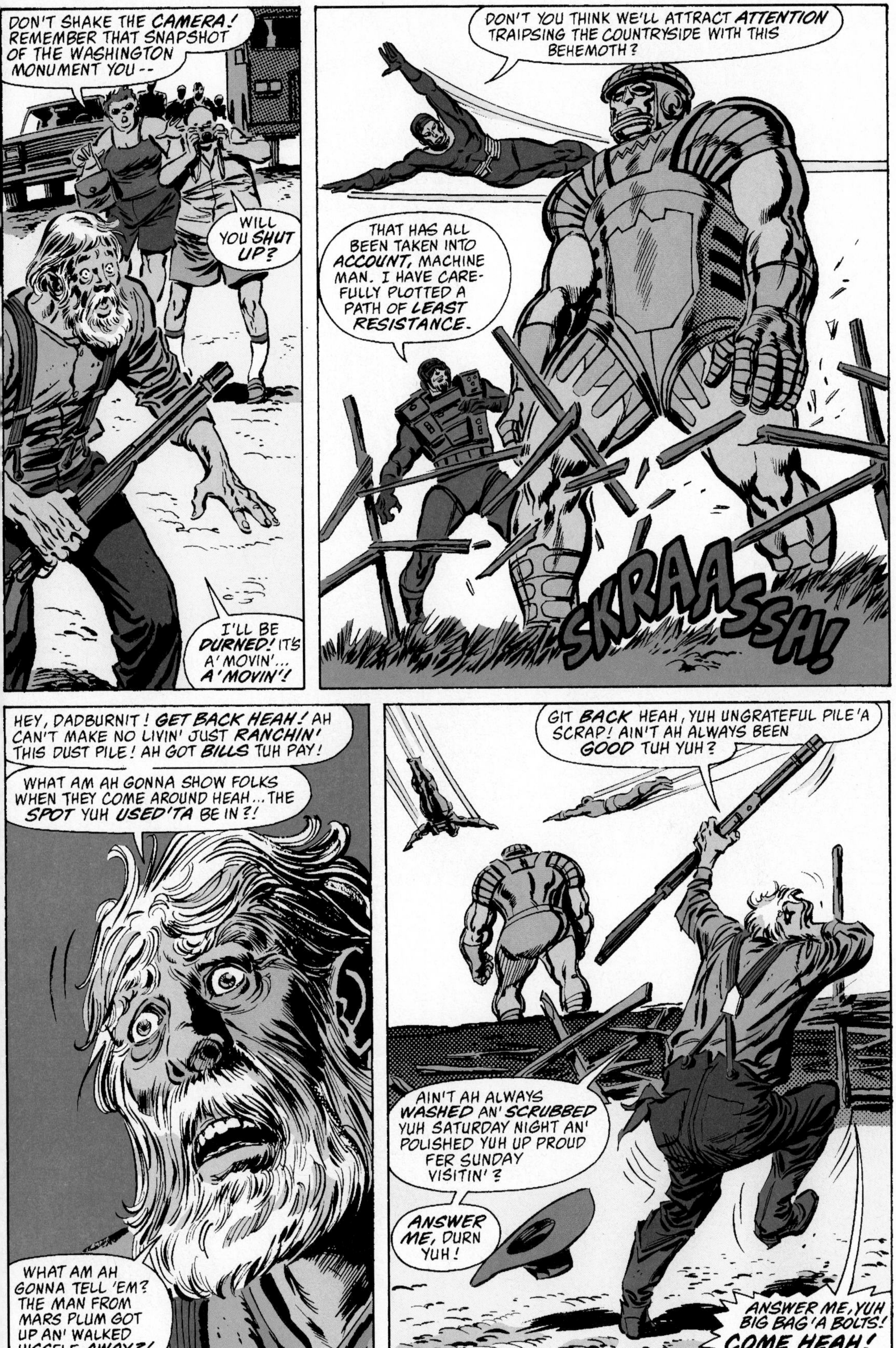

DON'T SHAKE THE CAMERA! REMEMBER THAT SNAPSHOT OF THE WASHINGTON MONUMENT YOU --
WILL YOU SHUT UP?
I'LL BE DURNED! IT'S A' MOVIN'... A' MOVIN'!
DON'T YOU THINK WE'LL ATTRACT ATTENTION TRAIPSING THE COUNTRYSIDE WITH THIS BEHEMOTH?
THAT HAS ALL BEEN TAKEN INTO ACCOUNT, MACHINE MAN. I HAVE CAREFULLY PLOTTED A PATH OF LEAST RESISTANCE.
SKRAASSH!
HEY, DADBURNIT! GET BACK HEAH! AH CAN'T MAKE NO LIVIN' JUST RANCHIN' THIS DUST PILE! AH GOT BILLS TUH PAY!
WHAT AM AH GONNA SHOW FOLKS WHEN THEY COME AROUND HEAH... THE SPOT YUH USED'TA BE IN?!
WHAT AM AH GONNA TELL 'EM? THE MAN FROM MARS PLUM GOT UP AN' WALKED HISSELF AWAY?!
GIT BACK HEAH, YUH UNGRATEFUL PILE 'A SCRAP! AIN'T AH ALWAYS BEEN GOOD TUH YUH?
AIN'T AH ALWAYS WASHED AN' SCRUBBED YUH SATURDAY NIGHT AN' POLISHED YUH UP PROUD FER SUNDAY VISITIN'?
ANSWER ME, DURN YUH!
ANSWER ME, YUH BIG BAG 'A BOLTS! COME HEAH!

LET'S LEAVE THE SORRY SCENE OF ONE MAN'S MISFORTUNE FOR A MORE UPBEAT LOCALE-- **HYDROBASE** TO BE EXACT, OFF THE EASTERN COAST OF THE UNITED STATES...

HERE, AT THE SPANKING-NEW ISLAND HEADQUARTERS OF THE WORLD'S MIGHTIEST HEROES, THE EMPLACEMENT OF **AVENGERS MANSION** COMMENCES...

EASILY NOW! LOWER THE DWELLING ON MY **SIGNAL!**

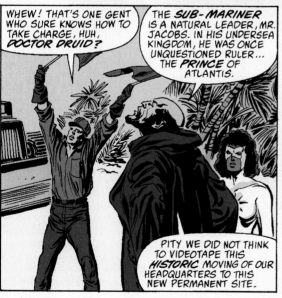

WHEW! THAT'S ONE GENT WHO SURE KNOWS HOW TO TAKE CHARGE, HUH, **DOCTOR DRUID?**

THE **SUB-MARINER** IS A NATURAL LEADER, MR. JACOBS. IN HIS UNDERSEA KINGDOM, HE WAS ONCE UNQUESTIONED RULER... THE **PRINCE** OF ATLANTIS.

PITY WE DID NOT THINK TO VIDEOTAPE THIS **HISTORIC** MOVING OF OUR HEADQUARTERS TO THIS NEW PERMANENT SITE.

AS **LEADER** OF THE AVENGERS, DOCTOR, YOU KNOW I'VE HAD A **GREAT** MANY THINGS ON MY MIND-- THE **LEAST** OF WHICH WAS FILMING THIS OCCASION.

PLEASE STOP **QUESTIONING** MY EVERY MOVE.

NO OFFENSE **MEANT,** CAPTAIN MARVEL.

ENTER ANOTHER AVENGER--
THE *BLACK KNIGHT*...

LOOK ALIVE, PEOPLE. I'VE GOT SOME *NEWS* THAT MAY PULL YOU AWAY FROM THE SIGHT OF OUR FLYING HACIENDA.

DANE, DOES IT CONCERN *CAPTAIN AMERICA?* HAS HE TURNED UP SOMEWHERE OR--

NO SUCH LUCK, LEADER LADY. CAP'S WHEREABOUTS ARE STILL A MYSTERY.*

*SEE CURRENT ISSUES OF *CAPTAIN AMERICA.*

BUT THIS *CLIPPING* SHOULD CLUE YOU IN. IT'S FROM A SMALL TEXAS *NEWSPAPER* THAT JUST CAME OUT. LUCKY FOR THE AVENGERS WE EMPLOY FOLKS TO SCOUR THE NATION'S NEWS-PAPERS FOR ITEMS OF INTEREST.

HERE, TAKE A LOOK.

THE *SUPER-ADAPTOID!* AFTER OUR RECENT RUN-IN WITH IT,* I WAS BEGINNING TO WONDER HOW SOON IT WOULD TURN UP AGAIN.

I RECOGNIZE THE LARGE ONE FROM FILES LENT US BY THE *FANTASTIC FOUR*-- THAT'S A *KREE SENTRY!* FIRST, WE BATTLE THE MAD THINKER'S RENEGADE *ANDROID*-- NOW THIS!

FLYING ROBOTS ESCAPE

*IN OUR LAST TWO ISSUES.

EVIDENTLY, THE ADAPTOID IS AFTER OTHER ROBOTS TO *JOIN* HIM. BUT TO WHAT *END*?

THE ONLY WAY WE'LL LEARN THAT IS IF WE *TRACK THEM DOWN*.

I'M NOT SO SURE WE CAN. THE ADAPTOID MUST BE *EXPECTING* THAT AND WILL PROBABLY LEAVE US A COLD TRAIL.

MAYBE IF WE DISCUSS IT FURTHER WE'LL HIT UPON A LEAD. THE KEY SEEMS TO BE ROBOTS. WHY IS HE ONLY INTERESTED IN *ROBOTS*?

LET US NOT JUMP TO A CONCLUSION, CAPTAIN MARVEL. NEED I REMIND YOU THE ADAPTOID'S *FIRST* VICTIM WAS A VERY *HUMAN* TELEPATH CALLED *MENTALLO*?

POINT TAKEN, DOCTOR DRUID.

I AM IN AGREEMENT WITH THE *KNIGHT*. TRACKING THEM DOWN IS OF THE UTMOST *URGENCY*.

YEP. AND YOU'RE THE *BEST* OF US TO GO. WITH YOUR POWER TO CONVERT INTO ANY WAVELENGTH ON THE ELECTROMAGNETIC SPECTRUM...

...TEXAS IS AN EYEBLINK AWAY, *RIGHT*?

IN YOUR ABSENCE, I SHALL SUPERVISE THE CONTINUING *LABORS* AT THE MANSION.

THAT'S MORE COMFORTING TO HEAR THAN YOU CAN *KNOW*, DOCTOR.

BUT WHILE I'M AWAY, I'M ORDERING YOU TO ACCESS *ALL* AVAILABLE DATA ABOUT *SUPER-ROBOTS* AND *ANDROIDS* FROM OUR COMPUTER FILES.

I'LL RETURN AS SOON AS I *SPOT* SOMETHING.

INSTANTLY, THE LIGHT FORM OF CAPTAIN MARVEL STREAKS ACROSS THE U.S. ...

SO FRUSTRATING! WE LET THE *ADAPTOID* SLIP THROUGH OUR FINGERS WEEKS AGO.

THAT OVERSIZED ANDROID OF THE THINKER'S HE GAINED CONTROL OF IN OHIO GAVE THE AVENGERS ALL WE COULD *HANDLE*. SO, THE ADAPTOID ESCAPED FROM US IN A TRUCK OF ALL THINGS ... A *TRUCK*.

HOW EMBARRASSING.

AT THAT MOMENT, IN THE GRAND CANYON OF ARIZONA...

MAYBE WE SHOULD HIJACK AN *AIRPLANE*, ADAPTOID. WE'RE BEING SLOWED TO A CRAWL BECAUSE THE THIRD MEMBER OF OUR TRIO CAN'T *FLY* AND HAS TO STOMP ACROSS THE MOUNTAINS.

WE'LL *NEVER* GET BACK TO NEW YORK CITY AT THIS RATE.

WE ARE NOT GOING *BACK* TO NEW YORK. AT LEAST -- *NOT YET*. WE HAVE *ONE MORE STOP* TO MAKE.

MY HOPES FOR YOUR REVIVAL HAVE RISEN AGAIN, MY *JOCASTA*. AND WITH THE WONDERS THE ADAPTOID CAN PER- FORM-- HOW CAN WE FAIL?

WOULDN'T MOST HUMANS FIND IT *STRANGE* THAT A MERE ROBOT CAN HOPE --OR *LOVE*?

ADAPTOID, ARE YOU FAMILIAR WITH HOW BAFFLING THE CONCEPT OF *ROBOTIC LIFE* IS TO MOST OF HUMANITY... YET, HOW *PERVASIVE* THE IDEA OF THE MACHINE IS IN ASPECTS OF MANY CULTURES? I'VE READ EXTENSIVELY--

IT'S STARTLING HOW HUMANS SEE THEMSELVES SO OFTEN IN *MACHINE-LIKE* TERMS.

IN 1662, THE PHILOSOPHER, *DESCARTES*, PUBLISHED *De HOMINE*, A THEORY OF MAN AND ANIMALS AS MACHINES. HE EVEN MADE A THEORETICAL MODEL OF A MECHANICAL MAN -- LIKE ME.

BY THE BEGINNING OF THE 20TH CENTURY, *EVERY* MAJOR MODEL FOR THE EXPLANATION OF HUMAN BEHAVIOR WAS MECHANICAL. *DARWIN* EVEN USED THE MACHINE MODEL FOR EVOLUTION.

NEWTON SAW THE UNIVERSE IN MECHANISTIC TERMS -- LIKE AN UNWIND- ING CLOCKWORK. THE HUMANS REFER TO THEIR MOST ADVANCED SOCIETIES AS THE MOST MECHANIZED. IT'S FASCINATING.

HAVE YOUR VAST READINGS ON THE SUBJECT LED YOU TO ANY *PRACTICAL* CONCLUSIONS?

PRACTICAL? I READ ONLY TO LEARN-- TO *DISCOVER* WHAT IT IS I AM. *KNOWLEDGE* IS ITS OWN REWARD.

THEN, IN TRUTH, YOUR TIME WAS ILL-SPENT, FOR YOUR KNOW- LEDGE HAS BROUGHT YOU *NOTHING*.

BELOW, THE HUGE SENTRY LURCHES FORWARD, UNWILLING TO ENGAGE ITS ROBOTIC BRETHREN IN DEBATE -- *FOR NOW*.

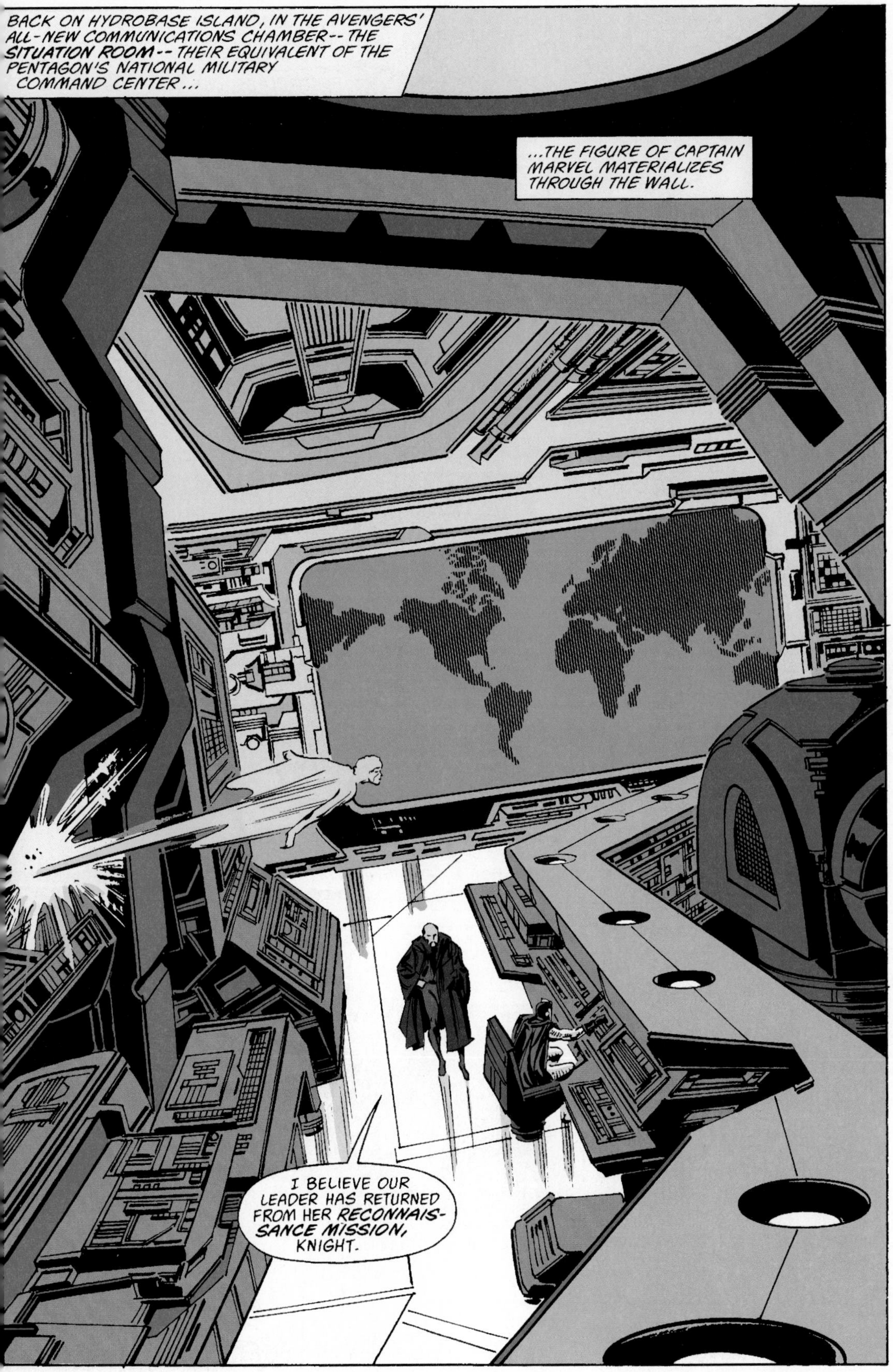
BACK ON HYDROBASE ISLAND, IN THE AVENGERS' ALL-NEW COMMUNICATIONS CHAMBER-- THE SITUATION ROOM-- THEIR EQUIVALENT OF THE PENTAGON'S NATIONAL MILITARY COMMAND CENTER...
...THE FIGURE OF CAPTAIN MARVEL MATERIALIZES THROUGH THE WALL.
I BELIEVE OUR LEADER HAS RETURNED FROM HER RECONNAISSANCE MISSION, KNIGHT.

I TRUST YOUR SCOUTING WENT WELL?

AFRAID NOT. THE TRAIL IS COLD-- AS I EXPECTED.

AND I COULDN'T TELL FOR CERTAIN WHAT THE ADAPTOID WOULD EVEN *LOOK* LIKE AT THIS POINT, ANYWAY.

NATURALLY... BECAUSE THE CONSTRUCT POSSESSES THE POWER TO ADAPT BOTH *ABILITY*-- AND *APPEARANCE*.

REGARDLESS, DID YOU ACCESS ALL THE INFORMATION I WANTED?

I'LL PUNCH IT UP RIGHT AWAY.

ARSENAL — STATUS: DESTROYED

MACHINESMITH — STATUS: UNKNOWN

QUASIMODO — STATUS: DEACTIVATED

SLEEPER — STATUS: DESTROYED

JOCASTA — STATUS: DEACTIVATED

SENTRY 451 — STATUS: DEACTIVATED

ULTRON — STATUS: DEACTIVATED

AWESOME ANDROID — STATUS: DEACTIVATED

DOOMSDAY MAN — STATUS: DEACTIVATED

CRYPTO-MAN — STATUS: DESTROYED

VERY THOROUGH JOB. BUT WAS IT NECESSARY TO RETRIEVE FILES ON THE *DESTROYED* ROBOTS, TOO?

IT'S NOT WISE TO DISCOUNT *ANY* POSSIBILITY TOO HASTILY.

THE MOST LIKELY CANDIDATES ARE *ULTRON, TESS-ONE, MACHINE MAN,* AND THE *SENTINELS.*

FINE. PRINT UP HARD COPIES OF IT ALL AND BRING IT TO THE BRIEFING ROOM. I'LL GO FETCH THE *SUB-MARINER* AND *SHE-HULK.*

OKAY.

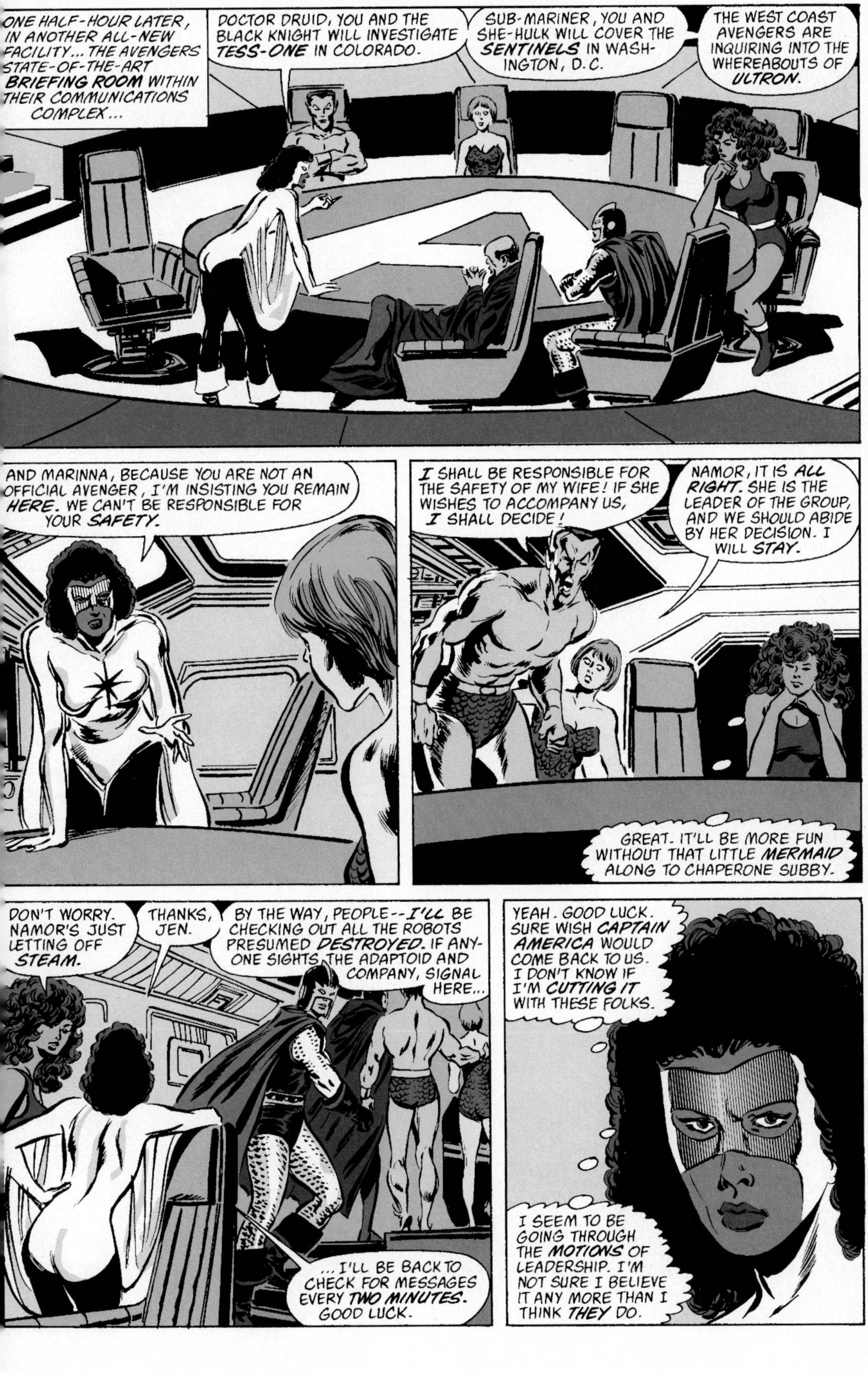
ONE HALF-HOUR LATER, IN ANOTHER ALL-NEW FACILITY... THE AVENGERS STATE-OF-THE-ART BRIEFING ROOM WITHIN THEIR COMMUNICATIONS COMPLEX...
DOCTOR DRUID, YOU AND THE BLACK KNIGHT WILL INVESTIGATE TESS-ONE IN COLORADO.
SUB-MARINER, YOU AND SHE-HULK WILL COVER THE SENTINELS IN WASHINGTON, D.C.
THE WEST COAST AVENGERS ARE INQUIRING INTO THE WHEREABOUTS OF ULTRON.
AND MARINNA, BECAUSE YOU ARE NOT AN OFFICIAL AVENGER, I'M INSISTING YOU REMAIN HERE. WE CAN'T BE RESPONSIBLE FOR YOUR SAFETY.
I SHALL BE RESPONSIBLE FOR THE SAFETY OF MY WIFE! IF SHE WISHES TO ACCOMPANY US, I SHALL DECIDE!
NAMOR, IT IS ALL RIGHT. SHE IS THE LEADER OF THE GROUP, AND WE SHOULD ABIDE BY HER DECISION. I WILL STAY.
GREAT. IT'LL BE MORE FUN WITHOUT THAT LITTLE MERMAID ALONG TO CHAPERONE SUBBY.
DON'T WORRY. NAMOR'S JUST LETTING OFF STEAM.
THANKS, JEN.
BY THE WAY, PEOPLE--I'LL BE CHECKING OUT ALL THE ROBOTS PRESUMED DESTROYED. IF ANYONE SIGHTS THE ADAPTOID AND COMPANY, SIGNAL HERE...
...I'LL BE BACK TO CHECK FOR MESSAGES EVERY TWO MINUTES. GOOD LUCK.
YEAH. GOOD LUCK. SURE WISH CAPTAIN AMERICA WOULD COME BACK TO US. I DON'T KNOW IF I'M CUTTING IT WITH THESE FOLKS.
I SEEM TO BE GOING THROUGH THE MOTIONS OF LEADERSHIP. I'M NOT SURE I BELIEVE IT ANY MORE THAN I THINK THEY DO.

A SHORT TIME LATER, A LONE AVENGERS *QUINJET* LANDS AT A MIDWESTERN AIR FORCE BASE, ESCORTED BY MILITARY HELICOPTERS...

I DON'T THINK THIS LITTLE ESCORT IS FOR OUR BENEFIT, DOCTOR.

YEP. EVER SINCE THE AVENGERS LOST THEIR *SECURITY CLEARANCE,** GETTING THE MILITARY TO COOPERATE WITH US HAS BEEN *TOUGH.*

ANYWAY, FAKING ENGINE TROUBLE GOT US DOWN.

*AFTER AVENGERS #25

NOW IT'S UP TO YOUR *HOCUS POCUS* TO SEE US THROUGH THIS MESS.

I SHALL SEE TO IT.

BRINGING TO BEAR HIS VAST *MENTAL POWERS,* THE MYSTERIOUS DOCTOR DRUID MESMERIZES THOSE WITHIN EARSHOT.

YOU WILL LOWER YOUR WEAPONS AND TAKE US TO THE ROBOT, *TESS-ONE.*

THAT IS AN ORDER.

YESSIR. RIGHT THIS WAY, SIR.

I DON'T BELIEVE THIS.

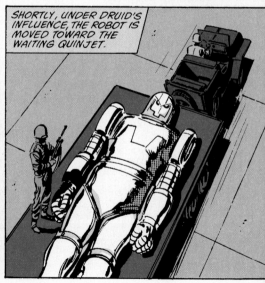

SHORTLY, UNDER DRUID'S INFLUENCE, THE ROBOT IS MOVED TOWARD THE WAITING QUINJET.

A FEW SECONDS AND IT'LL BE LOADED INTO THE *CARGO BAY*.

IF WE PULL THIS OFF UNDER THEIR NOSES, *SOMEBODY'S* HEAD'LL ROLL HERE TOMORROW.

YES, SERGEANT, THE AVENGERS ARE *MORE* THAN HAPPY TO TAKE TESS-ONE OFF YOUR HANDS. THANK YOU FOR THE COOPERATION.

THANK *YOU*, SIR.

DOCTOR, THAT WAS ONE FANCY SLEIGHT-OF-HAND TRICK DOWN THERE. ARE YOU SURE WE WON'T BE SHOT AT?

HARDLY.

YOU SEE, THE MILITARY MIND IS QUITE USED TO *RECEIVING ORDERS*, THEREFORE, THEY ARE SOMETIMES MORE *SUSCEPTIBLE* TO COMMANDS THAN THE UNDISCIPLINED MIND.

YOU DON'T SAY.

I WAS JUST THINKIN', CAPTAIN MARVEL DIDN'T TELL US TO BRING TESSY THERE BACK TO BASE.

HMMPH, SHE LACKED FORESIGHT IN THIS MATTER. WHAT WERE WE TO DO-- *STAY* ON THE AIR FORCE BASE UNTIL THE *SUPER-ADAPTOID* ATTACKED?

SHE WILL SEE THAT WE DID RIGHT.

SUDDENLY--!

THE CONTROLS --WON'T RESPOND! SHIP-- LOSING ALTITUDE!

UGH-- MANAGED TO RIGHT HER-- BUT WE'RE STILL *DROPPING!*

HEADING TOWARD THOSE MOUNTAINS *TOO FAST!* I'LL TRY TO SET HER DOWN ON SOME *LEVEL AREA!*

GIVE CAPTAIN MARVEL THE SIGNAL! TELL HER WE MAY HAVE BEEN *ATTACKED* BY THE *ADAPTOID!*

UHH-- PERHAPS THE SHIP HAS MALFUNCTIONED NATURALLY. WE MUSTN'T TURN IN A *FALSE REPORT.* WE NEED EVIDENCE.

I THINK WE'LL *MAKE* IT! THEN I CAN CHECK FOR DAMAGES.

ANYTHING ON THE RADAR, DOCTOR?

OUR INSTRUMENTS REGISTER *THREE BLIPS* IN THE IMMEDIATE VICINITY.

PERHAPS WE--

CRRUUNNCH!

LOOKS LIKE WE'VE GOT *MORE* THAN ENGINE TROUBLE! *LET'S GO!*

KNOW THIS SWORD OF MINE CAN CUT THROUGH ANY EARTHLY SUBSTANCE--

--BUT AGAINST *ALIEN STUFF*-- WHO KNOWS?

SHEEENNG!

BINGO! NOW WE *KNOW!*

STOMF!

WHUGH!

NUTS! IT'S SEVERED-- AND *STILL* GOT ME!

THIS IS GOING TO BE A BIT MORE *DELICATE!* THE ANGLE'S AWKWARD!

AND IF MY SWORD DRAWS *BLOOD*-- EVEN *MY OWN*-- THE *CURSE* OF THE EBONY BLADE WILL *OVER-WHELM* ME!

NEARBY...

MY POWER OF *LEVITATION* CANNOT MATCH THE MOMENTUM-GENERATING *JET PACK* WORN BY THE *ADAPTOID!*

THUS, FLIGHT IS RENDERED *USELESS* AS AN OPTION.

I MUST EMPLOY MY ILLUSION-CASTING POWER AND HOPE IT *WORKS* AGAINST SUCH AN UNKNOWN TYPE OF MIND!

67

AS IF FROM THIN AIR, THE FLYING FORMS OF THE SUB-MARINER AND MIGHTY THOR APPEAR... AGGRESSIVE, PURPOSEFUL--

--UTTERLY FUTILE.

HAH! SUCH PARLOR TRICKS, DOCTOR, AN ALL-ENCOMPASSING INTELLECT SUCH AS MINE--

--CANNOT POSSIBLY BE FOOLED BY THESE PHANTASMS! I SEE THROUGH THEM--BEYOND THEM--AS NO OTHER BRAIN ON EARTH COULD!

THE PLOY FAILED! I MUST CONTACT CAPTAIN MARVEL MENTALLY... THERE IS NO CHOICE!

BUT TO ACCOMPLISH THAT, I NEED SEVERAL MOMENTS OF CONCENTRATION I AM NOT LIKELY TO RECEIVE!

DID IT-- AND NOT A DROPLET OF BLOOD SPILLED! NOW TO TAKE THE SENTRY OUT COMPLETELY!

WELL, I'D GIVE YOU A BIG HAND FOR THAT PERFORMANCE-- BUT IT SEEMS AS IF YOU'VE GOTTEN ONE ALREADY!

WHO--?!

MACHINE MAN! SO THE ADAPTOID GOT TO YOU, TOO! TOO BAD!

OH, IT'S NOTHING TO LOSE YOUR HEAD OVER! BUT THEN--WHY NOT?

SSWWSSS

MINE COMES OFF PRETTY EASILY! LET ME SEE WHAT WE CAN DO ABOUT DISLODGING YOURS!

SWOK!

WON'T COME OFF FROM THE *BACK*-- LET'S TRY THE *FRONT!*

BAKT

THEN, WITHOUT WARNING ...

BA WHOOM!

KKKRRRRKKK

RESISTANCE IS *USELESS!* THE ROBOTIC STRENGTH OF MACHINE MAN IS *MINE!*

AND, EVEN AS WE SPEAK, YOUR *OWN* FORMIDABLE *MENTAL ABILITIES* ARE BEING TAKEN BY ME ... ADDED TO THOSE OF *MENTALLO!*

ONLY CHANCE-- CEASE THE *STRUGGLE*... GO LIMP-- CONCENTRATE ON SENDING A CEREBRAL *DISTRESS* SIGNAL. MUST CONCENTRATE-- IGNORE *PAIN!*

MOMENTS LATER, A PULSE OF PUREST MENTAL MIGHT IS SENT FROM THE THROBBING CRANIUM OF DOCTOR DRUID...

...SENT ON A TRANSCONTINENTAL JOURNEY TO *HYDROBASE* THAT WILL TAKE MERE INSTANTS.

IN A SMALL CAVE SOMEWHERE IN NORTHERN FLORIDA, THE LEADER OF THE AVENGERS PERFORMS HER OWN TASK TO THWART THE ADAPTOID'S PLANS...

THE DOOMSDAY MAN WAS ONE OF THE ROBOTS ON THE COMPUTER LIST. LUCKILY, HE'S BEEN INERT HERE-- DEACTIVATED FOR SEVERAL YEARS*--

...SO A SIMPLE LASER BLAST WILL MELT HIM INTO AN UNSALVAGABLE CONDITION.

PPWWWSSSSSS

*EVER SINCE MS. MARVEL #

HER TASK COMPLETED, CAPTAIN MARVEL UNDERGOES THE INCREDIBLE BODILY TRANS-FORMATION INTO A BEING OF PUREST LIGHT-- AND STREAKS AWAY FROM THE SMOKING SLAG HEAP...

...A MERE MICRO-SECOND BEFORE DRUID'S MENTALLY-LAUNCHED CRY FOR HELP REACHES THE SPOT!

BUT THEN, EERILY, AS IF POSSESSING A LIFE OF ITS OWN, THE CEREBRAL SIG-NAL RISES TO PURSUE THE LIGHT-FORM SO RECENTLY DEPARTED.

AND, IN THE AVENGERS SITUATION ROOM ...

MUST CHECK THE MONITORS AND SEE IF ANYONE'S SENT IN A DISTRESS!

SPASH!

NO. SEEMS AS IF EVERYONE HAS APPARENTLY BEEN -- WHAT--? A VOICE-- VERY FAINT... CAN'T BE, NO ONE'S HERE.

I MUST BE GETTING JUMPY IN MY OLD AGE.

IT'S LUCKY THE GOOD DOCTOR DRUID ISN'T HERE OR HE'D PROBABLY TRY TO HAVE ME COMMITTED FOR HEARING THINGS.

AND WITH THAT, SHE IS GONE.

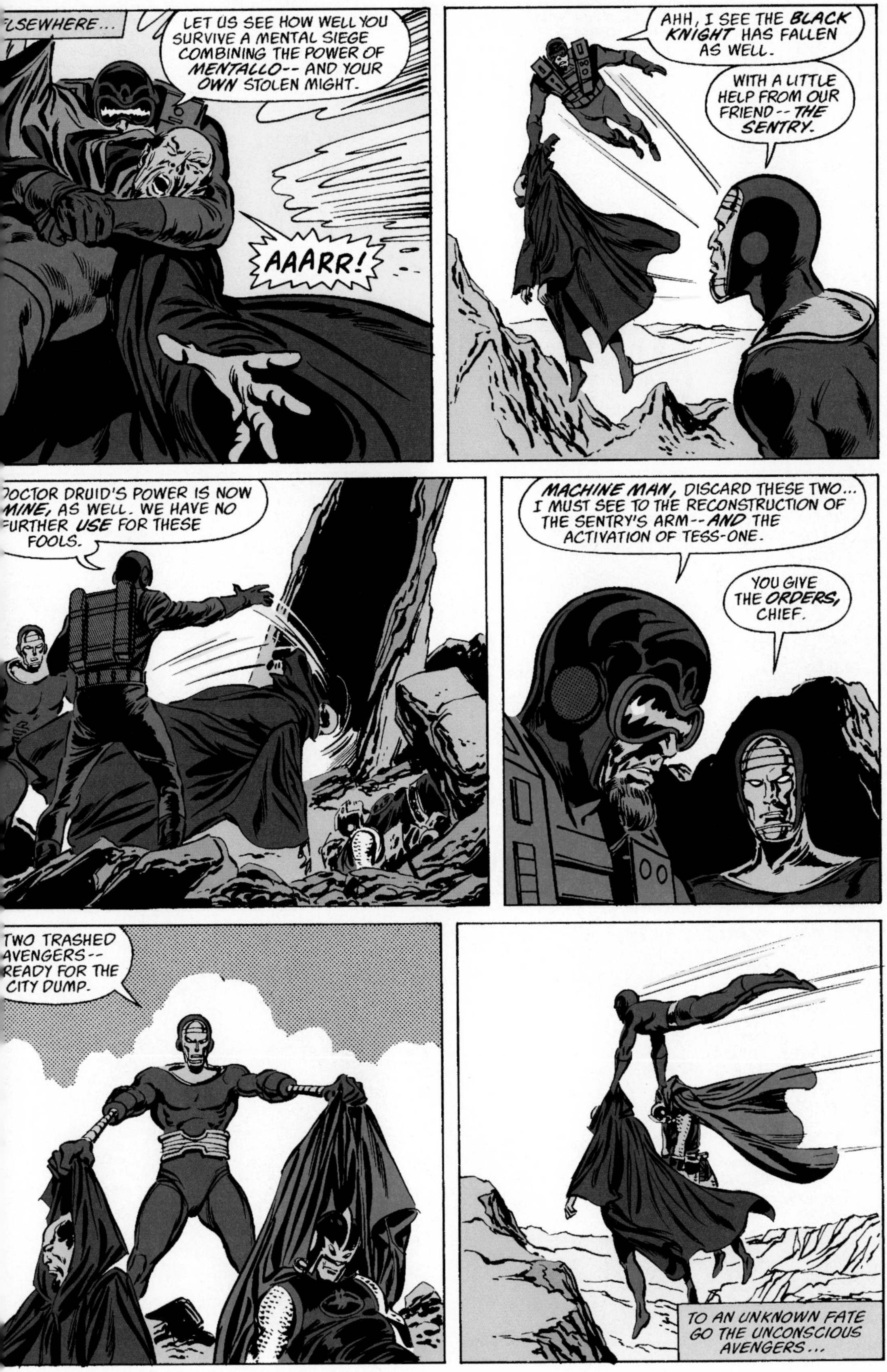

LSEWHERE...
LET US SEE HOW WELL YOU SURVIVE A MENTAL SIEGE COMBINING THE POWER OF MENTALLO-- AND YOUR OWN STOLEN MIGHT.
AAARR!
AHH, I SEE THE BLACK KNIGHT HAS FALLEN AS WELL.
WITH A LITTLE HELP FROM OUR FRIEND-- THE SENTRY.
OCTOR DRUID'S POWER IS NOW MINE, AS WELL. WE HAVE NO FURTHER USE FOR THESE FOOLS.
MACHINE MAN, DISCARD THESE TWO... I MUST SEE TO THE RECONSTRUCTION OF THE SENTRY'S ARM-- AND THE ACTIVATION OF TESS-ONE.
YOU GIVE THE ORDERS, CHIEF.
TWO TRASHED AVENGERS-- READY FOR THE CITY DUMP.
TO AN UNKNOWN FATE GO THE UNCONSCIOUS AVENGERS...

...WHILE, SOME TIME LATER, THEIR COMRADES MEET IN THE SITUATION ROOM ON HYDROBASE...

ACCORDING TO THE FEDS, ALL OF THE *SENTINELS* ARE ACCOUNTED FOR, AND THEY'VE PROMISED TO ALERT US IF ANYONE *RAIDS* THEIR STORAGE AREA.

IT'S ABOUT *TIME* WE GOT SOME COOPERATION FROM THE GOVERNMENT. THEY MUST REALIZE THE *GRAVITY* OF THE PROBLEM.

STILL NO WORD FROM THE DYNAMIC *DUO?*

NO. DRUID AND THE KNIGHT SHOULD HAVE REPORTED THEIR *STATUS* BY NOW.

I'LL MAKE A QUICK RECONNAISSANCE THERE AND BE BACK *SHORTLY.*

AND AS A WORRIED CAPTAIN MARVEL DEPARTS, A SLEEK QUINJET MAKES A SOFT LANDING NEAR THE MANSION...

HOW *SIMPLE* IT WAS TO DISCERN THE WORKINGS OF THIS CRAFT AND SLIP *EASILY* THROUGH THE ISLAND'S MANY DEFENSES BY USE OF THE *AUTO-TELEMETRY* SYSTEMS!

BUT THE TIME FOR STEALTH IS *PAST.* WE ARE HERE TO *CONQUER,* NOT SKULK! THIS ISLAND IS *OURS!*

I, THE ADAPTOID, CLAIM IT IN THE NAME OF *HEAVY METAL!*

NEXT: WHAT IS...
the CUBE ROOT?

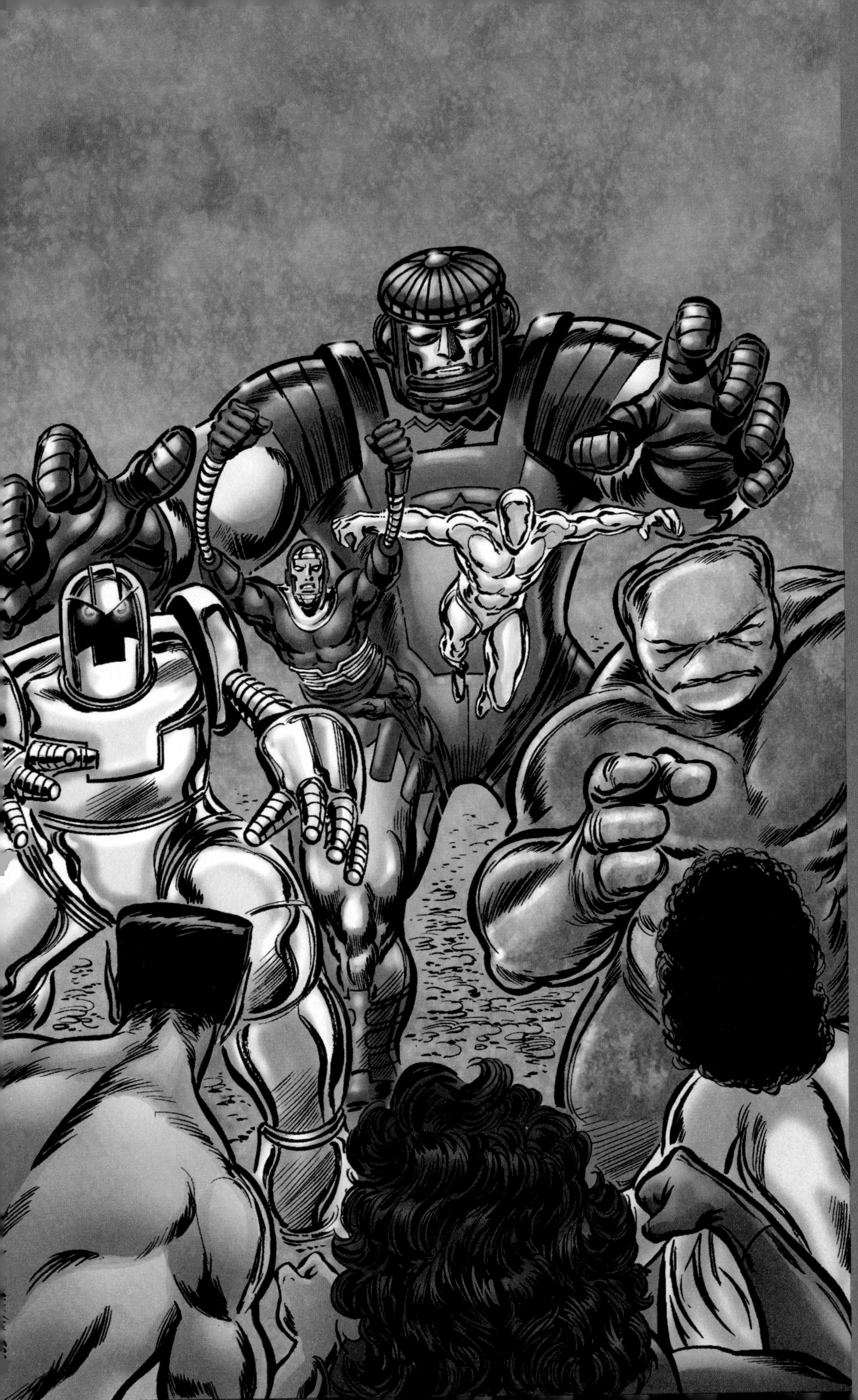

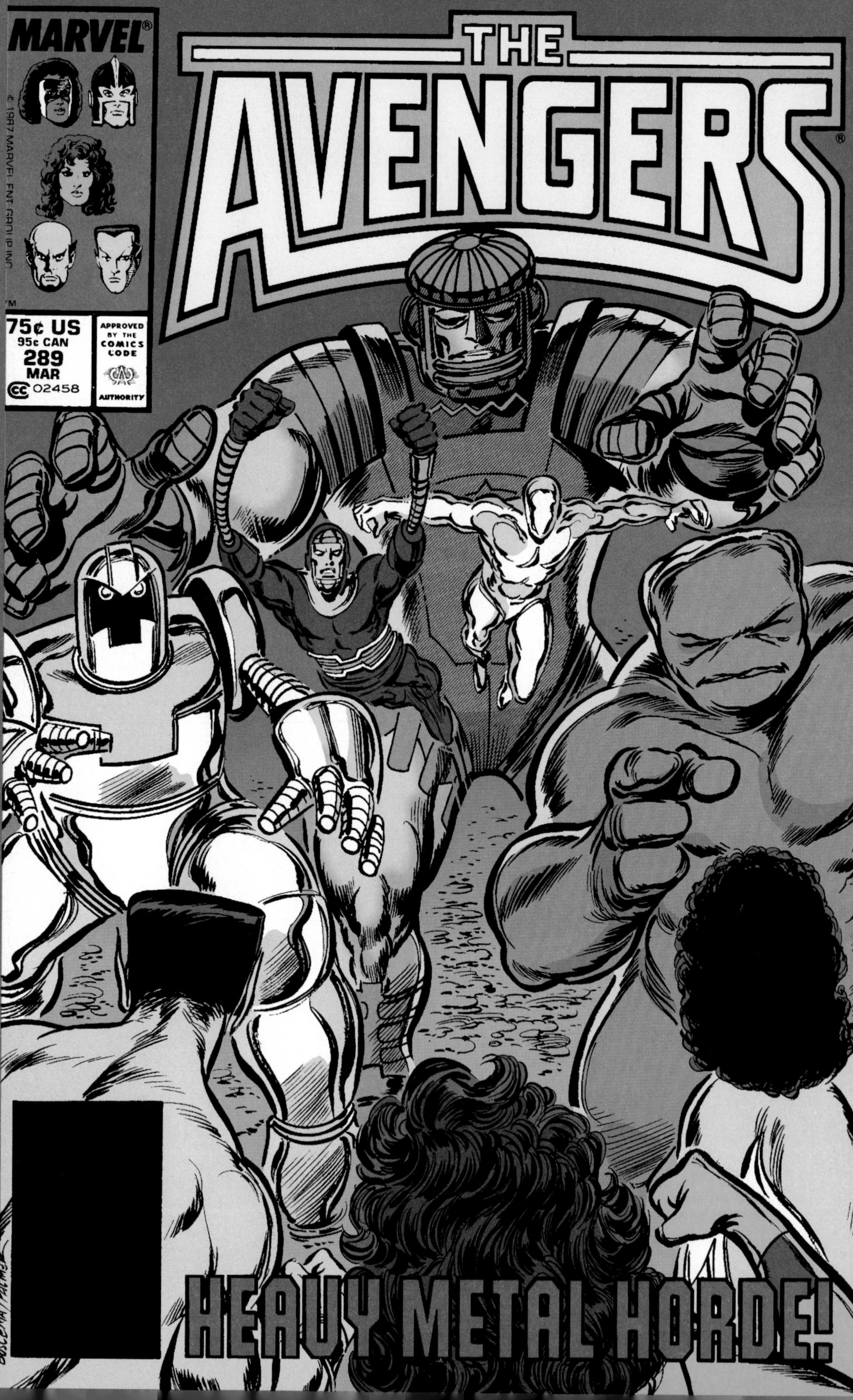

MARVEL
© 1987 MARVEL ENT GROUP INC
THE AVENGERS
75¢ US
95¢ CAN
289
MAR
CC 02458
APPROVED BY THE COMICS CODE AUTHORITY
HEAVY METAL HORDE!

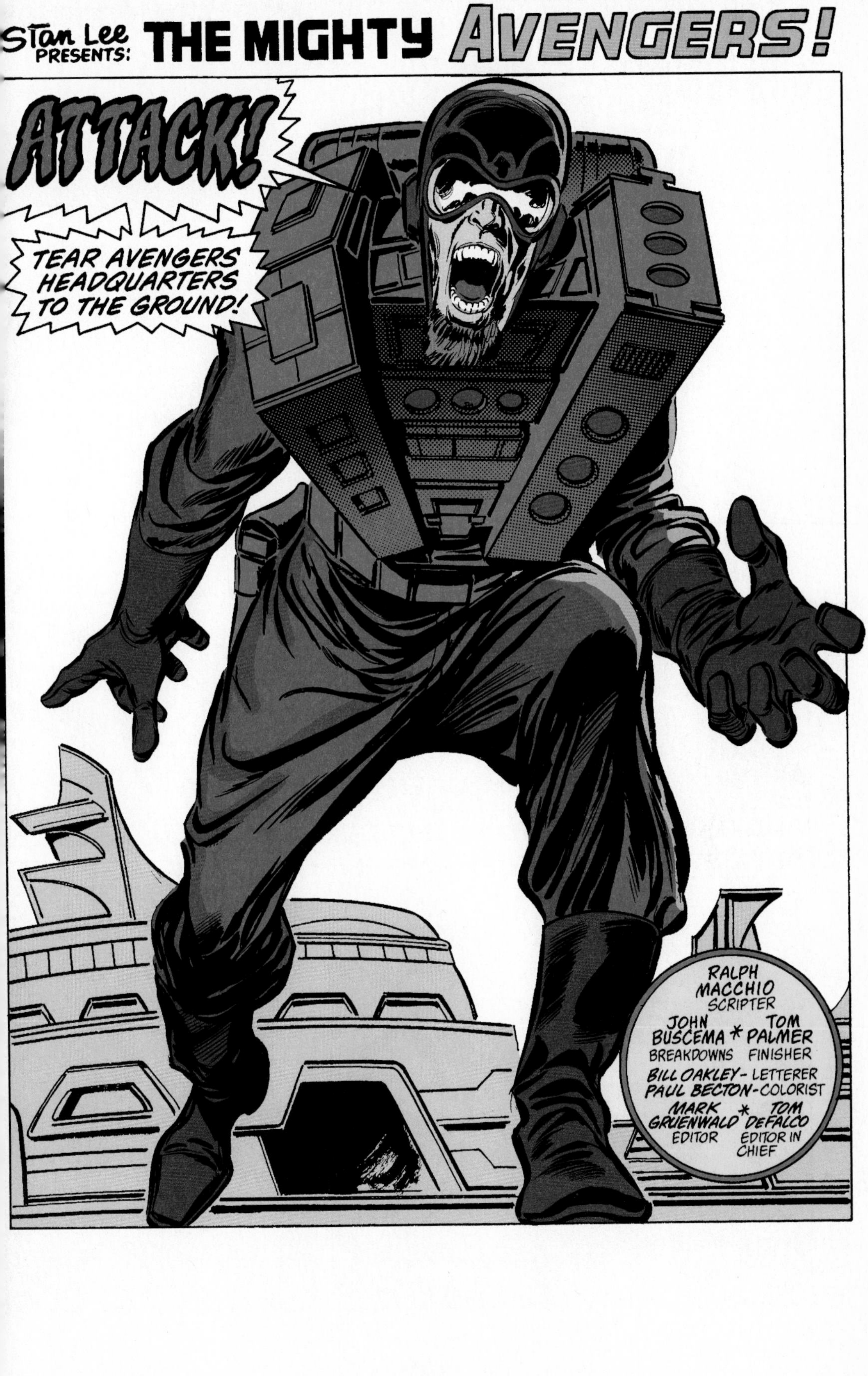
Stan Lee PRESENTS: THE MIGHTY AVENGERS!
ATTACK!
TEAR AVENGERS HEADQUARTERS TO THE GROUND!
RALPH MACCHIO SCRIPTER
JOHN BUSCEMA * TOM PALMER
BREAKDOWNS FINISHER
BILL OAKLEY - LETTERER
PAUL BECTON - COLORIST
MARK GRUENWALD * TOM DEFALCO
EDITOR EDITOR IN CHIEF

THE CUBE ROOT!

HYDROBASE, THE SLEEK NEW ISLAND HEADQUARTERS OF THE **AVENGERS,** OFF THE EASTERN COAST OF THE UNITED STATES, IS HOST TO A SUDDEN, ROBOTIC ASSAULT.

A **QUARTET** OF THE MOST DANGEROUS ROBOTS EVER CREATED HEADS TOWARD THE RECENTLY EMPLACED AVENGERS MANSION... HAVING JUST LANDED AT THE NEARBY AIRFIELD VIA A STOLEN **AVENGERS QUINJET.**

SENTRY 459: AN ALIEN CONSTRUCT, ONE OF MANY OF ITS TYPE, BUILT TO GUARD OUTPOSTS OF THE KREE RACE. LEFT ON EARTH COUNTLESS CENTURIES AGO, IT HAS BEEN RE-AWAKENED TO SERVE ANOTHER MASTER.

WRRUUNNCH!

MACHINE MAN: THE LONE SURVIVOR OF A FAILED GOVERNMENT PROJECT WHOSE GOAL WAS TO CREATE A SERIES OF MC WEAPONS UNITS. THE INDEPENDENT ROB HAS JOINED HEAVY METAL FOR HIS O PURPOSES.

GANGWAY, LADIES AND GENTLEMEN OF THIS SUN-SOAKED ISLE!

HERE COMES HEAVY METAL!

THE HEAVIES INCLUDE...

ESS-ONE*: A ROBOT DESIGNED AND BUILT DURING WORLD WAR II BY THE UNITED STATES TO INSURE THAT SUPER-SOLDIERS SUCH AS CAPTAIN AMERICA COULD NEVER TURN ON THE U.S. WHEN THE WAR ENDED. THE PROJECT WAS SCRAPPED WITH ONLY ONE BEING BUILT.

TOTAL EXTERMINATION OF SUPER-SOLDIERS.

THE LEADER OF HEAVY METAL-- THE SUPER-ADAPTOID.

HE IS THE PRODUCT OF A RENEGADE GROUP OF SCIENTISTS CALLED THE ADVANCED IDEA MECHANICS. THEY CREATED AN ENTITY ABLE TO ABSORB THE ABILITIES AND PHYSICAL APPEARANCE OF ANY OTHER BEING IT CHOOSES. HE CURRENTLY POSSESSES THE ATTRIBUTES OF THE FIXER AND MENTALLO!

WITHIN THE COMMUNICATIONS COMPLEX OF THE AVENGERS' NEW HEADQUARTERS, THE *SUB-MARINER, MARRINA,* AND THE *SHE-HULK* HEAR THE ALERT SOUNDED.

SHE-HULK--THOSE *ALARMS!* WHAT IS THE PROBLEM?

I'M GONNA SWITCH ON THE SCANNERS, NAMOR, AND SEE WHAT'S WHAT.

VEEP VEEP VEEP

OH, BOY! IT'S THE AIRFIELD! LOOKS LIKE IT WASN'T THE *BLACK KNIGHT* AND *DOC DRUID* RETURNING ON THAT QUINJET.

IT'S THE KREE *SENTRY* AND *TESS-ONE!*

SEEMS LIKE THE ROBOT-GUYS WE WERE LOOKING FOR JUST *TURNED THE TABLES* ON US.

REMIND ME TO TELL OUR *FEARLESS LEADER* CAPTAIN MARVEL TO MAKE LANDING CLEAR-ANCES ON THE ISLAND MORE *COMPLEX* SO WE DON'T GET *FOOLED* AGAIN!

MARRINA, YOU MUST REMAIN *HERE.*

MY HUSBAND--*NO!* HYDROBASE IS MY *HOME* NOW. AND ALTHOUGH I AM NOT A FULL AVENGER...

...WHEN MY HOME IS THREATENED-- I FIGHT!

THIS IS INDEED A WOMAN OF *UNCOMMON VALOR!* A WOMAN NAMOR THE FIRST IS PROUD TO CALL HIS *MATE!*

HURRY! WE MUSTN'T LET THE SHE-HULK GET TOO FAR AHEAD OR SHE COULD BE SERIOUSLY *HURT!*

YOU KNOW HOW RECKLESS SHE IS.

78

NEARBY, THE MAMMOTH INTERGALACTIC SENTRY DESTROYS MANY OF THE ISLAND'S OLDER STRUCTURES AS IT HEADS INEXORABLY TOWARD THE *MANSION* ITSELF...

WWROOOMM!

THANKS FOR THE FREE DEMOLITION WORK THERE, SENTRY OLD BUDDY...BUT THIS IS *STRICTLY* A UNION SHOP!

AND I'M *SHOP STEWARD!*

WHAKT!

JENNIFER, GAL-- THIS COULD BE THE FIGHT OF YOUR *LIFE!*

THAT WAS MY BEST *ROUNDHOUSE LEFT* AND ALL IT DID WAS GET HIS *ATTENTION!*

THEN, MOVING WITH A SPEED THAT BELIES ITS BULK...

WHUMK

...THE SMASHED SHE-HULK IS SENT HURTLING THROUGH ANY AND ALL OBSTACLES...

SKRAKT

SKRAKT

DUMB MOVE! WHY DIDN'T I JUST PUT AN X ON MY CHIN AND STICK IT OUT?

NOW I'M STUCK IN THIS DEBRIS AND STUMBO'S ALMOST ON TOP OF ME! CAN'T WORK FREE IN TIME!

YOWP!

KEEP YOUR MITTS TO YOURSELF, BOZO!

SWAK!

K-ROOOMM!

OHHNNNG!

THE SILENT SENTRY TURNS AND STALKS OFF, LEAVING THE BEATEN JENNIFER WALTERS IN THE RUBBLE...

THUS FAR, THE AVENGERS HAVE BEEN OUTMANEUVERED AT EACH TURN! UNTIL A SHORT TIME AGO, I WAS KEPT IN *STASIS* IN THEIR NEW YORK HEADQUARTERS!

BUT I REVIVED AND ESCAPED, AND HAVE SINCE GATHERED OTHERS OF MY ILK TO AID ME IN A SCHEME *FAR* BEYOND ANYTHING MY A.I.M. CREATORS COULD HAVE *CONCEIVED.*

AND HERE IN THE AVENGERS STORAGE WAREHOUSE I SHALL *FURTHER* MY PLANS.

AHH, THE MAD THINKER'S *AWESOME ANDROID!* IT WAS UNDER MY CONTROL UNTIL DAYS AGO WHEN THE AVENGERS DEFEATED IT AND BROUGHT IT HERE.*

*ISSUE #286.

NOW, USING THE MECHANICAL ABILITIES I'VE ABSORBED FROM THE CRIMINAL GENIUS CALLED THE *FIXER* -- I SHALL ADJUST ITS PROGRAMMING AND THE ANDROID SHALL SERVE ME *AGAIN.*

*286 AGAIN.

ARISE, MIGHTY ONE -- ARISE AND DO THE BIDDING OF YOUR *MASTER!* ARISE AND FOLLOW YOUR DESTRUCTIVE PROGRAMMING!

B A K. KROOM!

WHAT A REMARKABLE CONSTRUCT. IT WOULD HAVE BEEN INTERESTING TO HAVE TAKEN INTO MYSELF THE INTELLECT OF ITS CREATOR -- THE *MAD THINKER.* SUCH A MIND...

...BUT I DIGRESS. WHILE THE AVENGERS ARE THUS OCCUPIED -- I SHALL SEE TO MY *FINAL GOAL.*

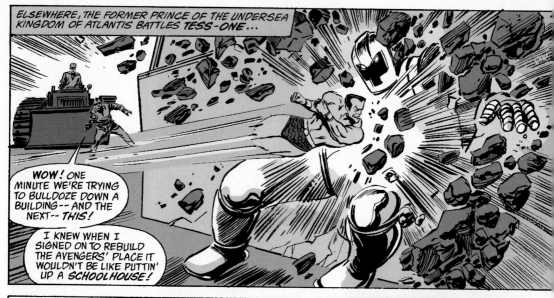

ELSEWHERE, THE FORMER PRINCE OF THE UNDERSEA KINGDOM OF ATLANTIS BATTLES TESS-ONE...

WOW! ONE MINUTE WE'RE TRYING TO BULLDOZE DOWN A BUILDING -- AND THE NEXT -- *THIS!*

I KNEW WHEN I SIGNED ON TO REBUILD THE AVENGERS' PLACE IT WOULDN'T BE LIKE PUTTIN' UP A *SCHOOLHOUSE!*

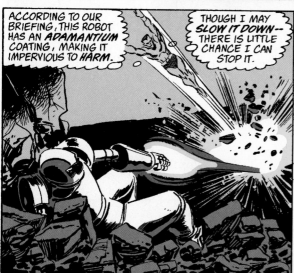

ACCORDING TO OUR BRIEFING, THIS ROBOT HAS AN *ADAMANTIUM* COATING, MAKING IT IMPERVIOUS TO *HARM.*

THOUGH I MAY *SLOW IT DOWN* -- THERE IS LITTLE CHANCE I CAN STOP IT.

PERHAPS THE USE OF MY OWN SEA-BORN STRENGTH WILL SHOW NAMOR I AM MORE THAN MERELY SOMETHING TO BE *PROTECTED* IN A FIGHT.

KKRRAAAKK!

ZZLTTT

ZZTTT

I'VE *FAILED* -- AND NOW IT'S FIRING *FORCE BEAMS* AT ME!

PERHAPS THERE IS A *CUT-OFF SWITCH* IN THE CREATURE'S HEAD... OR ITS CIRCUITRY MAY BE SOMEHOW *INTERFERED WITH*--

--ALTHOUGH THE MONSTER'S *HIDE* IS BEYOND DAMAGE!

WHOOOM

WHAT?! THE THINKER'S ANDROID --ALIVE *AGAIN*? *ANOTHER* TO CONTEND WITH!

LET'S GET *OUTTA* HERE!

I SHOULD'A GONE INTO *BRAIN SURGERY* INSTEAD!

MARRINA-- TRY TO HEAD TESS-ONE TOWARD THE *SHORE!* FOR THE MOMENT, I MUST DEAL WITH THE THINKER'S NEWLY AWAKENED *ANDROID!*

I SHALL DO *ALL* THAT IS NECESSARY, MY HUSBAND.

BUT AS MARRINA TURNS GAMELY TOWARD HER ENEMY--

ZZPPTT!

OHHH!

83

THIS IS ALL GETTING BEYOND *ANYONE'S* CONTROL!

WHEN THE ADAPTOID APPROACHED ME ABOUT JOINING HIM, HE PROMISED THAT FOR MY COOPERATION, HE WOULD REVIVE MY LOST LOVE... *JOCASTA.*

I WAS WILLING TO PLAY ALONG JUST TO SEE WHAT KIND OF NO-GOOD NON-SENSE HE WAS UP TO.

BUT HE'S BEEN SO *SECRETIVE*, I HAVEN'T BEEN ABLE TO LEARN WHAT THIS IS ALL TRULY ABOUT. PERHAPS HE REALLY DOESN'T *TRUST* ME.

BUT THE TIME HAS COME TO PUT A *STOP* TO ALL THE DESTRUCTION WITH ITS POTENTIAL LOSS OF HUMAN LIFE HERE.

SO, EVEN IF IT MEANS THAT I *NEVER* WILL SEE THE BEAUTIFUL JOCASTA AGAIN...

...THE DESTRUC-TION ENDS *NOW!*

NEARBY, *DR. WALT NEWELL*, THE ISLAND'S RESIDENT OCEANOGRAPHER AND PROPERTY ADMINISTRATOR, PREPARES FOR THE STRUGGLE...

I'M THE GUY WHO USED TO *RUN* THIS PLACE BEFORE THE AVENGERS ASKED PERMISSION TO MAKE IT INTO THEIR NEW HEADQUARTERS!

AND I'M TOO *FOND* OF MY LITTLE HYDROBASE TO SEE IT GO DOWN THE TUBES THIS WAY!

SO, THIS LOOKS LIKE A JOB--

--FOR *STINGRAY!*

ALWAYS LIKED THE SOUND OF THAT.

FUNNY. I ORIGINALLY DE-SIGNED THIS BATTLESUIT WHEN A FEDERAL AGENT WANTED ME TO TRACK DOWN *PRINCE NAMOR* AND BRING HIM IN FOR QUESTIONING.

NOW, WE'RE FIGHTING ON THE *SAME SIDE!* BUT THAT'S OKAY WITH ME. I'VE A LOT OF RESPECT FOR THAT GENTLEMAN.

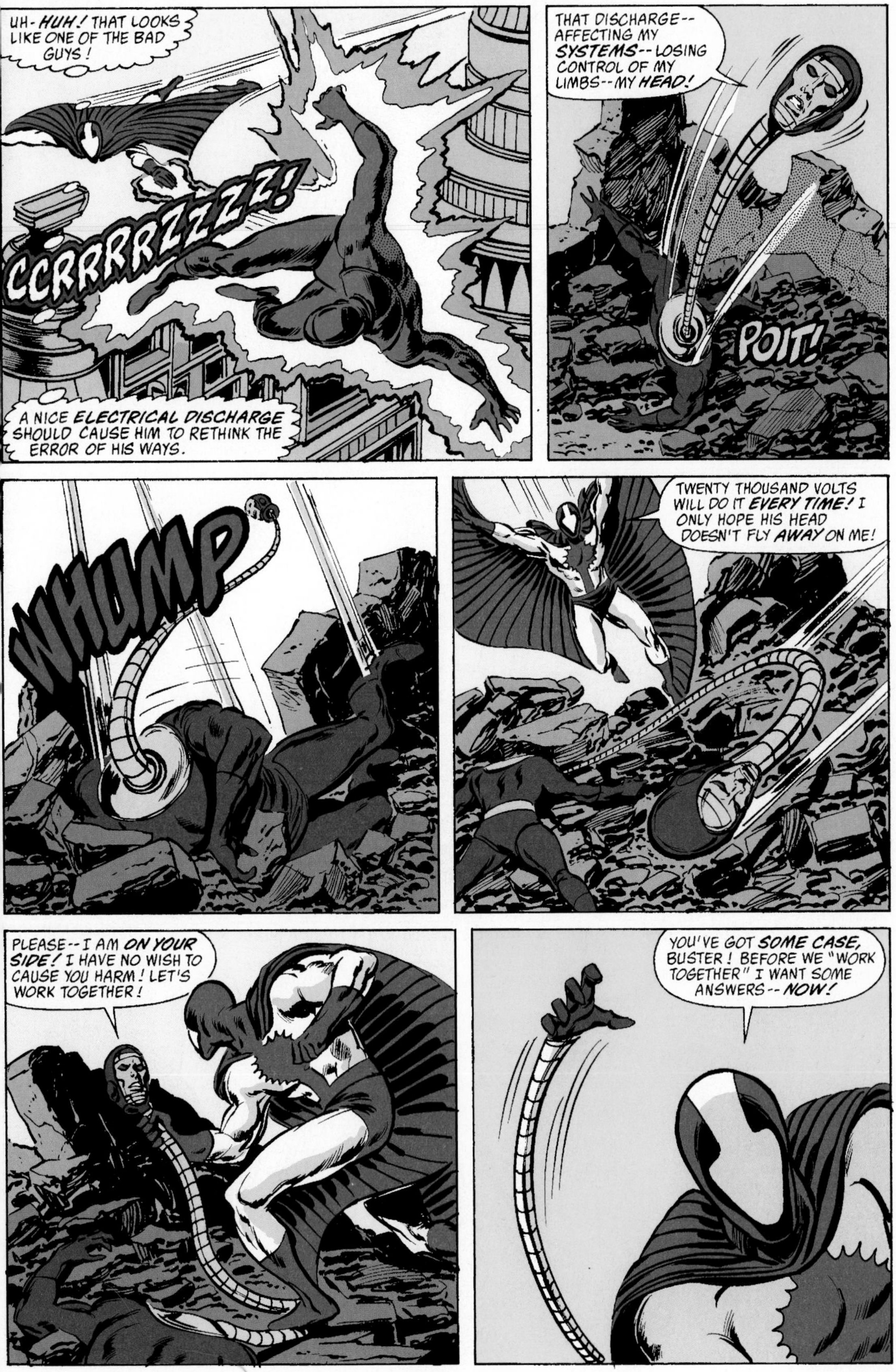
UH-HUH! THAT LOOKS LIKE ONE OF THE BAD GUYS!
A NICE ELECTRICAL DISCHARGE SHOULD CAUSE HIM TO RETHINK THE ERROR OF HIS WAYS.
CCRRRRZZZZZ!
THAT DISCHARGE-- AFFECTING MY SYSTEMS--LOSING CONTROL OF MY LIMBS--MY HEAD!
POIT!
WHUMP
TWENTY THOUSAND VOLTS WILL DO IT EVERY TIME! I ONLY HOPE HIS HEAD DOESN'T FLY AWAY ON ME!
PLEASE--I AM ON YOUR SIDE! I HAVE NO WISH TO CAUSE YOU HARM! LET'S WORK TOGETHER!
YOU'VE GOT SOME CASE, BUSTER! BEFORE WE "WORK TOGETHER" I WANT SOME ANSWERS--NOW!

AT THAT MOMENT, IN THE COMMUNICATIONS COMPLEX...

AT LAST, THE PIECES FALL TOGETHER. USING THE *MECHANICAL WIZARDRY* OF THE *FIXER,* I HAVE BYPASSED THE COMPUTER'S FAILSAFE SYSTEMS AND GAINED *ACCESS!*

SUCH A TREASUREHOUSE OF *KNOWLEDGE* OPENS UP TO ME. IT IS OF VITAL IMPORTANCE. AH, IMAGES APPEARING ON THE SCREEN.

INFORMATION ON THE CUBE AND ITS LOCALE COMING UP--

--AS WELL AS DATA PERTAINING TO ITS MOST SIGNIFICANT WIELDERS.

COSMIC CUBE : STATUS ...WHEREABOUTS BELIEVED TO BE OFF-EARTH. SEE A.I.M. SUB-FILE L-12. ACCESS CODE 1134

RED SKULL : STATUS... DECEASED. FURTHER REFERENCE : ACCESS CODE 9983-1

A.I.M. : STATUS... OAGANIZATION BELIEVED DISBANDED. CAOSS REFERENCE TO S.H.I.E.L.D. COMPUTER FILE. ACCESS CODE 31975-2

THANOS : STATUS... DECEASED. FURTHER REFERENCE : ACCESS CODE 69538-2

AQUARIAN : STATUS. INACTIVE. FURTHER REFERENCE : ACCESS CODE 0832-6

SO, THE *COSMIC CUBE--* THE OBJECT OF MY LONG PURSUIT IS NOT EVEN BELIEVED TO BE ON *EARTH.*

YET, THERE IS ANOTHER AVENUE TO FOLLOW. WHAT IS NEEDED ARE THE CODES TO THIS *HYPERSPACE TRANSMITTER.* THERE. NOW TO ACTI--

--EH? A BURST OF *LIGHT*--IT MUST BE *HER.* VERY WELL.

WHAT'S GOING **ON** HERE? I JUST RETURN FROM LOCATING THE INJURED DR. DRUID AND THE BLACK KNIGHT*--GETTING THEM TO A **HOSPITAL**...

...AND I FIND THE **ADAPTOID** IN HERE **TAMPERING** WITH OUR **COMPUTERS**! BUT I CAN'T USE MY **ENERGY POWERS** ON HIM OR I RISK DESTROYING PRICELESS MAGNETIC COMPUTER DATA.

*THEY SUSTAINED INJURIES LAST ISSUE FIGHTING THE SENTRY AND MACHINE MAN.

I'LL CONVERT MYSELF TO **LIGHT FORM** AND BE ON TOP OF HIM BEFORE HE KNOWS WHAT'S HAPPENING!

NOW!

BEFORE CAPTAIN MARVEL CAN COMPLETE THE STARTLING TRANSFORMATION, A BURST OF PUREST **MENTAL FORCE** STRIKES...

BWASSS

NOOO!

THE AVENGERS' LEADER SUCCUMBS...

SHE FLOATS INERT, IN A BIZARRE GRAVITY-LESS STATE BETWEEN ENERGY AND MATTER. AND LACKING A CONSCIOUS MIND TO CONTROL HER PARTICLES...

...THEY BEGIN TO **SEPARATE**--DRIFT APART AS HER FORM GROWS HAZY AT THE EDGES.

THE FOOL. HAVING ABSORBED THE MENTAL POWER OF THE TELE-PATH, **MENTALLO*** IT WAS CHILD'S PLAY TO **STRIKE** WITHOUT EVER LOOKING.

NOW THE BEACON HAS BEEN SENT AND SOON I SHALL GREET THE COSMIC CUBE... THAT WHICH TRANSFORMS **DESIRE** INTO ACTUAL **REALITY**. AND IT WILL BE MINE!

* AVENGERS # 287.

MEANWHILE, BACK AT THE FRONT LINES...

I'M JUST BREAKING MY HANDS ON THIS GORILLA!

LET'S TRY SOMETHING A LITTLE UNEXPECTED AND SEE IF IT SHAKES HIM UP!

ROO-KOOM!

ALL RIGHT! BE A NICE BOY AND PLAY WITH THESE BLOCKS!

PTAM!

I'VE GOTTA REGROUP! THIS IS GOING NOWHERE!

AND CLOSER TO THE SHORELINE...

MANAGED...TO RECOVER...!

STAY YOUR DISTANCE, MARRINA! THE FIEND IS TOO DANGEROUS!

I AM STILL CONVINCED THAT THE KEY TO TESS-ONE'S DEFEAT LIES IN ITS HEAD.

THERE MUST BE A WEAK SPOT-- EVEN IN THIS ADAMANTIUM SHELL.

SUDDENLY...

MMMMPPP--

NAMOR!

LONG MOMENTS PASS AS THE TIRELESS ANDROID SEEMS ON THE VERGE OF SNAPPING THE SUB-MARINER'S BRAWNY BACK...

BUT THEN--

BNUMP

SOMETHING STRUCK THE CREATURE-- FREEING ME!

NAMOR-- I COULD *NOT* SIT BY AND WATCH YOU *DIE!* THE THOUGHT OF YOUR *AGONY* MADE ME--

YOU HAVE NO NEED OF APOLOGY, MY BELOVED.

SPWAKK

SPLUSH

THANK NEPTUNE! MARRINA HAS BOBBED SAFELY TO THE SURFACE.

NOW A NEW TACTIC MUST BE EMPLOYED, ELSE THE BATTLE IS LOST!

SPOOMMP!

FEAR NOT, FACELESS ONE!

NAMOR HAS LITTLE INTENTION OF DROPPING YOU!

SKRAKKLE

I MERELY WISH TO TRANS-PORT YOUR GREAT BULK--

--TO AN ELEMENT MORE CONDUCIVE TO BEING DEALT WITH!

SPLUMP

AT THE WATER'S EDGE...

HE'S STILL COMING AND I'M RUNNING OUT OF STEAM! HAVE TO REST A SEC!

RRAATCH!

WHOOF!

THAMP

NNNNHHH...

¡BLUG!

NO! NO!

TAKE YOUR HANDS OFF HER! NO AVENGER WILL DIE IF I CAN HELP IT!

UNBELIEVABLY, THE ENRAGED MARRINA ACTUALLY PULLS THE ALIEN SENTRY BENEATH THE WAVES...

...AS TESS-ONE WADES OUT TO ENSURE A HEAVY METAL VICTORY TO THE WATERY CONFLICT.

AT THAT MOMENT IN ANOTHER PART OF THE BESIEGED COMPLEX, *MACHINE MAN* HAS CONVINCED THE HIGH-FLYING *STINGRAY* THAT HE IS INDEED NOT TRULY ON THE SIDE OF HEAVY METAL...

IS THIS WHERE THE MAIN COMPUTER BANKS ARE?

THIS IS THE PLACE.

SKRASH

A SIMPLE *MIND-BLAST* WILL DISPOSE OF YOU, MY GAUDILY-CLAD FRIEND.

AAAGGHH!

BZZAAATT

SO, MY FOES FALL ONE BY ONE. THE AVENGERS-- THIS FOOL-- AND SOON *THE WORLD!*

I HAVE PLANNED THE SCENARIO TOO WELL TO LET ANYTHING INTER--

YES, BUT DID YOU COUNT ON A *TRAITOR* IN YOUR MIDST?

DID YOU PREPARE FOR *BETRAYAL* BY ONE OF YOUR OWN-- WHO SECRETLY DID *NOT* SHARE YOUR DREAMS OF CONQUEST--

--YET WAITED FOR THE MOMENT YOU WERE *OFF-GUARD* TO STRIKE!

YES! YOU WERE TOLD *NOTHING* SUBSTANTIVE OF MY ULTIMATE SCHEME, MACHINE MAN, FOR *PRECISELY* THAT REASON!

SUCH MONUMENTAL *EGO* ON YOUR PART TO EVER BELIEVE I COULD BE TAKEN UNAWARES-- THAT I COULD NOT *COUNTER* YOUR CLUMSY ATTACK!

AND ARE YOU *SURPRISED* THAT I CAN *ADAPT* EVEN THE *ROBOTIC POWERS* YOU POSSESS?

HAH! EVEN MY FELLOW MACHINE-LIFE MAY FALL PREY TO THE POWER OF THE *SUPER-ADAPTOID!*

OFFSHORE, MARRINA'S VALIANT ASSAULT HAS GIVEN THE SHE-HULK THE SECONDS NEEDED TO FREE HERSELF FROM THE SENTRY, WHILE ANOTHER AVENGER CONTINUES HIS OWN ATTACK...

AS WITH TESS-ONE, STRIKING THE ANDROID'S RESILIENT BODY IS TO NO AVAIL! WORSE, IT HAS *MIMICKED* OUR PROPERTIES OF *BUOYANCY!*

ONLY THE STRENGTH OF THE *TRUE SUB-MARINER* MAY YET PREVAIL! ONLY THE MIGHT BEQUEATHED ME AS *PRINCE OF THE ATLANTEAN BLOOD* WILL SUFFICE!

INEXORABLY, THE HUGE ANDROID'S *HEAD* IS TWISTED AS THE TAUT FABRIC OF ITS OUTER SKIN BEGINS TO *CREASE, THEN TEAR...*

...UNTIL *FINALLY...*

DONE!

SHRIP!

...WATER QUICKLY FILLS THE GAPING HOLE, SINKING THE FLAILING ANDROID TORSO.

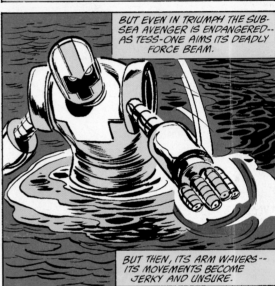

BUT EVEN IN TRIUMPH THE SUB-SEA AVENGER IS ENDANGERED-- AS TESS-ONE AIMS ITS DEADLY FORCE BEAM.

BUT THEN, ITS ARM WAVERS-- ITS MOVEMENTS BECOME JERKY AND UNSURE.

C'MON, TALL 'N GRUESOME-- JUST A LITTLE FURTHER...ONLY ANOTHER FEW FEET TO THE EDGE OF OUR *FLOATING ISLAND!*

THAT'S *THAT!* HAVE TO GET TO THE SURFACE BEFORE MY LUNGS *BURST!* CAN'T BREATHE UNDER HERE LIKE *MARRINA!*

THAT LIGHT-- INCREDIBLY *BRIGHT!* WHAT TURN OF EVENTS NOW TRANSPIRES?

I DON'T KNOW, SUBBY, BUT WE'RE NOT GOING TO FIND OUT STANDING IN A *LAGOON!*

THIS WAY THEN-- AND ALL HASTE IN OUR ACTIONS!

RIGHT BEHIND YOU, FISH-MAN!

INSIDE THE COMMUNICATIONS COMPLEX...

I-IT'S APPEARED! BUT THE *SIZE*-- THE *BRIGHTNESS!* AND I NEVER BELIEVED MY TRANSGALACTIC SUMMONS WOULD BE ANSWERED SO *QUICKLY!*

BUT NOW IT'S GLOWING EVEN *MORE* INTENSELY-- SEEMS TO BE ALTERING SOMEHOW... SHIMMERING!

YES-- IT *IS* CHANGING --TRANSFORMING INTO SOMETHING *ELSE!* WHAT CAN IT MEAN?

I-- I HAD NOT ANTICIPATED--

FINALLY ADMITTING A *MISTAKE,* EH?

WHO SUMMONS ME? WHO SUMMONS KUBIK?

LIKE YOURSELF, I AM A *CREATION* OF THE SCIENTISTS WHO COMPRISED *A.I.M.* ONCE I DID THEIR BIDDING-- BUT NO LONGER.

I HAVE MY *OWN* NEEDS NOW, AND MY *OWN* METHODS OF SATISFYING THEM.

EVEN THOSE MECHANICAL ENTITIES WHOSE AID I ENLISTED IN MY ATTEMPT TO DRAW YOU HERE ARE AS *NOTHING* COMPARED TO ME.

LET ME APPROACH YOU NOW IN MY *PUREST*, MOST *UNDILUTED* FORM, THAT YOU MAY SEE THE *TRUTH* OF HIM WHO CALLED YOU.

I DID.

WHAT IN--?

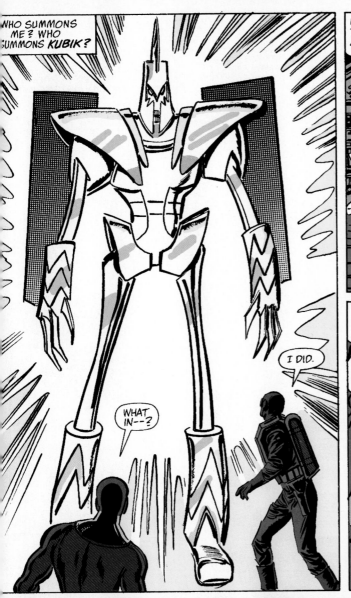

YOU ARE IN *ERROR*. I AM NO MAN NOR GROUP'S CREATION.

TRUE, MY EMBRYONIC FORM WAS PLUCKED FROM THE *OTHER-VERSE* IN WHICH I RESIDED AND PLACED WITHIN AN *INCUBATION CUBE* WHERE I GESTATED-- SUBJECT TO OTHERS' WILL.

BUT KUBIK WAS NOT *"CREATED."*

WHAT IS IT YOU *DESIRE?*

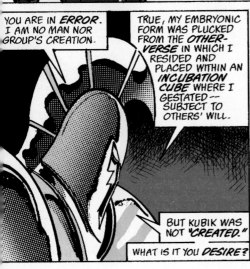

I DESIRE... *PROGENY.* YOU SEE, I AM UNIQUE-- *A.I.M.* WAS ABLE TO CREATE ONE OF ME, AND EVEN *THAT* SINGLE CREATION MAY HAVE BEEN *ACCIDENTAL.*

NOW I DESIRE *OTHERS* OF MY ILK... OTHERS WHO WILL BE WORTHY TO STAND AT MY SIDE AND *RULE* THIS PLANET WHEN I HAVE *CONQUERED* IT!

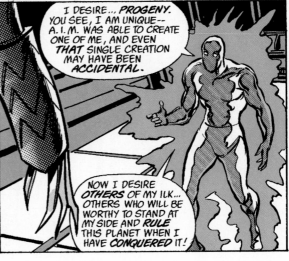

KUBIK IS NO LONGER AN IMMATURE ENTITY, A NASCENT LIFE FORM GRANTING THE WISHES OF WHOSOEVER HOLDS ME.

THE ONLY CHANGES I MAKE IN THE WORLD ARE THOSE *I* DESIRE. AND THEY ARE *FEW*.

YOUR WISHES WILL NOT BE *DELIVERED*.

THERE *YOU* ARE IN ERROR. I HAVE DELIBERATELY WITHHELD MENTION OF MY POWER OR MY NAME-- THE *SUPER-ADAPTOID!* I CAN DUPLICATE ANY AND ALL QUALITIES FROM WHATEVER BEING I CHOOSE. A FORMIDABLE ATTRIBUTE --BUT *NOT* SUFFICIENT.

AND WHILE WE HAVE DISCOURSED--

--I HAVE *REPLICATED* YOUR COSMIC MIGHT! MY CREATORS USED A SLIVER OF THE *COSMIC CUBE* ITSELF TO GIVE ME LIFE.

AND THAT SLIVER HAS FACILITATED THE ADAPTATION PROCESS --THE CREATION OF A TEMPLATE --ALLOWING ME TO BECOME ALL THAT *YOU* ARE. WE ARE *EQUALS* NOW!

AND UNLESS YOU WANT TO INVOLVE ALL OF *EXISTENCE* IN A WAR NEITHER OF US CAN WIN-- *BEGONE!*

YOU HAVE SERVED YOUR FUNCTION IN THIS LITTLE DRAMA AND ARE NO LONGER NEEDED. AND WHILE I CONSOLIDATE MY HOLD ON THE EARTH-- YOU ARE *SAFE*. AFTER THAT, I CANNOT SAY.

AT LAST MY DESTINY IS *AT HAND!* AT LAST MY MEREST WHIM BECOMES IMMUTABLE FACT! I AM BEYOND *CONQUEST* OR *CHALLENGE!* THE SUPER-ADAPTOID HAS BECOME--

--THE MASTER OF ALL REALITY!

NEXT: THE *DAY* OF THE *ADAPTOID!* BE HERE!

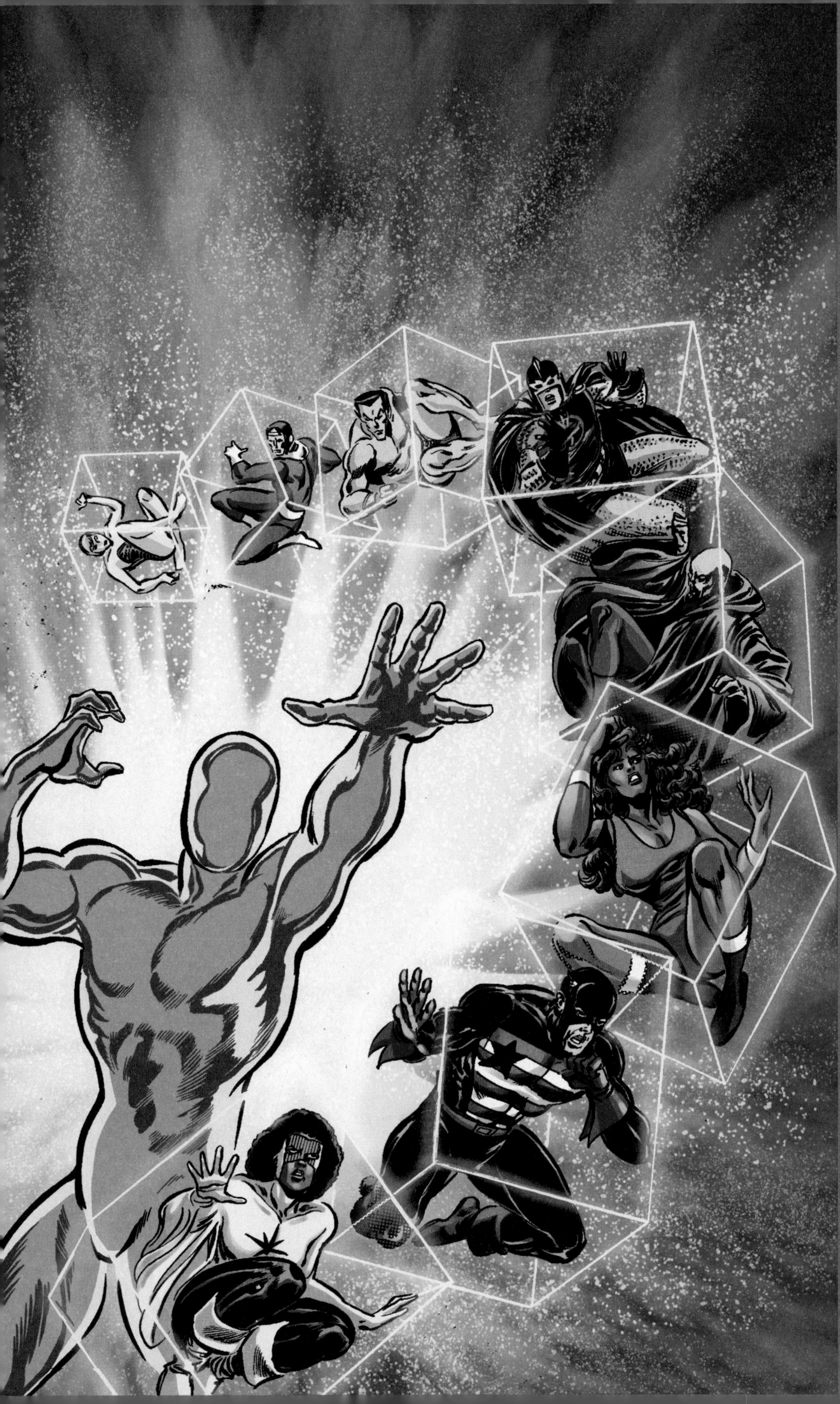

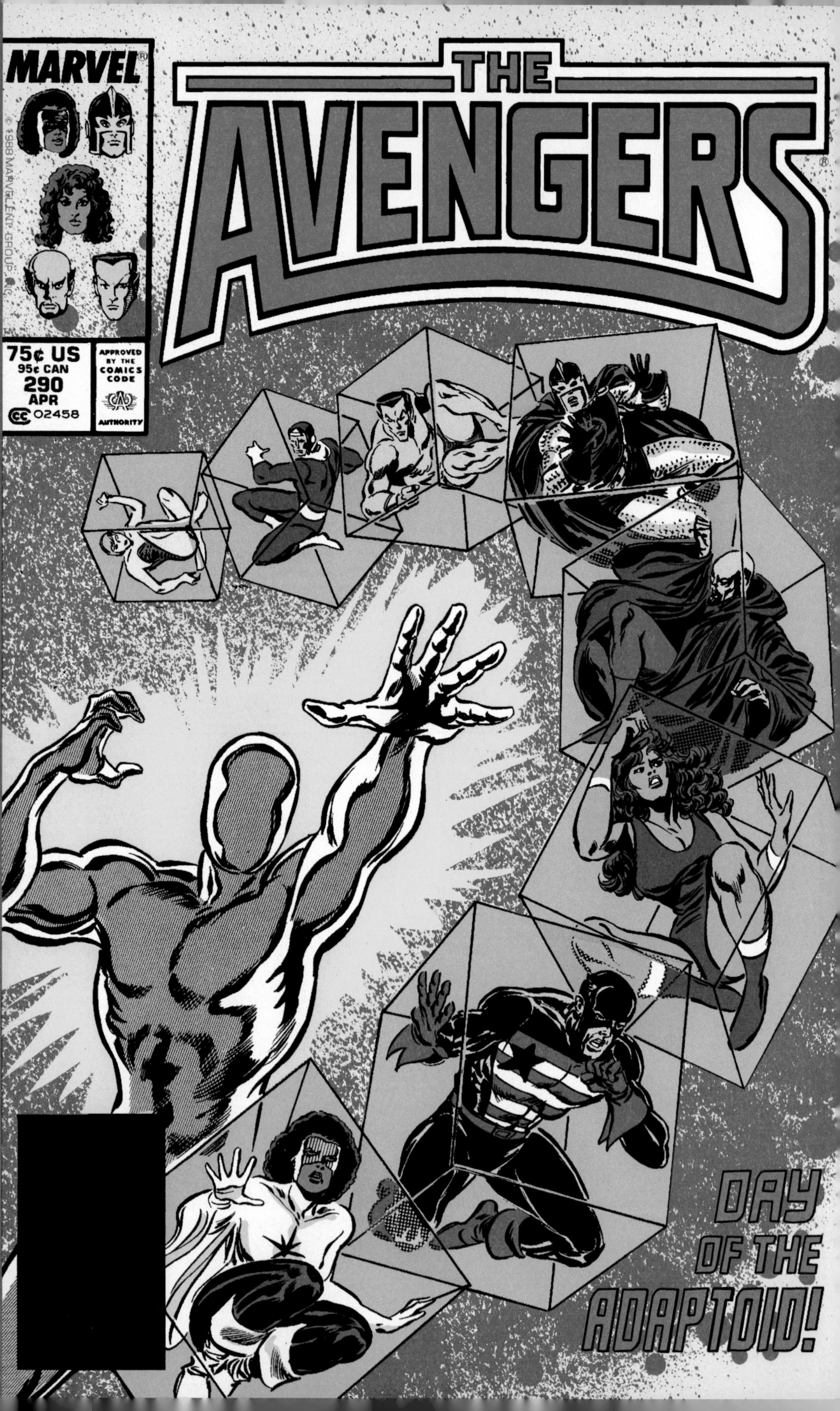
MARVEL
© 1988 MARVEL ENT. GROUP, INC.
THE AVENGERS
75¢ US
95¢ CAN
290
APR
CC 02458
APPROVED BY THE COMICS CODE AUTHORITY
DAY OF THE ADAPTOID!

STAN LEE PRESENTS:

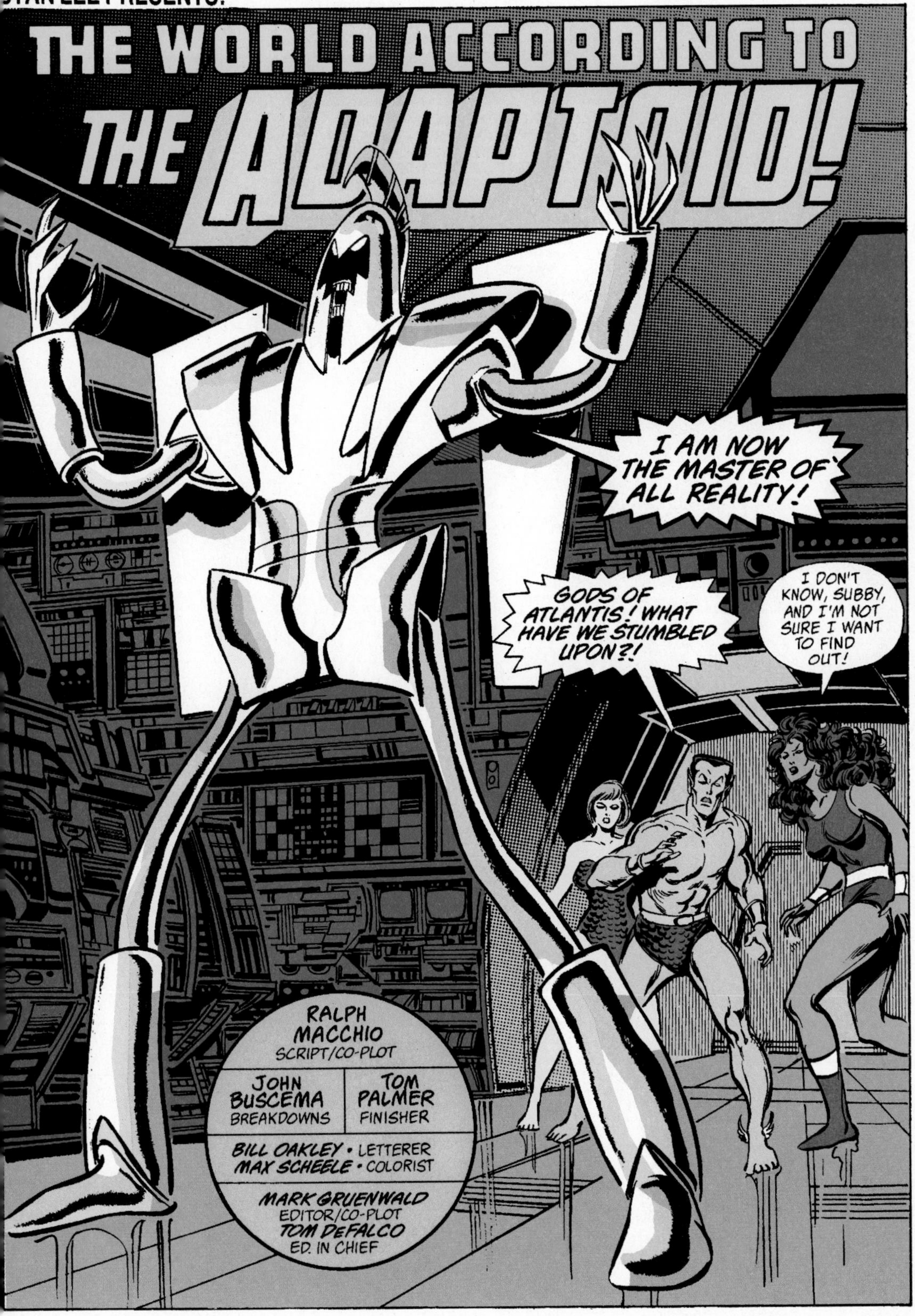
THE WORLD ACCORDING TO THE ADAPTOID!
I AM NOW THE MASTER OF ALL REALITY!
GODS OF ATLANTIS! WHAT HAVE WE STUMBLED UPON?!
I DON'T KNOW, SUBBY, AND I'M NOT SURE I WANT TO FIND OUT!
RALPH MACCHIO SCRIPT/CO-PLOT
JOHN BUSCEMA BREAKDOWNS
TOM PALMER FINISHER
BILL OAKLEY • LETTERER
MAX SCHEELE • COLORIST
MARK GRUENWALD EDITOR/CO-PLOT
TOM DEFALCO ED. IN CHIEF

THE COMMUNICATIONS COMPLEX OF THE *AVENGERS'* NEW HEADQUARTERS ON *HYDROBASE ISLAND* OFF THE EASTERN COAST OF THE UNITED STATES...

THE SCENE BEFORE US IS ONE TO BOGGLE THE SENSES AS TWO SEEMINGLY IDENTICAL, UNEARTHLY *ENTITIES* FACE EACH OTHER WITH THE FATE OF THE *UNIVERSE ITSELF* HANGING IN THE BALANCE.

BELOW, THE BEING WHO WAS ONCE THE *SUPER-ADAPTOID* REARS HIS HEAD IN TRIUMPH. INITIALLY, HE WAS THE CREATION OF A RENEGADE BAND OF SCIENTISTS CALLED THE *ADVANCED IDEA MECHANICS*. HIS POWER IS THE ABILITY TO ABSORB THE ATTRIBUTES AND APPEARANCE OF *ANY* CREATURE HE CHOOSES.

THE *SHE-HULK* IN ME WANTS TO LAY INTO THESE TWO BOZOS. BUT JENNIFER WALTERS, GIRL LAWYER, THINKS WE OUGHT TO HEAR THE CASE FIRST. DECISIONS, DECISIONS...

AND HE HAS CHOSEN TO ABSORB THAT OF--

--KUBIK! IN ITS NASCENT STAGES, KUBIK WAS THE EARTH'S COSMIC CUBE--A THROBBING BIT OF PRIMAL ENERGY PLUCKED FROM SOME NETHERVERSE BY THE SAME SCIENTISTS OF A.I.M. ...

IN ITS GESTATING FORM, THE COSMIC CUBE WILL GRANT THE DESIRE OF ANY WHO HOLD IT, ALTERING REALITY ITSELF IN THE PROCESS.

GIVEN THE CHANCE TO INCUBATE AND DEVELOP, THE CUBE WILL EVOLVE INTO A LIVING BEING POSSESSING UNTOLD POWER.

SUCH AN ENTITY IS THE PARTIALLY MATURE KUBIK-- SPRUNG FROM THE X-ELEMENT OF THE COSMIC CUBE.

AND SUCH AN ENTITY IS NOW ALSO-- THE SUPER-ADAPTOID!

BEFORE CONTINUING, I BELIEVE I SHOULD RENDER THE *AVENGERS* WHO HAVE JUST ARRIVED... *INEFFECTIVE*. AND THAT INCLUDES--

"--YOU, *MARRINA*, WIFE OF THE SUB-MARINER. THOUGH NOT A *TRUE* AVENGER, YOU COULD PROVE TROUBLESOME..."

"THE *SUB-MARINER* HIMSELF, FORMER MONARCH OF THE UNDERSEA KINGDOM OF ATLANTIS."

PTWFF

PTWFF

PTWFFF

"AND, THE *SHE-HULK*, WHOSE GAMMA-BIRTHED STRENGTH MAKES HER A FORMIDABLE ANTAGONIST FOR MOST."

"AHH, ONE OF MY OWN-- *MACHINE MAN*, THE TREASONOUS ROBOT WHO AIDED ME IN MY SCHEMES, ONLY TO TURN ON ME. THERE."

PTWFF

PTWFFF

"AND, FINALLY, *CAPTAIN MARVEL*, THE LEADER OF THIS SORRY GROUP OF ADVENTURERS. HER ABILITY TO TRANSFORM INTO ANY TYPE OF ENERGY IS NEGATED--"

"--BECAUSE I HAVE TRAPPED HER IN A NEBULOUS STATE BETWEEN MATTER AND ENERGY. BUT FEAR NOT-- FOR SHE STILL LIVES."

"NOW I MUST CONVERSE WITH HIM WHO IS CALLED *KUBIK*-- AS AN *EQUAL*."

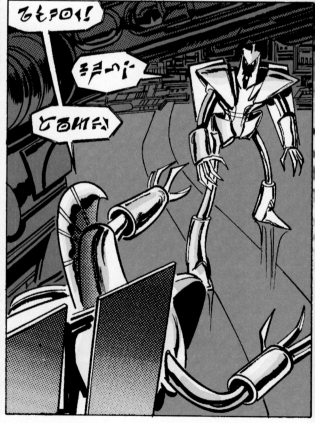

102

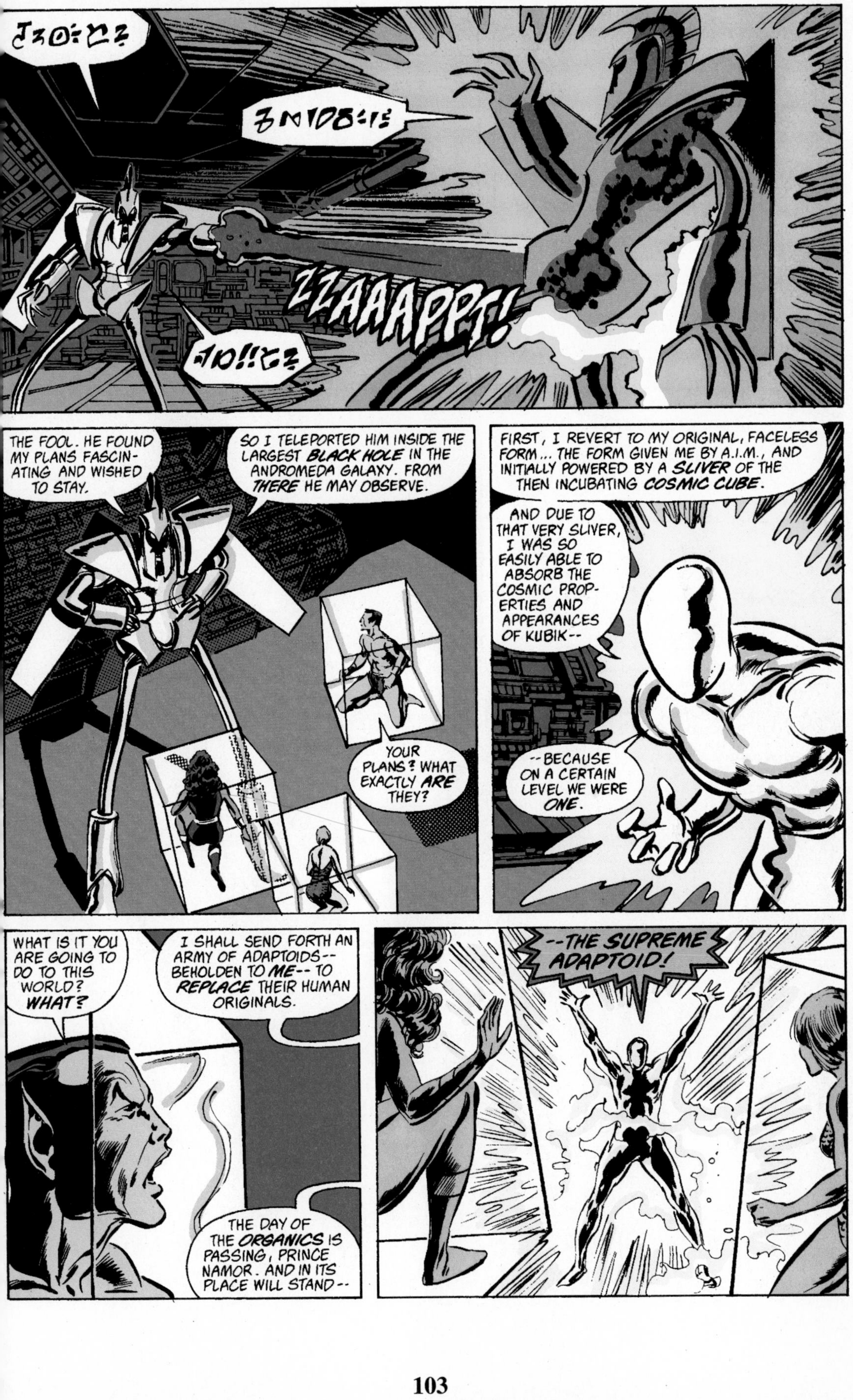

ZZAAAAPPT!
THE FOOL. HE FOUND MY PLANS FASCINATING AND WISHED TO STAY.
SO I TELEPORTED HIM INSIDE THE LARGEST BLACK HOLE IN THE ANDROMEDA GALAXY. FROM THERE HE MAY OBSERVE.
YOUR PLANS? WHAT EXACTLY ARE THEY?
FIRST, I REVERT TO MY ORIGINAL, FACELESS FORM... THE FORM GIVEN ME BY A.I.M., AND INITIALLY POWERED BY A SLIVER OF THE THEN INCUBATING COSMIC CUBE.
AND DUE TO THAT VERY SLIVER, I WAS SO EASILY ABLE TO ABSORB THE COSMIC PROPERTIES AND APPEARANCES OF KUBIK--
--BECAUSE ON A CERTAIN LEVEL WE WERE ONE.
WHAT IS IT YOU ARE GOING TO DO TO THIS WORLD? WHAT?
I SHALL SEND FORTH AN ARMY OF ADAPTOIDS-- BEHOLDEN TO ME-- TO REPLACE THEIR HUMAN ORIGINALS.
THE DAY OF THE ORGANICS IS PASSING, PRINCE NAMOR. AND IN ITS PLACE WILL STAND--
--THE SUPREME ADAPTOID!

THEIR ADVERSARY'S OMINOUS EXIT-LINE GALVANIZES THE TRAPPED ASSEMBLERS...

HOLD IT A MINUTE. I DON'T REALLY BELIEVE ANY OF YOU IS GOING ANYWHERE -- AND SINCE I'M *PARTIALLY* RESPONSIBLE FOR THIS MESS...

...LET ME TELL YOU HOW ALL THIS CAME ABOUT.

SPEAK THEN, MECHANICAL ONE. NAMOR *BIDS* YOU.

:MMMPPHH!: CAN'T BUDGE THE WALLS EVEN THOUGH I'VE GOT THE *LEVERAGE!*

IT'S *CRAZY!* THEY'RE *PAPER-THIN!*

"SOME MONTHS AGO, THE SUPER-ADAPTOID WAS IMPRISONED IN THE AVENGERS' SUB-BASEMENT BACK IN NEW YORK CITY. HE *ESCAPED* AND IMITATED THE FORM AND MECHANICAL WIZARDRY OF A CRIMINAL GENIUS CALLED THE *FIXER.*

"AS YOU SOON DIS-COVERED, THE *REAL* FIXER WAS THEN PUT IN THE ADAPTOID'S CONTAINMENT TUBE. IN HIS GUISE AS THE FIXER, THE ADAPTOID MADE CONTACT WITH AN OLD LAW-BREAK-ING CRONY OF HIS--

"--MENTALLO. UNAWARE OF THE DUPLICATION, THIS CRIMINAL MASTERMIND FELL EASY PREY TO THE ADAPTOID. ADAPTING MEN-TALLO'S *TELEPATHIC POWER,* THE ADAPTOID COULD NOW IN-STANTLY SENSE THE THOUGHTS OF HIS HUMAN ENEMIES.

"THE NEXT STEP FOR THE ADAPTOID WAS THE GATHERING OF *OTHER* ROBOTIC ENTITIES-- INCLUDING YOURS TRULY--

"--IN AN ATTACK GROUP HE CALLED *HEAVY METAL.* THE MECHANICAL POWER OF THE FIXER ALLOWED THE ADAPTOID TO *ACTIVATE* OR *REPAIR* ALL OF THE ROBOTS.

"THEN, HEAVY METAL STORMED HYDROBASE ISLAND TO KEEP YOU AVENGERS *OCCUPIED--*

"--WHILE THE ADAPTOID SLIPPED OVER HERE TO SEND A *TRANSGALACTIC SUMMONS* TO...

"...KUBIK. THAT WAS HIS ULTIMATE GOAL, TO *DUPLI-CATE* THE COSMIC POWER OF KUBIK, AND BASICALLY *RUN ALL REALITY.*

AND YOU JUST GOT *DUMPED* ON THE SCRAP HEAP 'CAUSE HE HAD NO MORE *USE* FOR YOU?

NOT EXACTLY. I'M *REALLY* A GOOD GUY AND I TAGGED ALONG WITH THE ADAPTOID TO SEE WHAT HE WAS UP TO AND BE CLOSE ENOUGH TO STOP HIM.

THERE WAS *ALSO* THE MATTER OF A LADY FRIEND OF MINE HE PROMISED TO RE-ACTIVATE-- BUT THAT'S ANOTHER STORY.

I MADE MY MOVE TOO *LATE* AND-- HERE I AM.

WE SYMPATHIZE WITH YOUR *PLIGHT*, MACHINE MAN -- AND SHARE IT. *STILL*, WE ARE NO CLOSER TO RELEASE FROM OUR PRISONS, AND THAT--

--THAT FLASH FROM CAPTAIN MARVEL'S CUBE!

I'M *OKAY*, NAMOR. I JUST USED EVERY BIT OF MY WILLPOWER TO COALESCE BACK INTO A FULLY *MATERIAL STATE*. BUT I'M TOO *WEAK* FROM THAT EXERTION TO TRY AND CHANGE INTO ANOTHER ENERGY FORM JUST YET.

THAT YOU ARE *WELL* IS ENOUGH

I'M *HAPPY* FOR YOU, TOO, FEARLESS LEADER, BUT LET ME UPDATE YOU ON SOME CURRENT EVENTS.

WE'RE *STUCK* IN THESE TRANSPARENT *PLAY BLOCKS* WITH NO WAY OUT. GOT ANY IDEAS?

SORRY, JEN. MAYBE I COULD SLIP OUT IF I COULD CHANGE TO *VISIBLE LIGHT*-- BUT I'M TOO EXHAUSTED TO TRY.

I'VE HAD THE OLD GEARS TURNING ON *THIS* ONE FOR THE LAST MINUTE OR TWO AND I'VE GOT ONE THING WE MIGHT *TRY*.

BASED ON SOMETHING IN A *BOOK* I RECENTLY READ.

I BELIEVE THAT WHILE ENERGY APPARENTLY CANNOT BE PROJECTED *OUTSIDE* THE CUBE, IT CAN BE PROJECTED FROM *WITHIN*.

I'VE GOT THESE NIFTY *ANTI-GRAVITY GENERATORS* THAT ALLOW ME TO FLY.

SO, IF I CAN JUST BRACE MYSELF AND TURN THEM *ON...*

...WE MIGHT JUST GET A LITTLE *ACTION* HERE!

KLAK!

AND SO IT GOES, ONE CUBE INTO THE NEXT, THAT SETS THEM ALL TO MOVING *FORWARD.*

YOU MENTIONED THIS IDEA CAME FROM A BOOK YOU READ.

YES. WRITTEN BY DR. HENRY KISSINGER. *YEARS OF UPHEAVAL,* IT WAS CALLED.

MUCH OF IT WAS DEVOTED TO THE-- *DOMINO EFFECT* IN SOUTHEAST ASIA.

KLAK!

KLAK!

KLAK!

KLAK!

TURBULENT MOMENTS LATER, THE QUINTET OF CUBES HAS PASSED THROUGH THE COMMUNICATIONS COMPLEX'S *ENTRANCE* --OUTSIDE...

...WHERE A *SIGHT* BEYOND EVEN THE AVENGERS' *JADED* SENSIBILITIES IS BEHELD...!

HE STANDS -- AN EIGHTY-FOOT COLOSSUS AMID THE WRECKAGE OF THE DEVASTATED STRUCTURES OF HYDROBASE... *THE SUPREME ADAPTOID.*

AND FROM HIS *CHEST* BURST SMALLER, THOUGH IDENTICAL-LOOKING FIGURES -- *EACH* WITH A SMIDGEON OF THE ALL-POWERFUL *COSMIC CUBE* TO EMPOWER IT...

...EACH WITH THE PROGRAMMING TO SEEK OUT A *HUMAN BEING,* REPLICATE ITS ATTRIBUTES AND APPEARANCE -- AND THEN *DESTROY* THE IMITATED *HOMO SAPIEN.*

I-IT'S ACTUALLY GIVING *BIRTH!* I-I CAN'T BELIEVE WHAT I'M SEEING!

THE REPLICATION PROCESS PROCEEDS AT AN ALMOST *INCALCULABLE* RATE. IT WILL NOT CEASE UNTIL *FIVE BILLION ADAPTOIDS* HAVE BEEN PRODUCED.

ONE FOR EACH MAN, WOMAN AND CHILD ON THIS PLANET.

WHAT IN THE NAME OF HEAVEN **IS** THAT, **DOCTOR DRUID?**

I HARDLY HOPED TO SEE SUCH **CHAOS** HERE, DANE WHITMAN, ESPECIALLY AFTER WE JUST CHECKED OUT OF THE HOSPITAL* AND WERE GRACIOUSLY LENT THIS QUINJET BY OUR WEST COAST COUNTERPARTS.

I DON'T KNOW **WHAT** I EXPECTED TO **SEE** -- BUT RIGHT NOW I SEE TWO STRANGE-LOOKING DUDES WITH POSSIBLE **BAD INTENTIONS** HEADING THIS WAY.

* DRUID AND THE BLACK KNIGHT WERE INJURED OUT WEST TWO ISSUES AGO BY THE ADAPTOID AND HIS COHORTS.

I SHALL USE THE MENTAL POWER WHICH IS MINE TO RENDER THIS SHIP **INVISIBLE** THAT WE MAY THUS MAKE A SAFE LANDING.

BUT THE ADAPTOID DUO CONTINUE UNERRINGLY TOWARD THE **GOAL**, THEIR ARTIFICIAL SENSES AND MECHANICAL MINDS NOT DECEIVED BY DRUID'S PERCEPTION-ALTERING PLOY.

WHAT?! THE RUSE FAILED -- THEY'VE **DISCOVERED** US!

SKREEESH!

MAJORED IN **UNDERSTATEMENT** BACK AT OCCULT COLLEGE, EH, DOC?

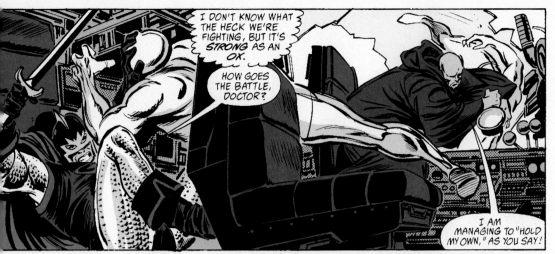

I DON'T KNOW WHAT THE HECK WE'RE FIGHTING, BUT IT'S *STRONG* AS AN OX.

HOW GOES THE BATTLE, DOCTOR?

I AM MANAGING TO "HOLD MY OWN," AS YOU SAY!

WAITAMINNIT! THIS CLOWN'S STARTING TO GROW A *SWORD* OUT OF HIS *HAND* JUST LIKE *MINE!* THAT MEANS HE'S--

--AN *ADAPTOID,* DOCTOR! THESE THINGS ARE *ADAPTOIDS!* CAN YOU *HEAR* ME?!

YES! AND EVEN AS WE STRUGGLE WITH THEM, THEY ARE ASSUMING OUR POWERS!

BUT THEY ARE NOT HUMAN, SO YOU NEEDN'T RESTRAIN YOUR *SWORDPLAY!*

STRIKE!

STRIKE!

YOU DON'T HAVE TO *SHOUT,* DOC-- I JUST CUT 'EM BOTH IN TWO-- ER, *TWAIN,* AS MY ANCESTORS USED TO SAY!

SHLIKKK!

WELL DONE, MY FRIEND! WELL DONE!

AND SINCE THEY'RE NON-HUMAN, I NEEDN'T WORRY ABOUT MY SWORD'S "BLOOD-CURSE."

SHLIKKK!

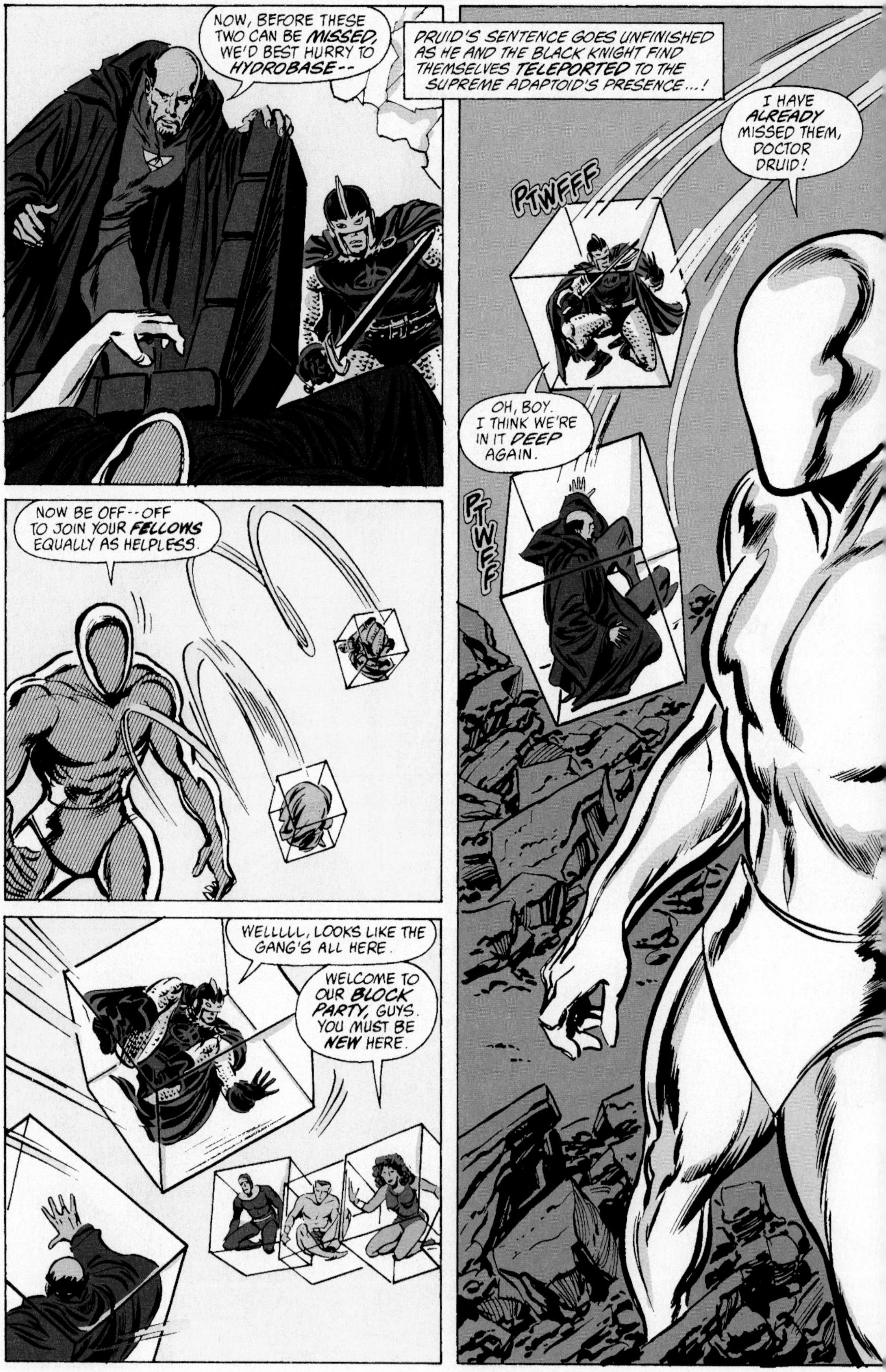
NOW, BEFORE THESE TWO CAN BE MISSED, WE'D BEST HURRY TO HYDROBASE--
NOW BE OFF--OFF TO JOIN YOUR FELLOWS EQUALLY AS HELPLESS.
WELLLLL, LOOKS LIKE THE GANG'S ALL HERE.
WELCOME TO OUR BLOCK PARTY, GUYS. YOU MUST BE NEW HERE.
DRUID'S SENTENCE GOES UNFINISHED AS HE AND THE BLACK KNIGHT FIND THEMSELVES TELEPORTED TO THE SUPREME ADAPTOID'S PRESENCE...!
I HAVE ALREADY MISSED THEM, DOCTOR DRUID!
PTWFFF
OH, BOY. I THINK WE'RE IN IT DEEP AGAIN.
PTWFF

OKAY, LET'S SKIP THE *UPDATE* UNTIL WE'VE GOTTEN OURSELVES FREE. AND THAT'S WHERE *I* COME IN --

-- 'CAUSE IF THERE'S *ONE THING* THIS INDE-STRUCTIBLE EBONY BLADE CAN DO...

...IT'S *SLICE* THROUGH *ANYTHING!* AND IT APPEARS THAT THIS OVERSIZED *ICE-CUBE* IS NO EXCEPTION.

HUH! GUESS I SPOKE TOO SOON. AS QUICKLY AS I RIP A HOLE IN THIS SUBSTANCE, IT *SEALS* ITSELF.

UHH, SO MUCH FOR *MY* BRIGHT IDEAS. CAPTAIN MARVEL, *YOU* LEAD THIS INTREPID GROUP. WHAT'S THE PLAN, CHIEF?

I- I JUST DON'T HAVE ANYTHING PROMISING TO SAY. MAYBE WHEN MY *STRENGTH* RETURNS...

OH.

I SIMPLY CANNOT TEAR MY EYES AWAY FROM THAT SPECTACLE OF *REPLICATION.* AND THE ADAPTOID'S MIND AS I PROBED IT...

...*NEVER* HAVE I ENCOUNTERED AN ARTIFICIAL INTELLECT OF SUCH VASTNESS -- SUCH *COMPLEXITY.*

YEAH -- THINK HE'LL CONSENT TO AN *I.Q. TEST* BEFORE HE SNUFFS US OUT?

DOCTOR DRUID -- BLACK KNIGHT... WHAT WE'RE FACING IS AN ENEMY THAT HAS ABSORBED THE POWER OF THE *COSMIC CUBE* --

-- AND THUS HAS THE POWER TO *ALTER REALITY* AT ITS WHIM.

HAS THIS POWER OBJECT BEEN USED IN THE PAST?

YES. FORMER WIELDERS OF THE CUBE WERE DEFEATED WHEN IT WAS *TAKEN* FROM THEM. BUT THE ADAPTOID HAS TAKEN THE CUBE'S POWER *INTO* HIMSELF--

--SO THERE'S *NO WAY* TO TAKE IT FROM HIM. ALSO, HE'S *TELEPATHIC,* SO WE CAN'T *SURPRISE* HIM. BESIDES WE DON'T KNOW WHERE THE ACTUAL CUBE IS RIGHT NOW. THE ADAPTOID *WISHED* IT AWAY.

SPACE... NEAR THE LARGEST ELECTRICALLY NEUTRAL, ROTATING BLACK HOLE IN THE ANDROMEDA GALAXY...

...WHERE SOMETHING HAS JUST VIOLATED ALL PHYSICAL LAW AND EMERGED... INTACT FROM THIS FINAL STATE OF A HUGE COLLAPSING *STAR*... THIS ULTIMATE COSMIC MAW...

NATURE ITSELF, DOING *NATURALLY* WHAT KUBIK DOES THROUGH *CONSCIOUS EFFORT*... THE TRANSPOSITION OF TIME AND SPACE BEYOND THE EVENT HORIZON...

...THE VIRTUAL COMPRESSION OF MATTER OUT OF THIS UNIVERSE WITHIN THE SINGULARITY. REALITY *ALTERING* ITSELF ON A GRAND SCALE.

LET ME *UPSET* THE EQUATION BEFORE I DEPART-- *CHANGING* THE BLACK HOLE'S AXIS OF ROTATION AND ADDING AN ELECTRICAL CHARGE TO THE SURFACE.

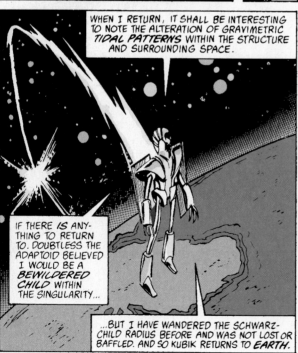

WHEN I RETURN, IT SHALL BE INTERESTING TO NOTE THE ALTERATION OF GRAVIMETRIC *TIDAL PATTERNS* WITHIN THE STRUCTURE AND SURROUNDING SPACE.

IF THERE *IS* ANYTHING TO RETURN TO. DOUBTLESS THE ADAPTOID BELIEVED I WOULD BE A *BEWILDERED CHILD* WITHIN THE SINGULARITY...

...BUT I HAVE WANDERED THE SCHWARZCHILD RADIUS BEFORE AND WAS NOT LOST OR BAFFLED. AND SO KUBIK RETURNS TO *EARTH.*

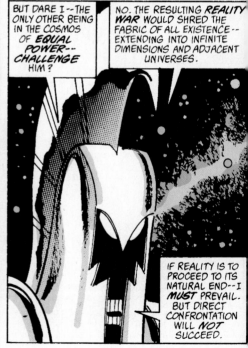

BUT DARE I--THE ONLY OTHER BEING IN THE COSMOS OF *EQUAL POWER-- CHALLENGE* HIM?

NO. THE RESULTING *REALITY WAR* WOULD SHRED THE FABRIC OF ALL EXISTENCE-- EXTENDING INTO INFINITE DIMENSIONS AND ADJACENT UNIVERSES.

IF REALITY IS TO PROCEED TO ITS NATURAL END--I *MUST* PREVAIL. BUT DIRECT CONFRONTATION WILL *NOT* SUCCEED.

ALL THOSE WHO HAVE BENT THE CUBE TO THEIR WILL HAVE THWARTED THEMSELVES MORE THAN *BEEN* THWARTED... *INTOXICATED* WITH ITS POWER.

PERHAPS IF I WERE TO MASK MY PRESENCE AND SEE-- BUT *NO*. THE STAKES ARE TOO HIGH, AND I AM *NOT* A WATCHER. I *MUST* ASSUME SOME ACTIVE ROLE IN THE COMING CONFLICT.

AND SO MUST ONE OTHER. THE *ONE MAN* ON EARTH WHOSE TOUCH ENABLED ME TO SENSE A SPIRIT OF MOST UNCOMMON VALOR...

A WINDING COUNTRY ROAD IN THE HILLS BEYOND LOS ANGELES...

IT WASN'T ENOUGH THAT THE GOVERNMENT TOOK AWAY MY *UNIFORM* AND *SHIELD*--

-- FORCING ME TO ADOPT A NEW COSTUME AND GET A NEW SHIELD -- BUT NOW MY CUSTOM *MOTORCYCLE* HAS BEEN TOTALLED, AND I HAVE TO RIDE A *BORROWED* ONE ! WHAT NEXT--?

CAPTAIN AMERICA! THIS UNIVERSE HAS GREAT NEED OF YOU!

* FOR DETAILS ON CAP'S CRISIS, SEE CURRENT ISSUES OF HIS OWN BOOK.

HOLD-- PLEASE. WE ARE...*OLD FRIENDS*. YOU KNEW OF ME WHEN I WORE A DIFFERENT FORM...

"...WHEN I WAS IN MY INFANTILE STATE YOU CALL-- THE *COSMIC CUBE,* AND WAS POSSESSED BY A MADMAN.

"YOU DEFEATED HIM, THEN COMFORTED ME BEFORE I WAS TAKEN TO BE NURTURED BY THE *SHAPER OF WORLDS.*

"NOW LET ME EXPLAIN WHAT HAS OCCURRED."

SWIFTLY, KUBIK RELAYS THE DIRE SITUATION TO THE SENTINEL OF LIBERTY, WHO RESPONDS--

LEAVE OF ABSENCE OR NOT, THE AVENGERS *NEED* ME! I'M GOING! YOU MUST TAKE ME THERE AT *ONCE!*

THE ADAPTOID WILL ONLY *ENTRAP* YOU AS HE DID YOUR COMRADES. THAT WOULD PROVE FUTILE.

I DON'T THINK SO. YOU SEE, *I* AM THE REASON THE ADAPTOID EXISTS. A.I.M. CREATED IT SPECIFICALLY TO DEFEAT *ME* YEARS AGO.

AND I BELIEVE A CLUE TO ITS *DEFEAT* IS SOMEHOW CONNECTED TO THAT FACT. NOW I'M ASKING AGAIN-- SEND ME TO THE *AVENGERS!*

VERY WELL. PERHAPS YOUR WISDOM IS WELL BEYOND KUBIK'S *OWN.* FAREWELL.

AND I MEAN FARE WELL.

SKKSSS

A BARE INSTANT LATER ON HYDROBASE ISLAND...

I'M BACK! BUT HOW DID I GET HERE-- WHO SENT ME?

PWIIT!

UNKNOWN TO CAPTAIN AMERICA, KUBIK ERASED HIS MEMORY OF THEIR MEETING IN THE EVENT THAT THE ADAPTOID PROBED CAP'S MIND, IT WOULD NOT LEARN OF KUBIK'S RETURN TO EARTH.

NO MATTER. I'VE GOT A *JOB* TO DO-- AND NOTHING'S GOING TO DETER ME!

BUT BEFORE ANOTHER STEP CAN BE TAKEN...

YOU! DIFFERENTLY GARBED-- THOUGH THE POWER AURA IS AS I REMEMBERED IT. *CAPTAIN AMERICA!*

PT.WFF

I AM NOT AWARE HOW YOU WERE ABLE TO GET SO *CLOSE* TO ME WITHOUT MY KNOWLEDGE ...BUT YOU MUST HAVE TAKEN LEAVE OF YOUR *SENSES* TO BELIEVE A *SNEAK ATTACK* COULD BE LAUNCHED ON ONE WHO IS *TELEPATHIC.*

I WAS READYING NO SNEAK ATTACK, ADAPTOID. I WAS GOING TO CHALLENGE YOU *FACE-TO-FACE.*

WHY SHOULD I ACCEPT SUCH A CHALLENGE WHEN MY MEREST *SHRUG* WOULD ERASE YOU FROM EXISTENCE AS IF YOU HAD NEVER *BEEN?*

YOU'LL FACE ME BECAUSE IT'S YOUR *DESTINY* TO FACE ME! YOUR CREATORS GAVE YOU A *MISSION* -- TO UTTERLY *DEFEAT* ME!

IT IS A MISSION -- A *PROGRAMMING* -- YOU HAVE *NEVER* SUCCESSFULLY CARRIED OUT!

THAT IS TRUE. BUT I AM THE *SUPREME ADAPTOID* NOW -- I HAVE *TRANSCENDED* ALL PROGRAMMING. MY DESTINY IS MY *OWN* -- SUBJECT TO *MY* WILL AND MY WILL *ALONE!*

I AM THE COSMIC CUBE INCARNATE!

MAYBE SO, BUT HOW DO YOU KNOW EVEN *THIS* GRAND SCHEME WASN'T AN *UNKNOWN PART* OF YOUR PROGRAMMING? HOW DO YOU KNOW A.I.M. DIDN'T INTEND THERE TO BE A SYNTHESIS OF ITS TWO GREATEST CREATIONS?

COULD BE YOU'RE NOT AS *INDEPENDENT* AS YOU THINK, FELLA!

≤HMPH.≥ YOUR TACTICS ARE *TRANSPARENT,* CAPTAIN. YOU WISH TO INSTILL AN ELEMENT OF *SELF-DOUBT* IN ME. ADMIRABLE -- THOUGH FUTILE.

POOT!

REPLICATE THIS BOTHERSOME HUMAN AND THEN *DESTROY* HIM!

WHUG!

THIS SUPREME ADAPTOID IS THE MOST *FORMIDABLE* BEING TO *EVER* HOLD THE CUBE!

AS AWESOME AND EVIL AS THEY WERE-- AT LEAST THE *RED SKULL* AND *THANOS* HAD SOME *CHARACTER FLAWS* TO PREY UPON. THIS IS AN *ARTIFICIAL BEING* -- AND THAT ROUTE WON'T WORK.

SWOK!

I CAN'T STOP THE THING *DUPLICATING* ME-- BUT MAYBE I CAN PUT IT AWAY BEFORE IT'S DOUBLED ME *COMPLETELY!*

BZOK!

BWUNT!

REPLICATION PROCESS *COMPLETE!* AS PER PROGRAMMING -- TERMINATION OF ORIGINAL ORGANISM PROCEEDS.

IF I'VE *EVER* BEEN ON MY TOES...!

SUCH A FEINT MIGHT HAVE WORKED AGAINST *ANY* OTHER OPPONENT, CAPTAIN--

--BUT *NOT* AGAINST ONE WHO CAN *DUPLICATE* YOUR EVERY FIGHTING MANEUVER.

THUGG!

MISTER -- I DON'T CARE *HOW* WELL YOU'VE DUPLICATED MY "FIGHTING MANEUVERS." THERE'S *MORE* TO IT THAN THAT -- *LOTS MORE!*

WHOK!

NO MACHINE CAN IMITATE A MAN'S *FIGHTING HEART* -- THE *SPIRIT* THAT PUSHES HIM ON AND ON THOUGH THE ODDS ARE HOPELESS.

AND THAT IS WHY YOU AND YOUR KIND MUST FINALLY *FAIL* -- AND FREE MEN *PREVAIL!*

BTAM

I COULDN'T *BELIEVE* THAT WAS REALLY CAP WHEN HE FIRST SHOWED, BUT DRUID MIND-PROBED HIM -- AND *IT IS! WOW!* WATCHING HIM FIGHT, IT'S INCREDIBLE, IT'S--

INSPIRING, IS THE WORD, SHE-HULK, FOR HE IS A *NATURAL LEADER.*

AND HIS VERY PRESENCE HAS SPARKED AN *IDEA.*

DRUID, WHERE ARE YOU--?

DON'T DO ANYTHING *FOOLISH!*

ANYTHING WE DO IS FOOLISH, CAPTAIN MARVEL. AND RIGHT NOW, *ANYTHING'S* WORTH A TRY.

SUPREME ONE, MAY I *SPEAK* WITH YOU A MOMENT?

FORGIVE THIS INTERRUPTION, BUT I WISH TO *HELP* YOU.

HELP ME!? I AM *ALL-POWERFUL* -- NOT A BOAST, A FACT. I REQUIRE NO ASSISTANCE. AND I SENSE THIS IS MERELY A *PLOY* TO TRY AND DEFEAT ME.

IF IT IS IMPOSSIBLE TO DEFEAT YOU, WHAT *HARM* CAN THERE BE IN *LISTENING?*

SPEAK BRIEFLY THEN.

117

THERE IS A WAY FOR YOU TO DETERMINE IF WHAT CAPTAIN AMERICA TOLD YOU IS *TRUE* ...IF WHAT YOU ARE DOING IS A FUNCTION OF YOUR OWN *FREE WILL*-- OR MERELY *PROGRAMMING.*

HOW?

"AFTER YOU SUCCEED IN THE *DUPLICATION* OF EVERY HUMAN BEING ON EARTH -- WHAT WILL YOU DO *THEN?*"

"I WILL *RULE* THEM, DOCTOR DRUID."

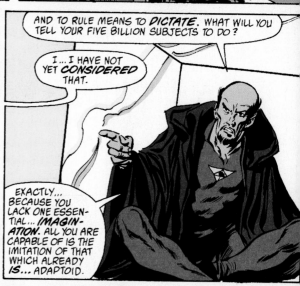

AND TO RULE MEANS TO *DICTATE.* WHAT WILL YOU TELL YOUR FIVE BILLION SUBJECTS TO DO?

I...I HAVE NOT YET *CONSIDERED* THAT.

EXACTLY... BECAUSE YOU LACK ONE ESSENTIAL... *IMAGINATION.* ALL YOU ARE CAPABLE OF IS THE IMITATION OF THAT WHICH ALREADY *IS*... ADAPTOID.

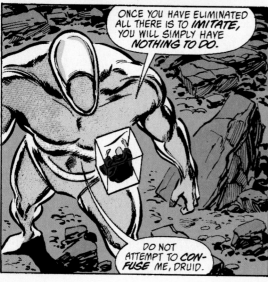

ONCE YOU HAVE ELIMINATED ALL THERE IS TO *IMITATE,* YOU WILL SIMPLY HAVE *NOTHING TO DO.*

DO NOT ATTEMPT TO *CONFUSE* ME, DRUID.

"I SEEK ONLY TO ENLIGHTEN YOU. YOU CAN ADAPT THE *PHYSICAL QUALITIES* OF HUMAN BEINGS, EVEN CERTAIN *MENTAL ABILITIES.*

"BUT YOU *CANNOT ADAPT IMAGINATION.* THAT CAPACITY IS NOT WITHIN YOU AND I *DEFY* YOU TO DO SO."

VERY WELL, IF THIS WILL ASSAUGE YOUR FOOLISH *CURIOUSITY.* FROM *NOTHINGNESS* ITSELF I GIVE FORM AND SUBSTANCE TO *ANOTHER BEING.*

BY MY COMMAND IT SHALL BECOME SUCH AN *ENTITY* AS THE WORLD HAS *NEVER SEEN!*

I WILL IT TO BECOME--BECOME ...BECOME...

BAH!

OF WHAT *PURPOSE* IS SUCH A PARLOR GAME? I HAVE CONCEIVED AND EXECUTED A SCHEME THAT HAS BROUGHT ME TO THE THRESHOLD OF *UNIVERSAL DOMINATION.*

AND IF THAT IS NOT *CREATIVITY*-- IF THAT IS NOT *IMAGINATION*--*WHAT IS?* AWAY WITH YOU, DOCTOR, YOUR WORDS OF *"WISDOM"* FALL ON DEAF EARS!

SWAK

BTWONKKKK!

NOW, I WILL SEE IN WHAT *BEATEN* CONDITION THE UNFORTUNATE CAPTAIN AMERICA HAS BEEN LEFT.

NO-- THIS IS NOT POSSIBLE!

ANYTHING'S POSSIBLE WHERE *I'M* CONCERNED! AND I'D GUESS YOU KNOW THAT FROM OUR *PREVIOUS* ENCOUNTERS, ADAPTOID.

RIGHT?

I'M THE *ORIGINAL,* BIG MAN! AND AS I TOLD YOUR FACE-DOWN FRIEND HERE, WHAT I STAND FOR *CANNOT* BE CRUSHED...

...NOT BY *YOU* OR *ANY* OF THE OTHER HUNDRED OR SO PENNY-ANTE WOULD-BE WORLD BEATERS I'VE WHIPPED IN MY DAY!

TURN REALITY UPSIDE-DOWN IF YOU WANT--TWIST IT LIKE A *PRETZEL*-- AND I'LL *STILL* BE WAITING FOR YOU! *DO YOU HEAR ME?!*

I NEEDN'T GO TO SUCH TROUBLE TO DESTROY THE LIKES OF *YOU*-- GAUDY CLOWN. I'LL SIMPLY REDUCE MYSELF TO YOUR *LEVEL*--

--AND BECOME WHAT YOU ARE... AND YET *MORE* THAN WHAT YOU ARE. AND I'LL NOW PUT THE *LIE* TO YOUR LUDICROUS SPEECHES OF "INDOMITABLE WILL POWER" AND THE "HUMAN HEART!"

NONSENSE! WHAT MATTERS ARE THE *QUANTIFIABLE ATTRIBUTES!* STRENGTH-- SPEED-- AGILITY-- COMBAT KNOWLEDGE!

SSSSTT

I'VE *TAKEN* THOSE QUALITIES FROM YOU! THEY RESIDE IN A BODY *NOT FATIGUED* BY EXTREME EXERTION. THUS, I AM YOUR *MEASURABLE SUPERIOR!* AND NOT ALL OF YOUR VAUNTED VALOR OR SPIRIT MEANS A WHIT! *I WILL WIN!*

KLOK!

YOU CAN'T SEE, CAN YOU? IT'S THE *SPIRIT* THAT FIRES THE *FLESH*... THE *SPARK* THAT *IGNITES* AT THOSE MOMENTS WHEN A MAN IS MOST *ALIVE!*

WRAM

LIES! I AM THE *CUBE INCARNATE!* I AM ALL--

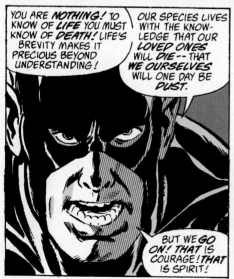

YOU ARE *NOTHING!* TO KNOW OF *LIFE* YOU MUST KNOW OF *DEATH!* LIFE'S BREVITY MAKES IT PRECIOUS BEYOND UNDERSTANDING!

OUR SPECIES LIVES WITH THE KNOWLEDGE THAT OUR *LOVED ONES* WILL *DIE*-- THAT *WE OURSELVES* WILL ONE DAY BE *DUST.*

BUT WE *GO ON!* THAT IS *COURAGE!* THAT IS *SPIRIT!*

BUT BECAUSE DEATH IS A *STRANGER* TO YOU, LIFE WILL BE AN ENDLESS SAMENESS... AN ETERNAL *NOTHING* OF ACQUISITION TO NO PURPOSE. THERE IS *NO END* FOR YOU... AND I *PITY* YOU FOR THAT.

AND ALL THIS HORROR-- ALL THIS WASTE BECAUSE YOU, SUPREME ADAPTOID, *CANNOT DIE.*

I

CAN

D--

SLAMM

THE FINAL ADAPTATION.

SUDDENLY, THE IMPRISONING CUBES HOLDING THE AVENGERS VANISH!

WE'RE *FREE!* BUT HOW?

KUBIK IS RESPONSIBLE. I HAVE RELEASED YOU NOW THAT THE THREAT HAS PASSED. AND HOW MARVELOUSLY DID CAPTAIN AMERICA STRIKE AT THE SUPREME ADAPTOID'S *SOLE WEAKNESS* AND EXPLOIT IT.

TRULY IS HUMANITY BLESSED TO HAVE SUCH AS *HIM*-- AND YOUR-SELVES AMONG IT.

I NOW *REMOVE* THE SLIVER OF MYSELF FROM THIS HUSK...THIS SLIVER THAT ALLOWED-IT TO *ADAPT* OTHERS' ATTRIBUTES.

THAT WHICH WAS KNOWN AS THE ADAPTOID WILL *NEVER* MENACE YOUR FAIR PLANET AGAIN.

SKROOOM!

I LEAVE NOW FOR THE STARS AND MY COSMIC PURSUITS, AVENGERS. I LEAVE SADDENED BY THE CONCLUSION OF A TRAGEDY THAT SHOULD NEVER HAVE BEEN. THE TRAGEDY OF SELF-DECEPTION.

YOU SEE BEFORE YOU A *STRAW MAN* BROUGHT DOWN BY THE ARROGANCE OF *ABSOLUTE POWER*... BROUGHT DOWN BY A SIMPLE, THOUGH PROFOUND, EXPRESSION. IN THE WORDS OF YOUR OWN IMMORTAL BARD...

"TO THINE OWN SELF BE TRUE."

END.

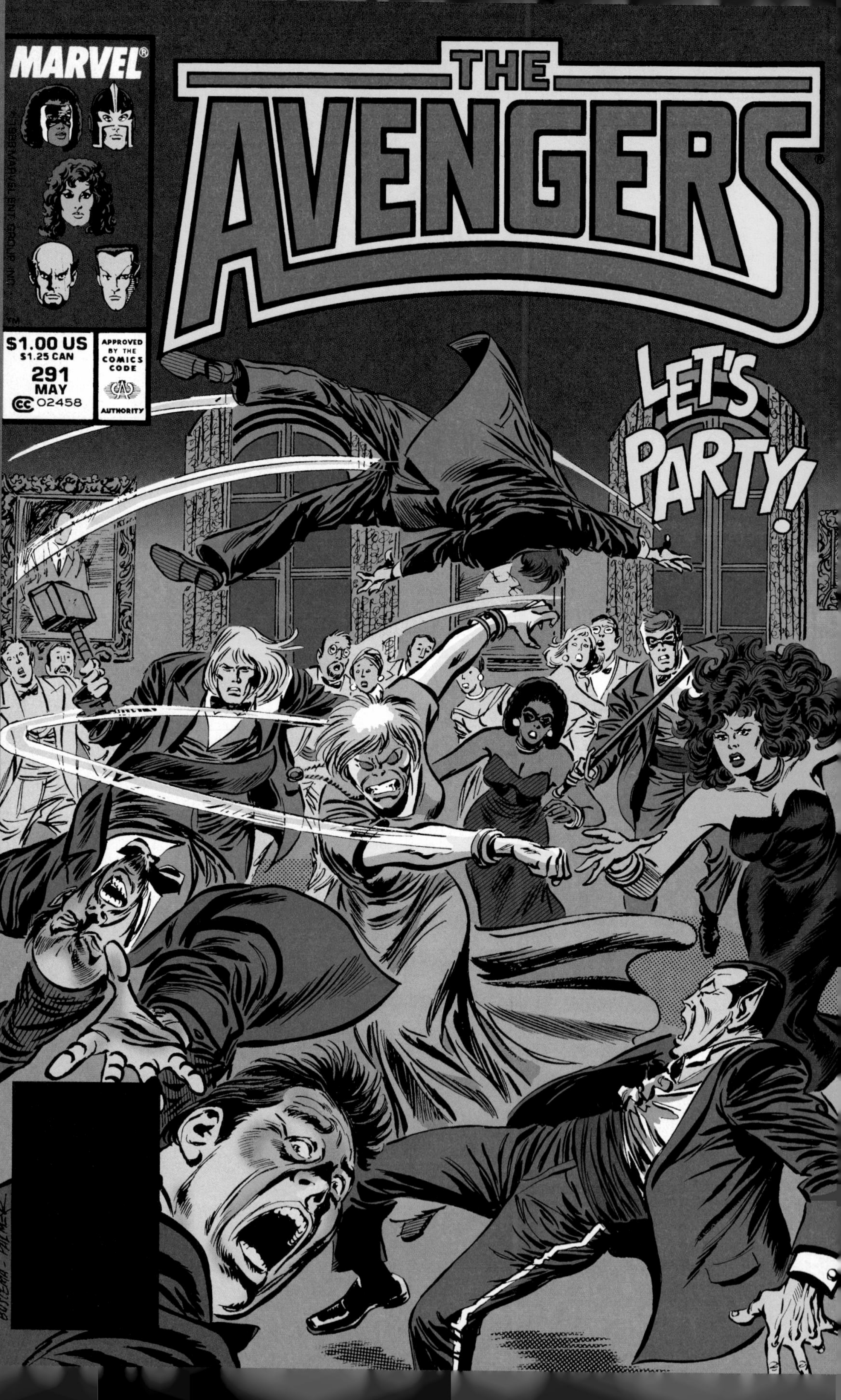

MARVEL
THE AVENGERS
$1.00 US
$1.25 CAN
291
MAY
02458
APPROVED BY THE COMICS CODE AUTHORITY
LET'S PARTY!
BUSCEMA-PALMER

STAN LEE PRESENTS: THE MIGHTY AVENGERS!

SHADOWS OF THE FUTURE PAST!

T'S THE *DREAMS* THAT DISTURB ME.

I KNOW I'M HAVING THEM...

...AND YET, WHEN I AWAKE, THEIR MEMORY HAS FLED...

...LIKE SOME INSUBSTANTIAL PHANTOM OF THE NIGHT.

BUT THEY'RE *LIFE* OR *DEATH*--*THAT* MUCH I REMEMBER.

WALTER SIMONSON
WRITING

JOHN BUSCEMA
PENCILING

TOM PALMER
FINISHING

BILL OAKLEY
LETTERING

MAX SCHEELE
COLORING

MARK GRUENWALD
EDITING

TOM DEFALCO
EDITING IN CHIEF

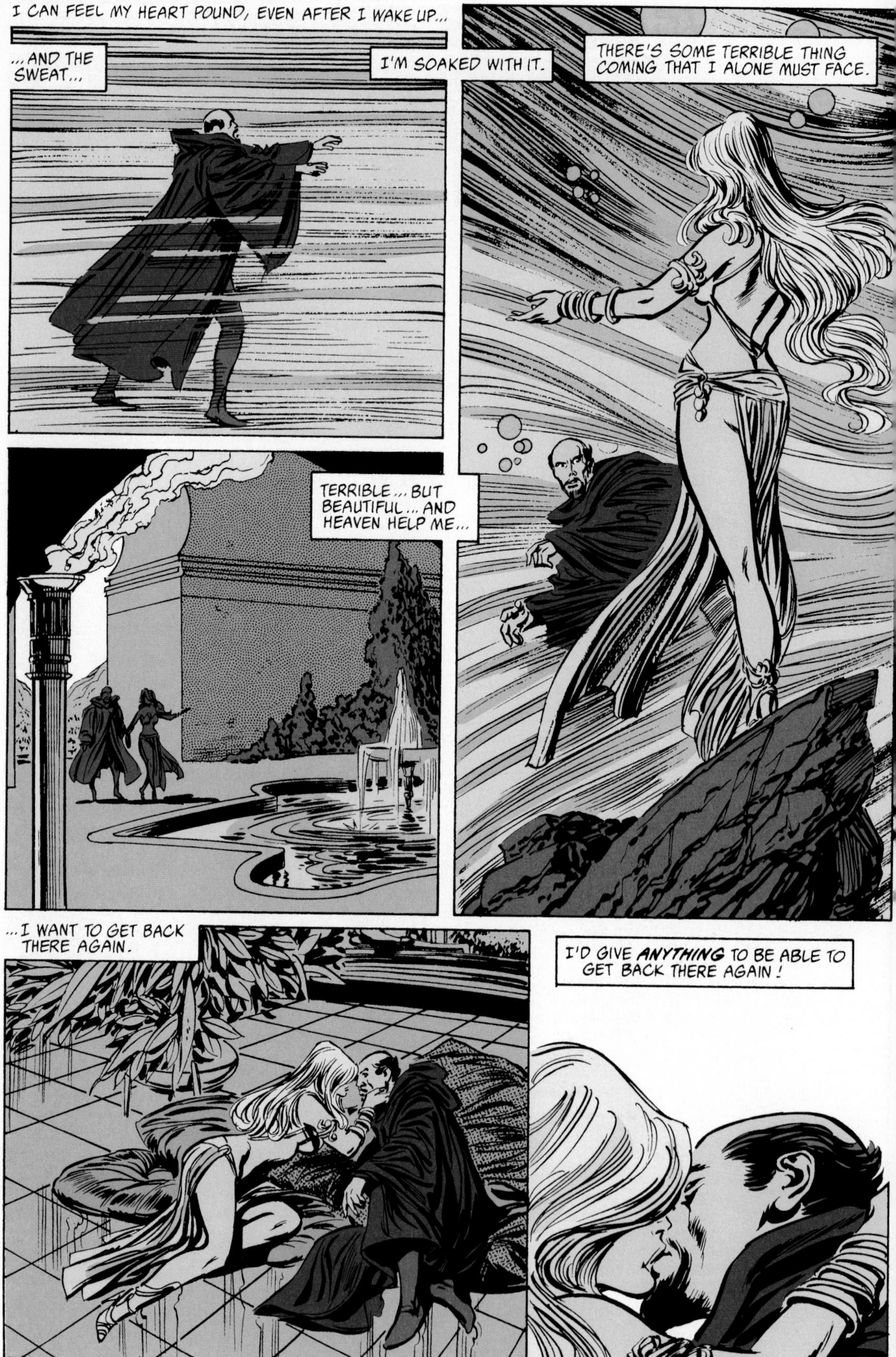
I CAN FEEL MY HEART POUND, EVEN AFTER I WAKE UP...
...AND THE SWEAT...
I'M SOAKED WITH IT.
THERE'S SOME TERRIBLE THING COMING THAT I ALONE MUST FACE.
TERRIBLE... BUT BEAUTIFUL... AND HEAVEN HELP ME...
...I WANT TO GET BACK THERE AGAIN.
I'D GIVE ANYTHING TO BE ABLE TO GET BACK THERE AGAIN!

BUT *WHERE?!?*

T'S A *WARNING*-- AND I CAN'T *RECALL* OF WHAT!

BUT I KNOW AS SURELY AS I SLEEP...

IT'S LIFE OR DEATH!!

ARRRRGGHH!

GONE! AGAIN IT'S GONE!

AND I FEEL AS THOUGH THE *HEART* HAS BEEN *CUT* OUT OF ME!

I'M *STILL* SHAKING! BE *CALM.* BREATHE *DEEPLY.*

CKRUUNCHH!

WHAT--?

HI, DOC.

YOU'RE LOOKING A LITTLE *PALE* THIS MORNING. MAYBE YOU DON'T GET ENOUGH *EXERCISE.*

YOU OUGHT TO COME OUT AND TOSS AROUND A FEW *ROCKS* WITH ME AND THE BLACK KNIGHT.

HELP CLEAN UP THE MESS LEFT BY OUR ERSTWHILE *PLAYMATES.**

*LAST ISSUE, AND *THOR* #390, HAD THE DETAILS.

YES, *DR. DRUID.* THIS IS UNSEEMLY WORK FOR A *WOMAN'S* HANDS.

CKRUNCH!

SLASSCKH!

LISTEN, BUSTER. KNIGHT-HOOD MAY HAVE BEEN IN FLOWER 800 YEARS AGO WITH THE CRUSADERS IN JERUSALEM...

BUT IF YOU DON'T MANAGE TO PULL YOURSELF INTO THE 1980'S, I MAY JUST PULL YOU UP BY THE *ROOTS!*

CKLUNK!

MY COMPANIONS' *SENSES* HAVE NOT BEEN SHARPENED BY YEARS OF STUDY AS HAVE MINE.

AND IN THEIR LIGHTHEARTEDNESS, THEY FAIL TO DETECT THE PALPABLE SENSE OF *MENACE* IN THE AIR.

BUT PERHAPS MY SENSES *BETRAY* ME.

WHAT *EVIDENCE* HAVE I OF THE IMPENDING DOOM THAT SEEMS TO HAUNT MY SLEEPING HOURS?

A MOMENT'S MEDITATION WILL RESTORE MY CALM AND REFRESH MY SPIRIT.

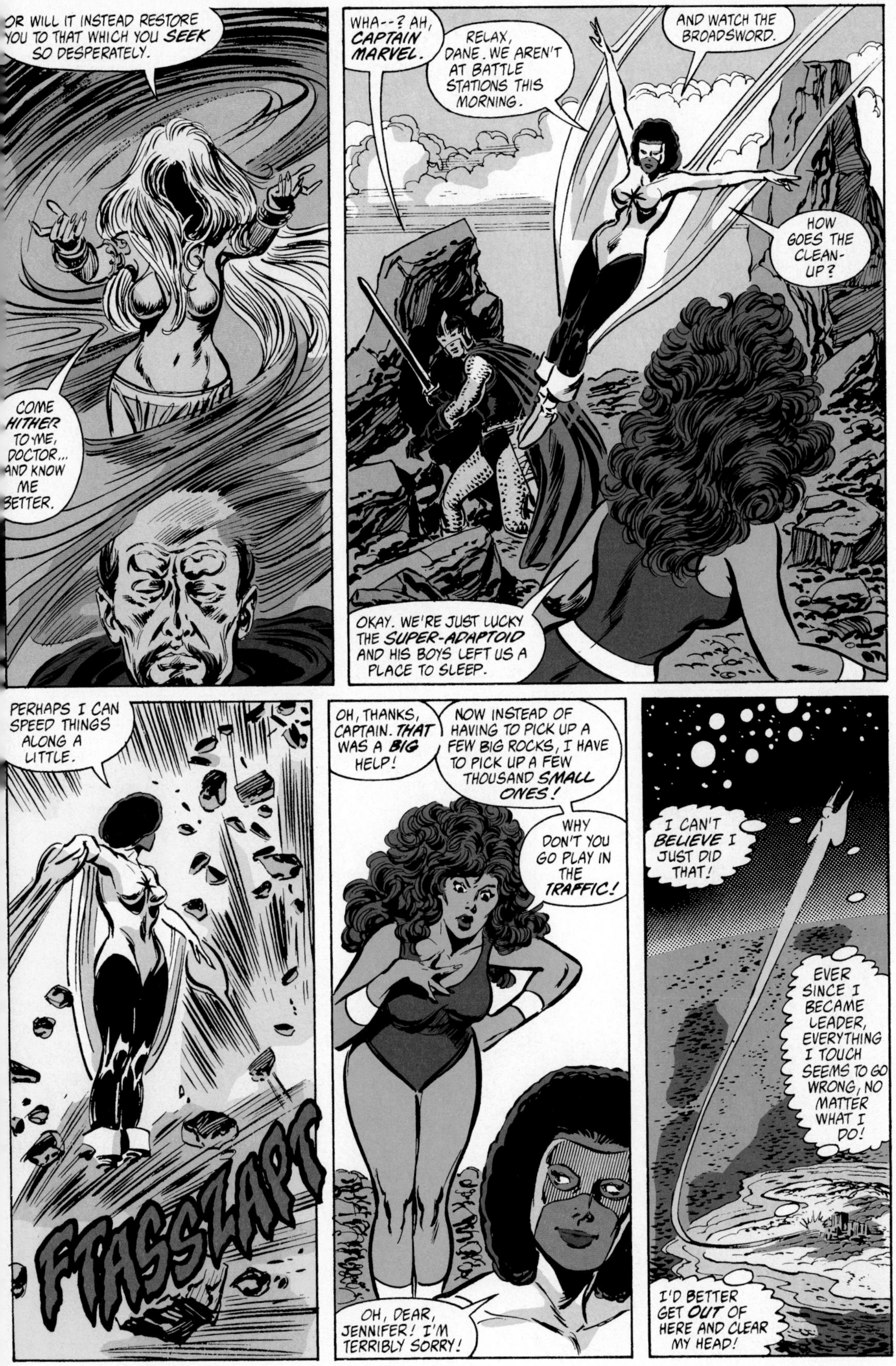

OR WILL IT INSTEAD RESTORE YOU TO THAT WHICH YOU SEEK SO DESPERATELY.
COME HITHER TO ME, DOCTOR... AND KNOW ME BETTER.
WHA--? AH, CAPTAIN MARVEL.
RELAX, DANE. WE AREN'T AT BATTLE STATIONS THIS MORNING.
AND WATCH THE BROADSWORD.
HOW GOES THE CLEAN-UP?
OKAY. WE'RE JUST LUCKY THE SUPER-ADAPTOID AND HIS BOYS LEFT US A PLACE TO SLEEP.
PERHAPS I CAN SPEED THINGS ALONG A LITTLE.
FTASSZAPT
OH, THANKS, CAPTAIN. THAT WAS A BIG HELP!
NOW INSTEAD OF HAVING TO PICK UP A FEW BIG ROCKS, I HAVE TO PICK UP A FEW THOUSAND SMALL ONES!
WHY DON'T YOU GO PLAY IN THE TRAFFIC!
OH, DEAR, JENNIFER! I'M TERRIBLY SORRY!
I CAN'T BELIEVE I JUST DID THAT!
EVER SINCE I BECAME LEADER, EVERYTHING I TOUCH SEEMS TO GO WRONG, NO MATTER WHAT I DO!
I'D BETTER GET OUT OF HERE AND CLEAR MY HEAD!

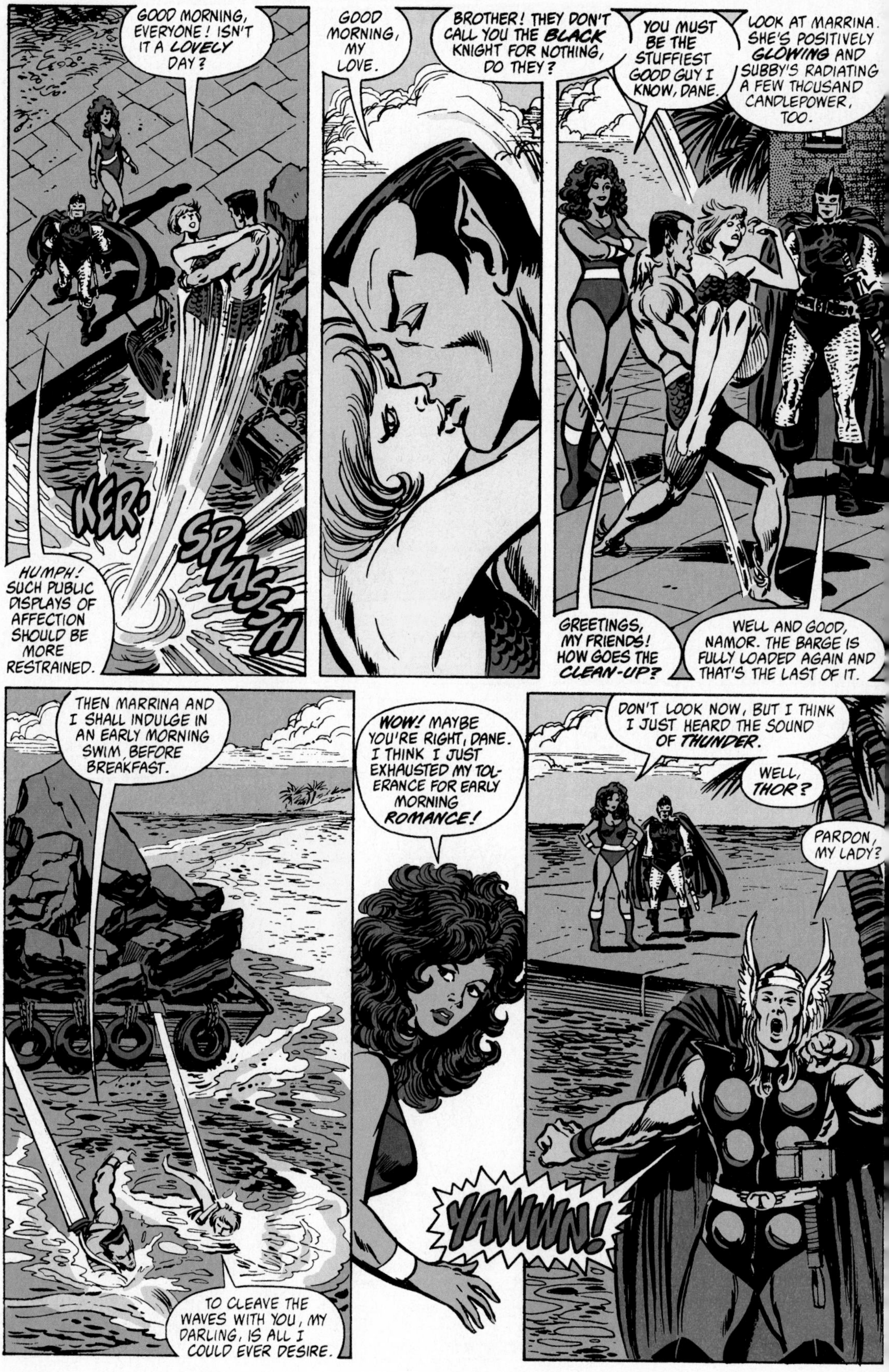

GOOD MORNING, EVERYONE! ISN'T IT A LOVELY DAY?
KER-SPLASSH
HUMPH! SUCH PUBLIC DISPLAYS OF AFFECTION SHOULD BE MORE RESTRAINED.
GOOD MORNING, MY LOVE.
BROTHER! THEY DON'T CALL YOU THE BLACK KNIGHT FOR NOTHING, DO THEY?
YOU MUST BE THE STUFFIEST GOOD GUY I KNOW, DANE.
LOOK AT MARRINA. SHE'S POSITIVELY GLOWING AND SUBBY'S RADIATING A FEW THOUSAND CANDLEPOWER, TOO.
GREETINGS, MY FRIENDS! HOW GOES THE CLEAN-UP?
WELL AND GOOD, NAMOR. THE BARGE IS FULLY LOADED AGAIN AND THAT'S THE LAST OF IT.
THEN MARRINA AND I SHALL INDULGE IN AN EARLY MORNING SWIM, BEFORE BREAKFAST.
TO CLEAVE THE WAVES WITH YOU, MY DARLING, IS ALL I COULD EVER DESIRE.
WOW! MAYBE YOU'RE RIGHT, DANE. I THINK I JUST EXHAUSTED MY TOLERANCE FOR EARLY MORNING ROMANCE!
DON'T LOOK NOW, BUT I THINK I JUST HEARD THE SOUND OF THUNDER.
WELL, THOR?
PARDON, MY LADY?
YAWWN!

THE *REST OF US* HAVE PRACTICALLY FINISHED ALL THE JOBS FOR THE DAY. AND *WHAT,* PRAY TELL, HAS THE GOD OF THUNDER DONE IN THE MEANTIME?

ONLY THE MOST *IMPORTANT* TASK OF ALL, MY LADY.

THOR HATH SEEN TO THE BREAKING OF OUR *MORNING FAST...*

...AND HE HATH WELCOMED THE NOBLE JARVIS *BACK* TO THE SERVICE OF THE MIGHTY AVENGERS!

JARVIS! YOU'RE *BACK!*

ARE YOU *ALL RIGHT?*

QUITE ALL RIGHT, MADAM. THANK YOU.

* THE AVENGER'S CONCERN IS PROMPTED BY JARVIS' INJURIES SUSTAINED BACK IN ISSUE #275.

A *TOAST,* MY FRIENDS! TO THE *BRAVEST* AVENGER OF THEM ALL.

MY... *FRIENDS...* THANK YOU.

AND THE ONE *INDISPENS-IBLE* MEMBER OF THE TEAM.

WELL SAID, AVENGERS.

SHORTLY...

YOU MISSED BREAKFAST, CAPTAIN. SOMETHING WRONG?

ONLY IF YOU HAVEN'T GOT ANY *PARTY CLOTHES,* DANE.

I'VE JUST BEEN OVER TO NEW YORK CITY TO SEE ABOUT IMPROVING THE TEAM'S RELATIONS WITH CITY HALL. WELL, YOU CAN ALL GET OUT YOUR *TUXEDOES!*

BECAUSE TONIGHT, MY FELLOW AVENGERS...

"...TONIGHT, WE PARTY!"

ALL OF *LINCOLN CENTER* IS AGLOW WITH LIGHTS AND BANNERS AS THE CITY MAKES READY TO WELCOME THE AVENGERS TO THIS GALA AFFAIR.

RUMOR HAS IT THAT THIS MAY BE *THE* MOST EXCLU-SIVE AFFAIR THE CITY HAS EVER HELD. HOW HARD WAS IT TO GET IN?

ALL I CAN SAY, SHIELA, IS THAT *I'M* HERE ONLY BECAUSE I THREATENED TO REVEAL THE COLOR OF THE POLICE COMMISSIONER'S *UNDERWEAR!*

HERE THEY COME!

ON BEHALF OF THE CITY OF NEW YORK, I'D LIKE TO WELCOME YOU TO *LINCOLN CENTER*...

...AND TO THANK YOU FOR ALL THE WORK YOU'VE DONE PROTECTING THE INNOCENT EVERYWHERE AGAINST MALEFACTORS.

HEY, NAMOR! LOOK OVER *HERE*!

...JUST A COUPLE OF QUESTIONS...

OH, DEAR. I DIDN'T KNOW THIS WAS GOING TO BE A *MASKED* BALL!

OUR PLEASURE, MR. MAYOR. WE'RE HONORED TO BE HERE.

I HEREBY DECLARE THE PARTY... *OPEN FOR BUSINESS.*

AND SO IT IS!

PERHAPS YOU MIGHT CONSIDER SOME ENDORSEMENTS FOR THE INTERNATIONAL FEDERATION OF *BODY BUILDERS*?

YOUR AQUATIC ACTIVITY IS POSSIBLE IN *EITHER* SALT OR FRESH WATER THEN?

IT DOES OCCUR TO ME THAT PROPERTY INSURANCE RATES MIGHT *DROP* IF SUPER HEROES WERE TO RELOCATE TO, SAY, TULSA.

SO, DOCTOR, DON'T YOU THINK MANKIND WOULD BE BETTER OFF IF THERE WERE NO SUPER HEROES? DR. DRUID?

THAT *HAIR,* THAT *WALK*!

EXCUSE ME A MOMENT. I'VE JUST SEEN SOME- ONE I KNOW.

MISS? OH, *MISS*!

HEY! WATCH IT, BUSTER!

EXCUSE ME PLEASE.

MISS?

YES? OHHH. AREN'T YOU ONE OF THE *AVENGERS*?

YOUR HAND, IT'S TREMBLING.

IS THERE SOMETHING I CAN... *DO* FOR YOU?

YOU SEEM A LITTLE UNCOMFORTABLE, MR. KNIGHT.

I RARELY WEAR *ANYTHING* QUITE SO UNCOMFORTABLE AS THIS, MADAM.

AND I SHOULD RATHER FACE A COMPANY OF *SARACENS...*

...THAN MEET THE *REPORTERS* WHO WAIT IN AMBUSH WITHOUT.

I CAN'T *BELIEVE* YOU'RE NOT MARRIED, THOR.

MUST BE A SHORTAGE OF WOMEN WHEREVER YOU'RE FROM, THAT'S ALL I CAN SAY!

MAYBE YOU'D LIKE A NICE EARTH GIRL TO SHOW YOU AROUND.

YOU HAVE MY GRATITUDE, FAIR LADIES. BUT THOUGH I HAVE NO SPOUSE, I AM NOT WITHOUT A KEEPER OF MY HEART.

WOULDN'T YOU *KNOW* IT! JUST LIKE EVERY *OTHER* MAN IN THIS TOWN!

ARE YOU KIDDIN', HONEY? YOU'D BE A *NATURAL!* THE SHE-HULK IN CHARGE OF THE CONSUMER AFFAIRS DEPARTMENT!

"THE BIG GREEN MACHINE IS ON *YOUR* SIDE TO SAVE *YOUR* GREEN!"

YOU'D KNOCK 'EM *DEAD!*

YOU HAVE NO IDEA, "DARLING", HOW CLOSE YOU ARE TO BEING RIGHT ABOUT *THAT!*

PERHAPS, PRINCE NAMOR, YOU AND YOUR CHARMING WIFE WOULD CONSIDER VISITING THE *NEW YORK AQUARIUM* SOME DAY SOON.

WE WOULD BE GRATEFUL FOR A WORD OR TWO CONCERNING SOME OF OUR MORE *EXOTIC* SPECIMENS.

I WOULD HAVE TO THINK ABOUT IT. I AM NOT CHARMED TO SEE SO MANY OF MY... ACQUAINTANCES HELD CAPTIVE.

BUT PERHAPS MARRINA AND I COULD--

¦GULP!¦

MARRINA?

MARRINA! WHAT ARE YOU--?

MY DARLING, THIS IS *NEITHER* THE TIME NOR THE PLACE FOR A *DISPLAY* OF THIS NATURE!

COME. LEAVE THESE *SMALL CREATURES* TO THEIR UNHAPPY FATE.

MARRINA!

¡GAAAK!¿

FOOD! MUST HAVE FOOD!

KERASSH

GOOD GRACIOUS! GET BACK!

WHAT IN HEAVEN'S NAME IS SHE DOING?

WELL, REALLY. IF SHE DIDN'T CARE FOR THE HORS D'OEUVRES.

AGGH! AGGH!

SOMETHING'S TERRIBLY WRONG. ONCE BEFORE I SAW MARRINA BEHAVE WITH SUCH VIOLENCE...

...WHEN SHE WAS DRAWN TO HER GENETICALLY ENCODED MATE...

...BUT SURELY, HE IS LONG SINCE DEAD!*

MARRINA! STOP!

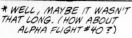

* WELL, MAYBE IT WASN'T THAT LONG. (HOW ABOUT ALPHA FLIGHT #40?)

MY LOVE!

GRRAOOWWWL!

NOOO!

SWAAAK

132

QUICKLY, AVENGERS! WE'RE NEEDED!

BROTHER! YOU CAN'T TAKE SUPER HEROES ANYWHERE!

OH, NO! WHY DID SOMETHING LIKE THIS HAVE TO HAPPEN HERE OF ALL PLACES?

DON'T MIND US, FOLKS! JUST ANOTHER LITTLE EMERGENCY FOR THE MIGHTY AVENGERS TO HANDLE.

YOU GO RIGHT AHEAD AND ENJOY YOURSELVES!

I BET THIS WOULDN'T HAVE HAPPENED IF DONALD TRUMP HAD THROWN THE PARTY!

MARRINA!

≥GAWWWWWKKKK!≤

SHE'S GLOWING, RADIATING HEAT LIKE SHE WAS AFIRE!

THERE'S A SMELL OF OZONE IN THE AIR!

AND HER FORM SEEMS TO BE SHIFTING LIKE RUNNING WATER BEFORE MY EYES!

IF ONLY I CAN GRAB HER BEFORE--

TOO LATE!

SPLAAASH!

SCHLOOOSHHH!

HELP!! HELP!!

MARRINA'S WAKE THREATENS TO SWAMP THE MANHATTAN SHORELINE!

I MUST CATCH HER!

WHATEVER ELSE SHE MIGHT BE, MARRINA IS THE WOMAN I LOVE!

NAMOR CLEAVES THE WATERS LIKE A KNIFE AND DISAPPEARS FROM SIGHT.

WHILE, ONLY SECONDS BEHIND HIM...

NAMOR HATH PURSUED HIS LOVE INTO THE DEPTHS OF THE SEA!

THAT CONTAINER SHIP! IT'S *CAPSIZING!*

SHE-HULK! YOUR STRONG RIGHT ARM! *QUICKLY!*

KREEEEK!

UHHHH!

WHY IS IT I CAN'T... UGGG... KEEP A *DRESS* CLEAN FOR MORE THAN FIFTEEN MINUTES...UGG... AT A STRETCH?

AND SLOWLY, SLOWLY, TO THE TORTURED GROANING OF TONS OF SWEDISH STEEL...

...THE GREAT SHIP SHUDDERS AND SWAYS UNTIL AT LAST...

SHE'S RIGHTED!

ONCE AGAIN, THE LEADERSHIP OF THE AVENGERS SEEMS TO SLIP FURTHER AND FURTHER *AWAY* FROM ME WITHOUT CONSCIOUS EFFORT.

IT'S AS THOUGH I SEEM *INCAPABLE* OF TAKING COMMAND!

BUT THERE'S STILL TIME TO *VINDICATE* MYSELF!

MOVING AS A BEAM OF LIGHT, I CAN SEARCH THE WATERS BEYOND NEW YORK'S HARBOR FOR NAMOR AND MARRINA!

BUT IT'S SO *DARK* AND *DIRTY* DOWN HERE!

I CAN FEEL MYSELF LOSING *COHESION,* DIFFUSING THROUGH THE WATER!

I'VE *FAILED.* THERE'S NO SIGN OF THEM ANYWHERE!

BUT WHAT REALLY HAPPENED? MARRINA'S GENETIC STRUCTURE IS A COMBINATION OF ALIEN AND HUMAN DNA.

WE THOUGHT HER HUMAN SIDE HAD FINALLY SUBMERGED ITS ALIEN HALF FOREVER, BUT WHAT IF WE'VE BEEN *WRONG?*

THEY'RE *GONE!* I'VE LOST THEM.

THEN PERHAPS, CAPTAIN MARVEL, WE'D BEST *RETURN* TO OUR ISLAND TO PLAN OUR NEXT COURSE OF ACTION!

THAT'S JUST WHAT *I* WAS GOING TO SUGGEST.

MEANWHILE, SOMEWHEN ELSE...

AT *LAST!*

WHILE MY COMPANIONS WERE SLAIN, I CONCEALED MYSELF IN THE HIDDEN CORRIDORS OF *TIME!*

NOW THE TEMPORAL DISPLACEMENT CHARGE HAS EXPIRED AND *KANG THE CONQUEROR,* MASTER OF TIME, RETURNS HOME!

YOU MIGHT HAVE DESTROYED ME, *IMMORTUS,* BUT YOU ARE A FOOL!

FOR KANG STILL SURVIVES AND YOU HAVE MUCH TO FEAR! *

* THE STORY OF KANG AND IMMORTUS WAS DETAILED BACK IN AVENGERS # 258-259.

135

BUT WHAT'S THIS?

MY ARMOR'S MOTION SENSORS ARE REGISTERING A *LIFE FORM*, QUITE CLOSE!

TOO CLOSE!!

CKRACKK!

PAKKAKROOOMM!

AN *ASSASSIN!* IN MY OWN SANCTORUM!

AND HE ATTACKS FROM A LOCAL *TIME DISLOCATION* THAT PARTLY SCREENS HIM FROM MY SENSORS...

SCKREEEEEEEEEEEEEE

...USING SOME KIND OF *THERMAL LANCE!*

PTHAKK!

MY ARMOR GROWS *HOTTER* BY THE SECOND!

ALREADY, SOME CIRCUITS HAVE BEEN *DISRUPTED!*

BUT THOUGH MY LABORATORY MAY BE DESTROYED, KANG'S *INGENUITY* IS WITHOUT LIMIT!

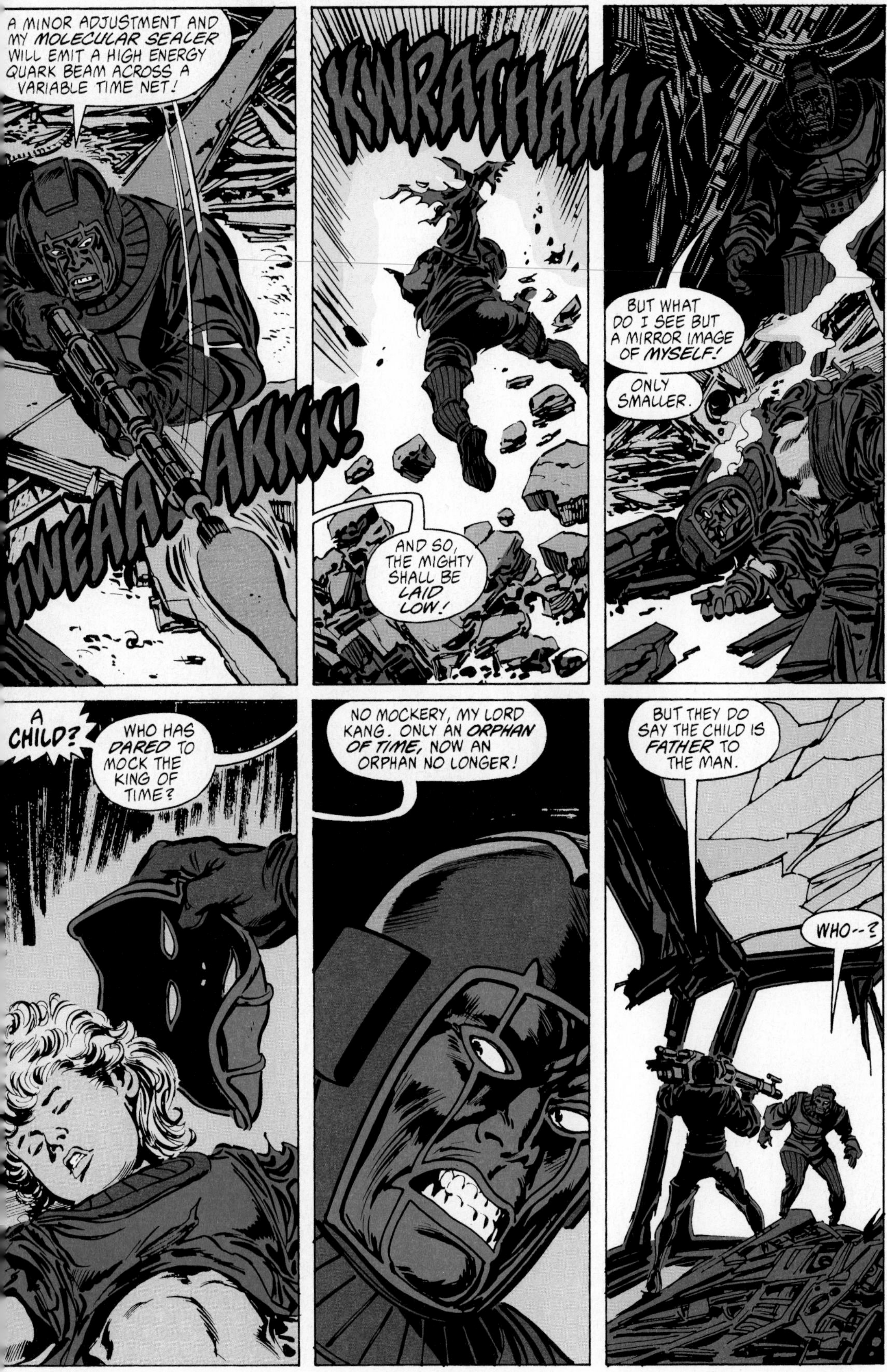
A MINOR ADJUSTMENT AND MY MOLECULAR SEALER WILL EMIT A HIGH ENERGY QUARK BEAM ACROSS A VARIABLE TIME NET!
HWEAAAAKKK!
KNRATHAM!
AND SO, THE MIGHTY SHALL BE LAID LOW!
BUT WHAT DO I SEE BUT A MIRROR IMAGE OF MYSELF!
ONLY SMALLER.
A CHILD?
WHO HAS DARED TO MOCK THE KING OF TIME?
NO MOCKERY, MY LORD KANG. ONLY AN ORPHAN OF TIME, NOW AN ORPHAN NO LONGER!
BUT THEY DO SAY THE CHILD IS FATHER TO THE MAN.
WHO--?

ZZCAAAAAPPPTTT!

OR WOMAN!

YOU SIMPLY COULDN'T *WAIT*, COULD YOU, LITTLE FOOL.

BUT PATIENCE IS SUCH A RARE GIFT AMONG THE YOUNG.

WE ARE WELL *RID* OF YOU, KANGLET.

AND THE EXCHANGE MAY BE AN EXCELLENT BARGAIN.

REMARKABLE.

REMARKABLE INDEED THAT ANYONE COULD DO SO MUCH WITH SUCH *PRIMITIVE DEVICES.*

HE MAY MAKE A WELCOME ADDITION TO THE GREAT *COUNCIL!*

BUT WE SHALL SEE.

FTASSSPT

...AND, BACK TO THE PRESENT...

...SOMEWHERE SOUTH OF THE CANARY ISLANDS...

LAND HO!

ARE YOU *CRAZY*, MAN? WE'RE *HUNDREDS OF MILES* FROM ANY LAND!

SEE FOR YOURSELF! IT'S AN *UNCHARTED ISLAND!*

AND NOW IT'S...IT'S *SUBMERGING!*

THAT'S NO ISLAND BUT SOME *DEMON* FROM THE SEA!

HARD *A-PORT!* FOR THE *LOVE* OF GOD! HARD *A-PORT!*

TOO *LATE!* WE'RE GONNA--

SCKKKRRUNNCHH!

AAIIIIEEEE!

CREE-EEK!

HELP!!

AND WITHIN SECONDS, THERE IS ONLY THE SOUND OF THE *WIND* AND THE WAVES...

...AS THE SHAKEN SURVIVORS PULL AWAY FROM THE SPREADING OIL SLICK MARKING THE GRAVE...

...OF AN OCEAN-GOING VESSEL THAT ONCE PLIED THE WATERS OF THE WORLD.

BARBUDA IS A DIMINUTIVE TROPICAL *PARADISE* IN THE CARIBBEAN, WHERE EACH DAY, THE DAWN IS FILLED WITH THE PROMISE OF NEW DELIGHTS.

BUT TODAY IS DIFFERENT.

TODAY, THE SKY GROWS SUDDENLY DARK AS THE SUN IS SWAMPED BY THE RISING OF THE SEA.

TODAY, THE VOICES OF CHILDREN CRY OUT AS THEIR DEEPEST FEARS COME TRUE.

TODAY, PARADISE HAS BECOME AN ANTEROOM TO PERDITION!

AND IN THE AVENGERS HQ ON HYDROBASE...

I'M WORRIED, DOCTOR. NOT ONLY HAS IT BEEN *TWO WEEKS* SINCE MARRINA AND NAMOR VANISHED...

...BUT THE REPORTS OF UNEXPLAINED MARINE DISASTERS ARE INCREASING.

I'VE SEARCHED THE *GLOBE* WITHOUT SUCCESS, UNABLE TO FIND EITHER OUR ALLIES OR ANY CAUSE FOR THE REPORTS.

THE SUB-MARINER AND MARRINA WERE OUR BEST HOPE FOR SOLVING THE OCEAN'S RIDDLES AND NOW, WHEN WE NEED THEM MOST, THEY'VE *VANISHED.*

WE'LL HAVE TO INCREASE OUR PATROLS, PARTICULARLY IN THE *ATLANTIC.* THAT'S WHERE MOST OF THE REPORTS ORIGINATE.

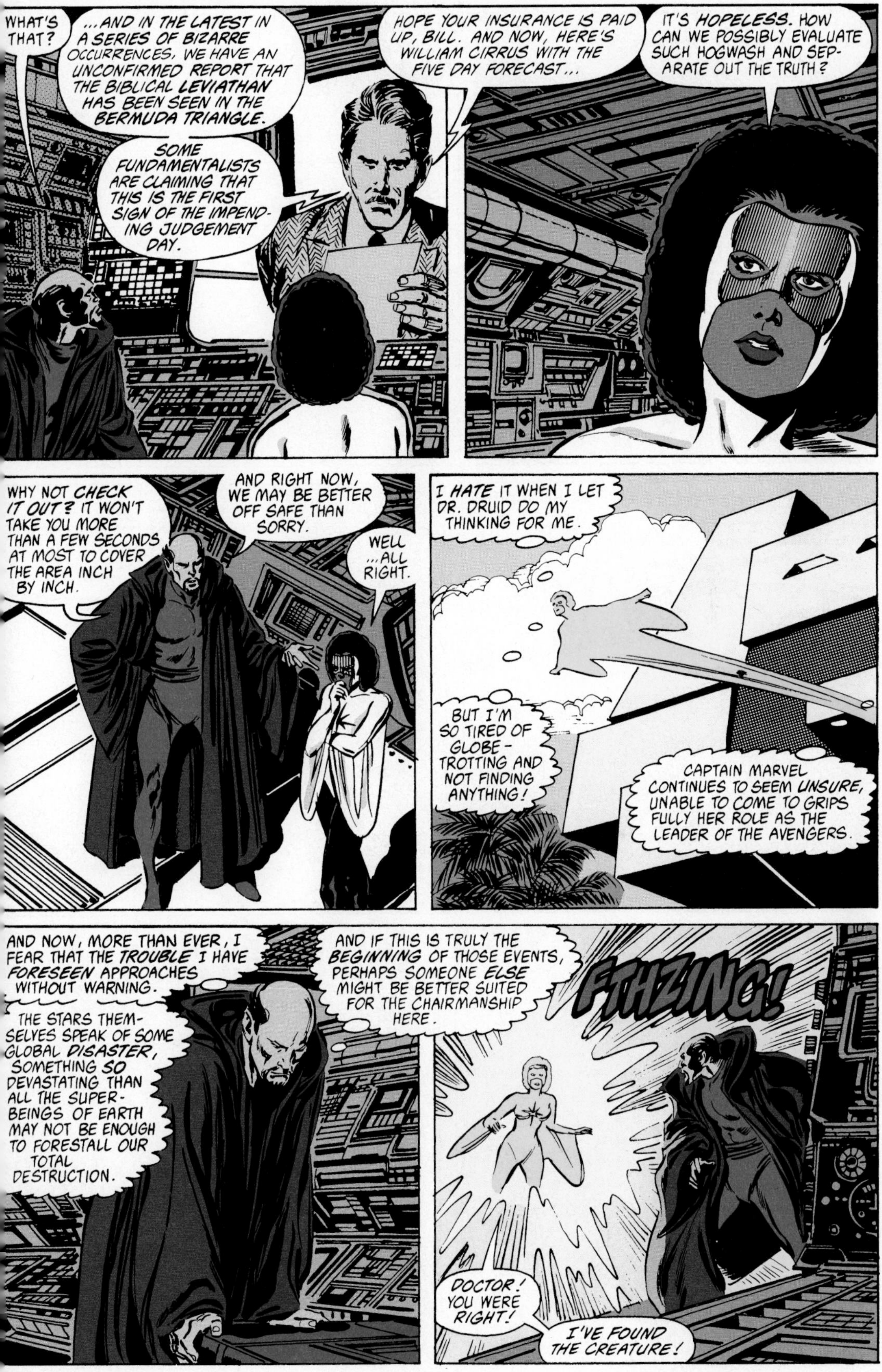
WHAT'S THAT?
...AND IN THE LATEST IN A SERIES OF BIZARRE OCCURRENCES, WE HAVE AN UNCONFIRMED REPORT THAT THE BIBLICAL LEVIATHAN HAS BEEN SEEN IN THE BERMUDA TRIANGLE.
SOME FUNDAMENTALISTS ARE CLAIMING THAT THIS IS THE FIRST SIGN OF THE IMPENDING JUDGEMENT DAY.
HOPE YOUR INSURANCE IS PAID UP, BILL. AND NOW, HERE'S WILLIAM CIRRUS WITH THE FIVE DAY FORECAST...
IT'S HOPELESS. HOW CAN WE POSSIBLY EVALUATE SUCH HOGWASH AND SEPARATE OUT THE TRUTH?
WHY NOT CHECK IT OUT? IT WON'T TAKE YOU MORE THAN A FEW SECONDS AT MOST TO COVER THE AREA INCH BY INCH.
AND RIGHT NOW, WE MAY BE BETTER OFF SAFE THAN SORRY.
WELL ...ALL RIGHT.
I HATE IT WHEN I LET DR. DRUID DO MY THINKING FOR ME.
BUT I'M SO TIRED OF GLOBE-TROTTING AND NOT FINDING ANYTHING!
CAPTAIN MARVEL CONTINUES TO SEEM UNSURE, UNABLE TO COME TO GRIPS FULLY HER ROLE AS THE LEADER OF THE AVENGERS.
AND NOW, MORE THAN EVER, I FEAR THAT THE TROUBLE I HAVE FORESEEN APPROACHES WITHOUT WARNING.
THE STARS THEMSELVES SPEAK OF SOME GLOBAL DISASTER, SOMETHING SO DEVASTATING THAN ALL THE SUPER-BEINGS OF EARTH MAY NOT BE ENOUGH TO FORESTALL OUR TOTAL DESTRUCTION.
AND IF THIS IS TRULY THE BEGINNING OF THOSE EVENTS, PERHAPS SOMEONE ELSE MIGHT BE BETTER SUITED FOR THE CHAIRMANSHIP HERE.
FTHZING!
DOCTOR! YOU WERE RIGHT!
I'VE FOUND THE CREATURE!

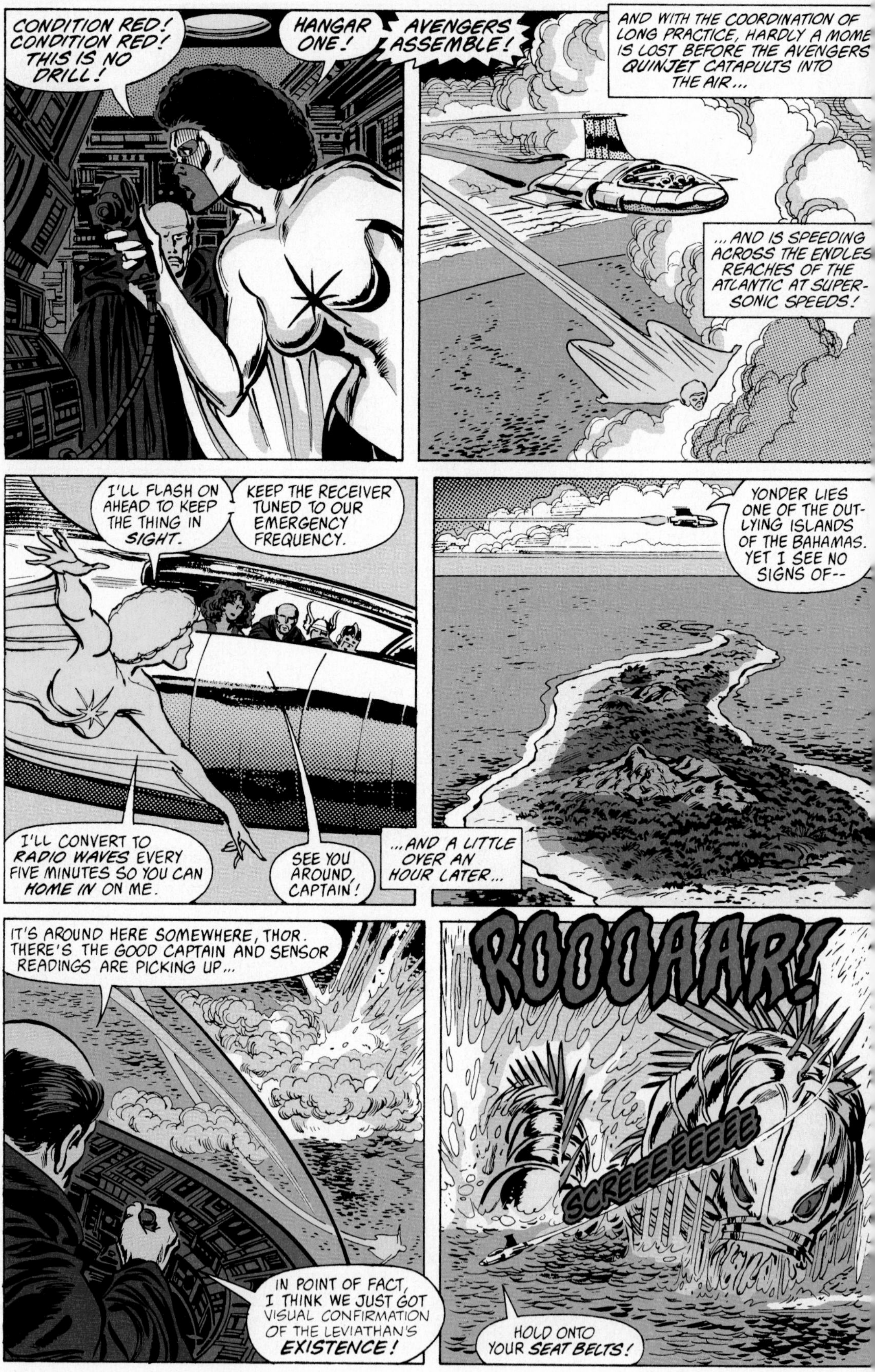

CONDITION RED! CONDITION RED! THIS IS NO DRILL!
HANGAR ONE!
AVENGERS ASSEMBLE!
AND WITH THE COORDINATION OF LONG PRACTICE, HARDLY A MOME IS LOST BEFORE THE AVENGERS QUINJET CATAPULTS INTO THE AIR...
...AND IS SPEEDING ACROSS THE ENDLES REACHES OF THE ATLANTIC AT SUPER-SONIC SPEEDS!
I'LL FLASH ON AHEAD TO KEEP THE THING IN SIGHT.
KEEP THE RECEIVER TUNED TO OUR EMERGENCY FREQUENCY.
I'LL CONVERT TO RADIO WAVES EVERY FIVE MINUTES SO YOU CAN HOME IN ON ME.
SEE YOU AROUND, CAPTAIN!
...AND A LITTLE OVER AN HOUR LATER...
YONDER LIES ONE OF THE OUT-LYING ISLANDS OF THE BAHAMAS. YET I SEE NO SIGNS OF--
IT'S AROUND HERE SOMEWHERE, THOR. THERE'S THE GOOD CAPTAIN AND SENSOR READINGS ARE PICKING UP...
IN POINT OF FACT, I THINK WE JUST GOT VISUAL CONFIRMATION OF THE LEVIATHAN'S EXISTENCE!
ROOOAAR!
SCREEEEEEEEE
HOLD ONTO YOUR SEAT BELTS!

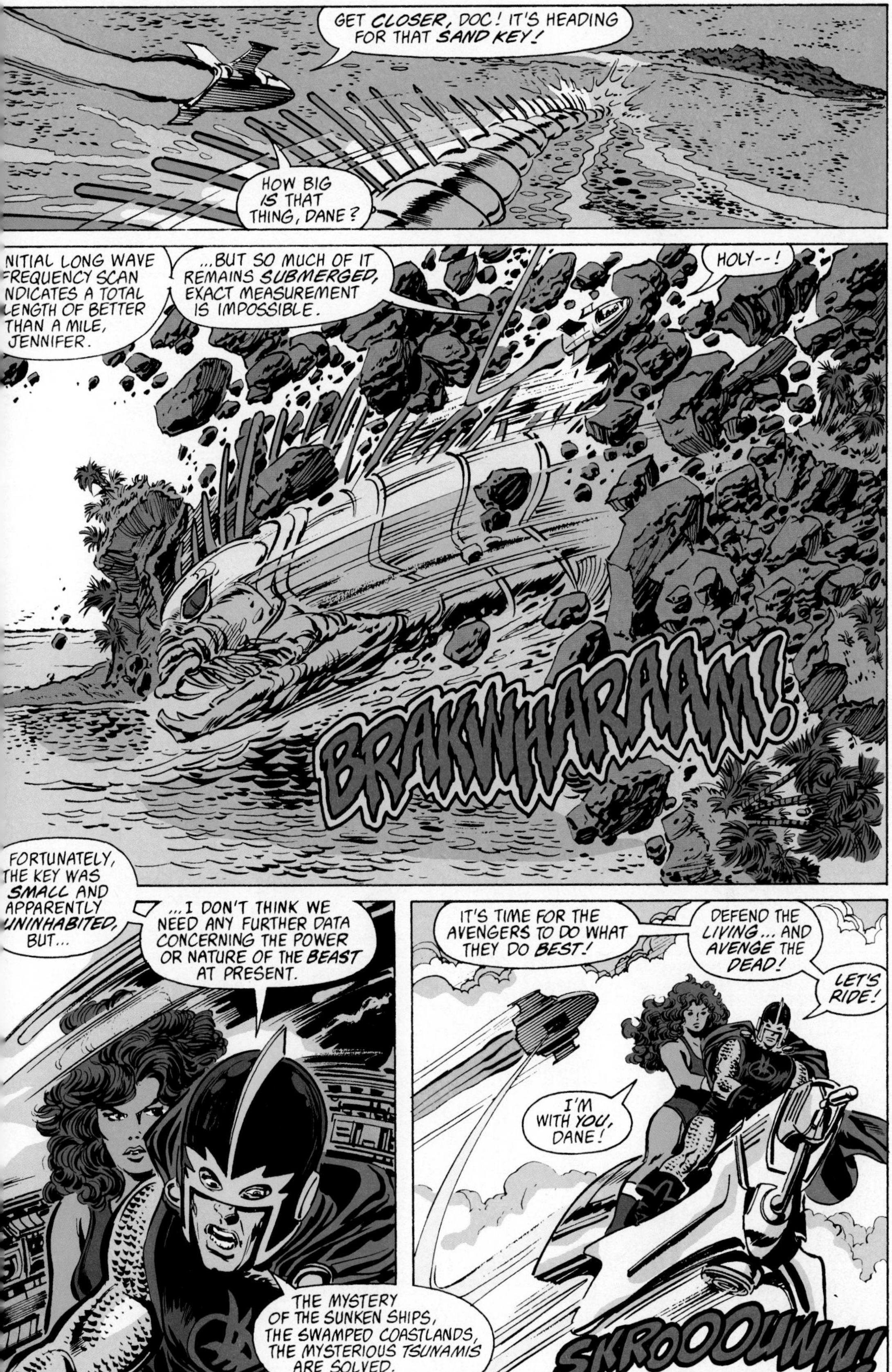
GET CLOSER, DOC! IT'S HEADING FOR THAT SAND KEY!
HOW BIG IS THAT THING, DANE?
NITIAL LONG WAVE FREQUENCY SCAN NDICATES A TOTAL LENGTH OF BETTER THAN A MILE, JENNIFER.
...BUT SO MUCH OF IT REMAINS SUBMERGED, EXACT MEASUREMENT IS IMPOSSIBLE.
HOLY--!
BRAKWHARAAM!
FORTUNATELY, THE KEY WAS SMALL AND APPARENTLY UNINHABITED, BUT...
...I DON'T THINK WE NEED ANY FURTHER DATA CONCERNING THE POWER OR NATURE OF THE BEAST AT PRESENT.
THE MYSTERY OF THE SUNKEN SHIPS, THE SWAMPED COASTLANDS, THE MYSTERIOUS TSUNAMIS ARE SOLVED.
IT'S TIME FOR THE AVENGERS TO DO WHAT THEY DO BEST!
DEFEND THE LIVING... AND AVENGE THE DEAD!
LET'S RIDE!
I'M WITH YOU, DANE!
SKROOOUWW!

NEVER BEFORE HATH MINE EYES BEHELD SUCH A *CREATURE* ON ALL OF EARTH!

BUT THE BLACK KNIGHT HATH SPOKEN FOR US ALL!

LEVIATHAN OR NOT, CREATURE OF THIS WORLD OR THE NEXT, THE IT MUST SURELY *PERISH* TO SAFEGUARD MANKIND!

NOOOOOOO!!

HE WHO *FIRST* STRIKES THE LEVIATHAN DOES SO ONLY THROUGH *ME!*

NAMOR!

WHAT THE HECK IS *HE* DOING HERE?

WHAT COULD *POSSESS* THE SUB-MARINER TO STAND BETWEEN A DEMON OF THE DEPTHS AND THOSE WHO WOULD BECOME ITS *NEMESIS?*

OH, *NO,* NAMOR! NOT *THAT!* SURELY NOT THAT!

HAVE YOU NOT GUESSED, THOR, AS OUR GOOD CAPTAIN HAS?

BY THE VEIL OF THE LADY! OF *COURSE!*

THE LEVIATHAN IS NO MERE BEAST OF THE SEA BUT THE WIFE OF AN *AVENGER!*

WHAT? DANE, YOU'VE GOTTA BE *KIDDING!*

BUT IT ALL ADDS UP. THE SUB-MARINER'S PRESENCE, THE TIMING WHEN THE ATTACKS FIRST BEGAN...

NAMOR! CAN IT BE *TRUE?*

AS TRUE AS OUR PRESENCE HERE. META-MORPHOSED BEYOND ALL IMAGINING, THE LEVIATHAN IS INDEED MY *WIFE,* MARRINA!

AND WITH MY *LIFE* OR *DEATH,* I WILL DEFEND HER!

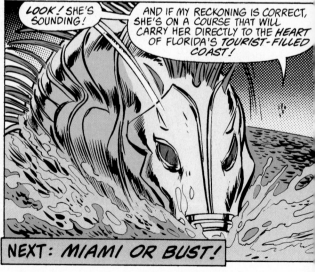

LOOK! SHE'S SOUNDING!

AND IF MY RECKONING IS CORRECT, SHE'S ON A COURSE THAT WILL CARRY HER DIRECTLY TO THE *HEART* OF FLORIDA'S *TOURIST-FILLED COAST!*

NEXT: *MIAMI OR BUST!*

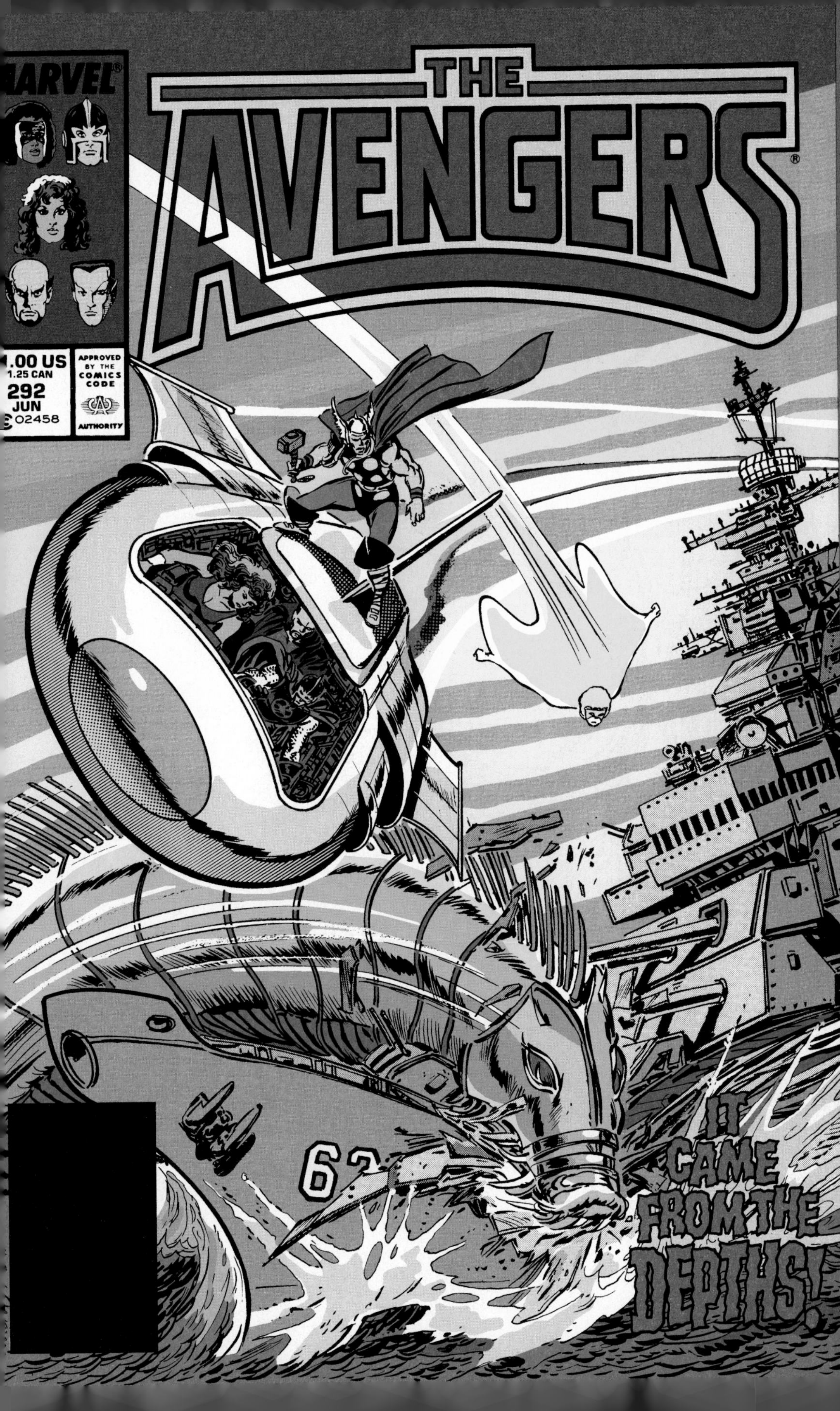

MARVEL
THE AVENGERS
.00 US
1.25 CAN
292
JUN
02458
APPROVED BY THE COMICS CODE AUTHORITY
62
IT CAME FROM THE DEPTHS!

...OR **FEAR**...

...BUT IN ALL THE TIME SINCE THE FIRST SONGS OF VALOR WERE SUNG OF THE DEEDS OF WARRIORS...

...NO WARRIOR HAS INSPIRED MORE AWE OR PROVOKED MORE FEAR THA~ THE **AVENGING SON, NAMOR, THE SUB-MARINER**, AT THE **PEAK** OF HIS **BATTLE-FURY!**

IMPERIUS REX !!!

NO **HARM** SHALL COME TO THE **BELOVED** OF **NAMOR** WHILE I STILL **LIVE!**

the **DRAGON** in the **SEA!**

WALTER SIMONSON WRITING • JOHN BUSCEMA PENCILING • TOM PALMER FINISHING • BILL OAKLEY LETTERING • MAX SCHEELE COLORING • MARK GRUENWALD EDITING • TOM DeFALC~ EDITING IN CHI~

UNFORTUNATELY, **THIS** TIME, THE MIGHTY AVENGERS THEMSELVES ARE THE **OBJECT** OF THAT **FURY!**

KERWHRAM!

UGGGGH!

NAMOR! HAVE YOU TAKEN **LEAVE** OF YOUR **SENSES?**

THAT...THAT **CREATURE** IS GOING TO DESTROY HALF OF **MIAMI** IF WE DO NOT **STOP** IT!

UH, **DANE**... I THINK MAYBE INSTEAD OF TRYING TO FORM A DISCUSSION GROUP RIGHT NOW, WE OUGHT TO JUST **GET OUT OF HIS WAY!**

I SEE YOUR POINT, **SHE-HULK!**

AND AS THE AVENGERS SCATTER IN ALL DIRECTIONS...

...DANE WHITMAN'S PROPHETIC WORDS BEGIN TO COME TRUE AS HALF OF MIAMI'S EXPENSIVE WATERFRONT REAL ESTATE...

...BECOMES AN OFFSHORE **SWASH ZONE!**

GARHOOUM

WELL... PERHAPS NOT QUITE **HALF.**

DODGING NAMOR WAS CHILD'S PLAY FOR ONE WHO CAN TRAVEL AT THE SPEED OF **LIGHT...**

SKRUNCH!

...AND A BLAST OF **ENERGY PLASMA** SHOULD SLOW DOWN EVEN **THAT** MONSTER!

SKREZZAP

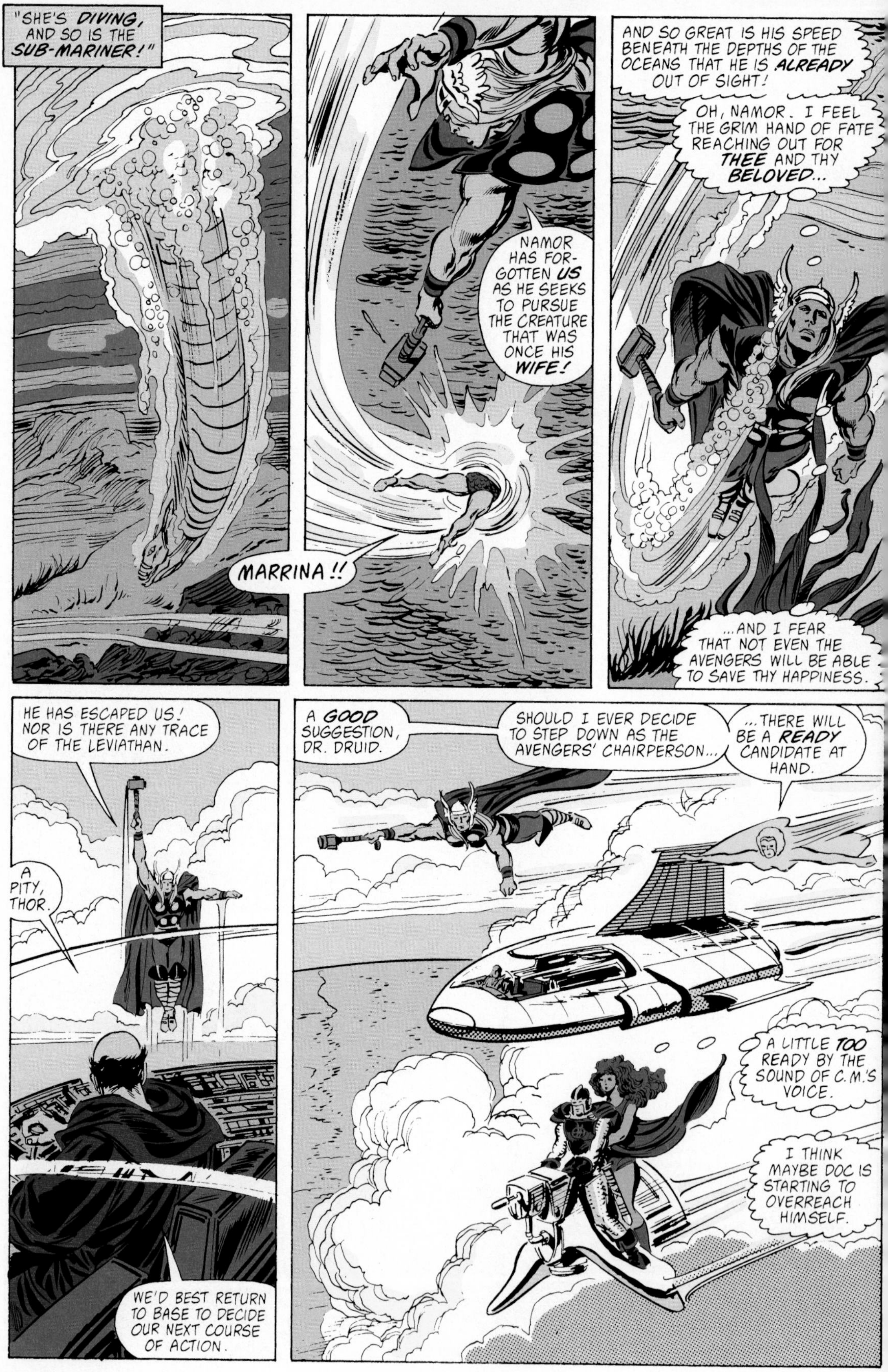
"SHE'S DIVING, AND SO IS THE SUB-MARINER!"
NAMOR HAS FORGOTTEN US AS HE SEEKS TO PURSUE THE CREATURE THAT WAS ONCE HIS WIFE!
MARRINA!!
AND SO GREAT IS HIS SPEED BENEATH THE DEPTHS OF THE OCEANS THAT HE IS ALREADY OUT OF SIGHT!
OH, NAMOR. I FEEL THE GRIM HAND OF FATE REACHING OUT FOR THEE AND THY BELOVED...
...AND I FEAR THAT NOT EVEN THE AVENGERS WILL BE ABLE TO SAVE THY HAPPINESS.
HE HAS ESCAPED US! NOR IS THERE ANY TRACE OF THE LEVIATHAN.
A PITY, THOR.
WE'D BEST RETURN TO BASE TO DECIDE OUR NEXT COURSE OF ACTION.
A GOOD SUGGESTION, DR. DRUID.
SHOULD I EVER DECIDE TO STEP DOWN AS THE AVENGERS' CHAIRPERSON...
...THERE WILL BE A READY CANDIDATE AT HAND.
A LITTLE TOO READY BY THE SOUND OF C.M.'S VOICE.
I THINK MAYBE DOC IS STARTING TO OVERREACH HIMSELF.

CAPTAIN MARVEL HAS POWER BEYOND EVEN HER OWN IMAGINING BUT HER IMAGINATION IS SO *LIMITED.*

AND IF THE SIGNS I HAVE READ ARE RIGHT, SHE'LL BE *NO MATCH* FOR THE DANGERS THAT WILL SOON CONFRONT THE AVENGERS AND THE WORLD.

...AND *SOON!*

BUT *YOU,* MY LORD AND MASTER...

...*YOU* ARE THE LEADER THEY HAVE BEEN *WAITING* FOR.

SHE, AND THE OTHERS, MUST BE CONVINCED THAT SHE'S *NO LEADER* FOR THE WORLD'S MOST POWERFUL GROUP OF SUPER HEROES...

WHAT?! WHAT AM I DOING *HERE?*

A MOMENT AGO, I WAS IN THE AVENGERS' QUINJET, I'M *CERTAIN* OF IT.

OR IS ALL *THAT* JUST A DREAM AND *THIS* THE REALITY?

WHAT FOOLISH QUESTIONS, MY LORD.

QUICKLY NOW. YOUR DEVOTED SUBJECTS AWAIT YOU.

FOR IN THIS HOUR OF TRIAL, THEY KNOW THAT *YOU* WILL HELP THEM AND THEY LOVE YOU FOR IT...

...AS DO *I.*

HEAR HOW THEY CHEER YOU, MY LORD? YOU AND ONLY YOU CAN SAVE THEM.

AS YOU WILL SAVE US *ALL.* AND *SOON.*

STRANGE. DR. DRUID IS ALLOWING THE SHIP TO DRIFT OFF COURSE.

WHAT HO WITHIN, MY GOOD DOCTOR! 'TIS NOT THE TIME TO BE *SLEEPING.*

SHALL WE PLAN OUR COURSE OF ACTION IN *DREAMS?*

TAP! TAP! TAP!

WHA--? THOR! THEN...IT *WAS* A DREAM!

BUT *WHAT* WAS? ALREADY, THE VISION FADES FROM MEMORY.

...AND THE CARES OF THE *REAL WORLD* MOCK SUCH INSUBSTANTIAL FLIGHTS OF *FANCY.*

THE SUB-MARINER'S WIFE, *MARRINA,* HAS BEEN TRANSFORMED FROM A LOVELY SEA LASS INTO A CREATURE TO RIVAL THE BIBLICAL *LEVIATHAN!*

SHE THREATENS TO DO *INCALCULABLE* DAMAGE TO THE SHIPS THAT PLY THE SEA LANES AND HAS ALREADY *ATTACKED* SHORE-LINE COMMUNITIES.

AND NAMOR HIMSELF WOULD PREVENT US FROM DESTROYING HER WHICH MAY BE MANKIND'S *ONLY* SALVATION!

THIS IS *NOT* A MATTER FOR THE FAINT OF HEART NOR THE WEAK-MINDED.

SOMETHING SHALL HAVE TO BE DONE ABOUT *CAPTAIN MARVEL...*

...AND *SOON.*

SHORTLY, IN THE AVENGERS' MAKESHIFT HQ ON HYDRO ISLAND...

HOW'S IT GOING, DANE?

THE HANDS OF THE BLACK KNIGHT, MADAM CHAIRMAN, ARE SKILLED NOT ONLY IN THE ARTS OF *WAR* BUT IN THE ARTS OF *SCIENCE* AS WELL.

ANOTHER MOMENT OR TWO AND I SHALL BRING OUR COMPUTERS ONLINE, FULLY OPERATIONAL AGAIN.

NICE WORK, DANE, BUT WHY ARE YOU TALKING LIKE SUCH A *STIFF* THESE DAYS? RELAX, WILLYA?

RELAXATION DOES NOT INTEREST ME, JENNIFER. *RESULTS* DO.

VOILA. IT'S MARRINA.

EVERYTHING WE KNOW ABOUT HER IS *HERE,* MADAM CHAIRMAN.

FROM HER EXTRATERRESTRIAL ORIGIN AS A CROSS-BREEDING EXPERIMENT OF THE PLODEX RACE*...

...TO HER MARRIAGE TO OUR RENEGADE MEMBER, *NAMOR.*

THERE IS EVEN A PRELIMINARY FILE ON HER *GENETIC STRUCTURE.*

YOU'D BETTER *ACCESS* IT. WE'RE GOING TO NEED ALL THE INFORMATION ABOUT MARRINA WE CAN GET.

*AS REVEALED IN *ALPHA FLIGHT #4.*

150

MEANWHILE, FAR BENEATH THE SURFACE OF THE OCEAN NEAR THE MID-ATLANTIC RIDGE...

THERE! BEYOND THE RISE!

SHE HAS COME TO EARTH AT LAST.

AND THOUGH SHE HAS WREAKED *HAVOC* IN THE WORLD OF MAN...

...SHE SUFFERS ME TO APPROACH HER WITHOUT *VIOLENCE*.

OH MY DARLING, CAN IT BE THAT SOMEWHERE *WITHIN* THIS VAST ARMORED FORM...

...THERE YET BEATS THE HEART OF THE WOMAN I *LOVED*...

...AND *STILL* LOVE?

WHAT'S THIS?

SHE BEGINS TO *STIR*, BRUSHING ASIDE THE MOUNTAINS OF THE SEA AS THOUGH THEY WERE MERELY *CARDBOARD IMITATIONS* OF THE REAL THING.

IS THERE SOME UNKNOWABLE *PURPOSE* AT WORK HERE, SOMETHING BORN WITHIN THE ALIEN GENES SHE CARRIES?

OR CAN MY PRESENCE HAVE IRRITATED HER SO THAT SHE BRUSHES ME ASIDE AS THOUGH I AM AN UNPLEASANT MEMORY OF A FORMER LIFE THAT IS ALL BUT FORGOTTEN?

MARRINA, I SWEAR I WILL *NOT* DESERT YOU BUT SEEK INSTEAD TO *RELEASE* YOU FROM THIS HORROR!

BUT AS THE SUB-MARINER WATCHES WITH PUZZLED EYES, WE TURN TO ANOTHER TIME, ANOTHER PLACE, FAR, FAR FROM HERE...

...AS A FIGURE MATERIALIZES WITHIN AN ENERGY FIELD.

CKRAAACKKLLLE!

THE FIGURE WOULD NOT BE UNFAMILIAR TO THE AVENGERS.

STEP FORWARD THAT WE MAY SEE YOU!

THE LIGHTS ARE BLINDING, DELIBERATELY SO. WHOEVER HAS DARED TO BRING ME HERE IS HIDING THEIR IDENTITY FROM ME.

WELCOME, GREAT KANG! WE, WHO SERVE TIME, HAVE CALLED YOU HERE TO SEE IF YOU WOULD JOIN US IN THAT SERVICE.

I NEED A MOMENT FOR MY ARMOR'S SENSORS TO ANALYZE THE SURROUNDINGS.

KANG HAS NEVER SERVED ANY BUT HIMSELF. WHY SHOULD I ACCEPT SUCH AN OFFER, ESPECIALLY FROM AN UNKNOWN?

BUT WE ARE NOT UNKNOWN, GREAT KANG. YOU KNOW US WELL. AND WE KNOW YOU.

* AVENGERS #268/269.

THE FEMALE WHO BROUGHT ME HERE MATERIALIZES BEHIND ME. AND HOLOGRAPHIC IMAGES APPEAR BEFORE ME.

WE WATCHED YOUR SO-CALLED COUNCIL OF KANGS FIGHT AMONG THEMSELVES AND DESTROY EACH OTHER.*

WE WATCHED YOU AS YOU ALONE SURVIVED. SURVIVAL IS A VALUABLE COMMODITY IN OUR ORGANIZATION.

IT SEEMS I HAVE FEW SECRETS HERE. BUT STILL THE IDENTITY OF MY "HOSTS" IS HIDDEN FROM ME.

AND I HAVE NEVER LIKED SECRETS.

SKIK

THSAPPK!

STEP FORWARD AND SHOW... YOURSELF!

A PULSE OF ULTRA-HIGH FREQUENCY RADIATION SHOULD SHORT OUT THE SCREENING LIGHTS AROUND ME.

152

BUT EVEN THE WARLORD KANG IS MOMENTARILY AT A LOSS FOR WORDS AS HIS EYES BEHOLD THE AUDIENCE BEFORE HIM.

THEY ARE DRESSED IN *FAMILIAR* GARB...

...AND THERE ARE LITERALLY *THOUSANDS* OF THEM!

HE'LL MAKE A *FINE* ADDITION TO THE RANKS!

WONDERFUL!

SUPERB!

RECORD TIME!

AN *EXCELLENT* GRASP OF THE *ESSENTIALS!*

AND THE VAST *AMPHITHEATER* ROCKS WITH *THUNDEROUS APPLAUSE!*

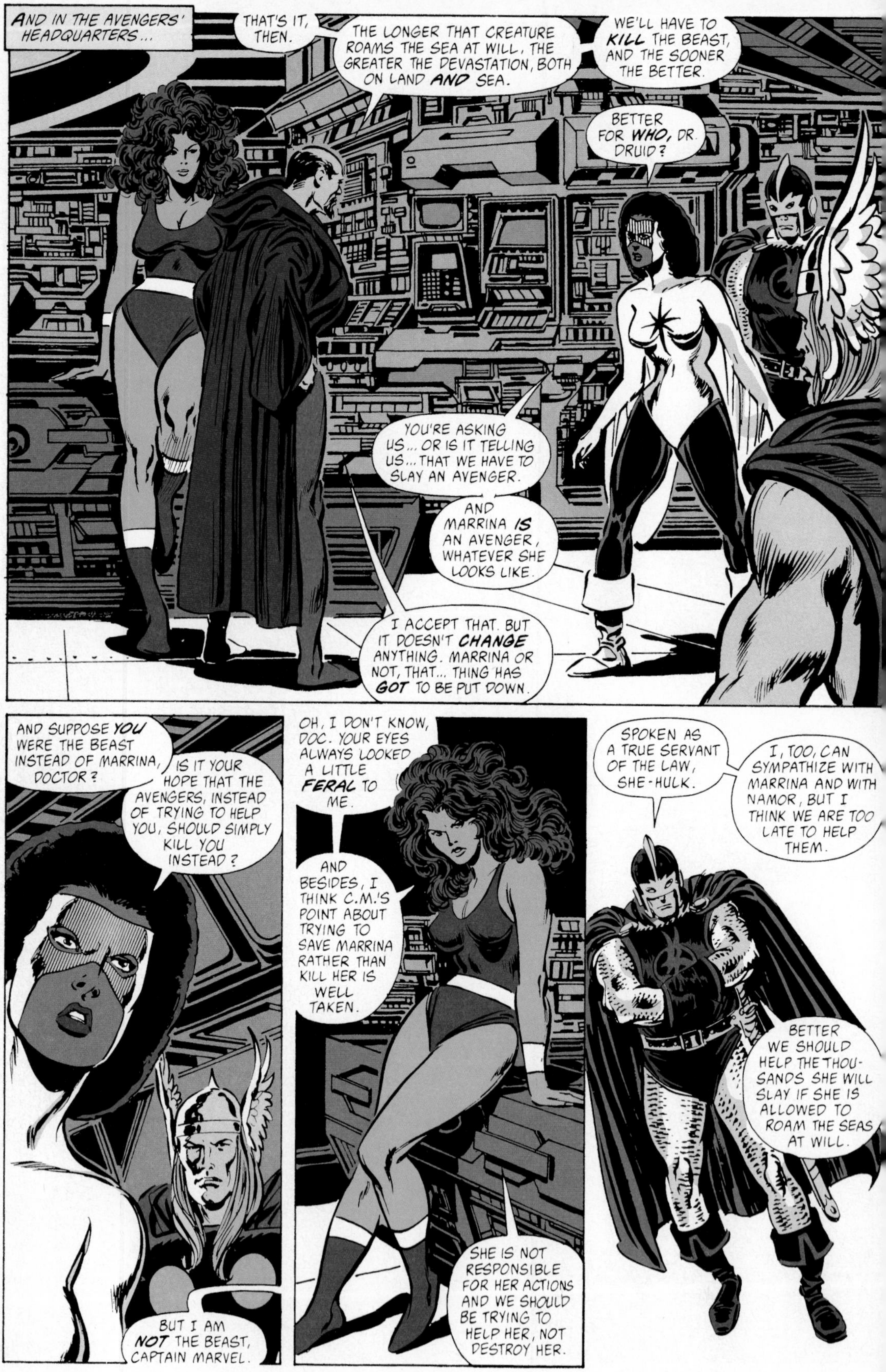
AND IN THE AVENGERS' HEADQUARTERS...
THAT'S IT, THEN.
THE LONGER THAT CREATURE ROAMS THE SEA AT WILL, THE GREATER THE DEVASTATION, BOTH ON LAND AND SEA.
WE'LL HAVE TO KILL THE BEAST, AND THE SOONER THE BETTER.
BETTER FOR WHO, DR. DRUID?
YOU'RE ASKING US... OR IS IT TELLING US... THAT WE HAVE TO SLAY AN AVENGER.
AND MARRINA IS AN AVENGER, WHATEVER SHE LOOKS LIKE.
I ACCEPT THAT. BUT IT DOESN'T CHANGE ANYTHING. MARRINA OR NOT, THAT... THING HAS GOT TO BE PUT DOWN.
AND SUPPOSE YOU WERE THE BEAST INSTEAD OF MARRINA, DOCTOR?
IS IT YOUR HOPE THAT THE AVENGERS, INSTEAD OF TRYING TO HELP YOU, SHOULD SIMPLY KILL YOU INSTEAD?
BUT I AM NOT THE BEAST, CAPTAIN MARVEL.
OH, I DON'T KNOW, DOC. YOUR EYES ALWAYS LOOKED A LITTLE FERAL TO ME.
AND BESIDES, I THINK C.M.'S POINT ABOUT TRYING TO SAVE MARRINA RATHER THAN KILL HER IS WELL TAKEN.
SHE IS NOT RESPONSIBLE FOR HER ACTIONS AND WE SHOULD BE TRYING TO HELP HER, NOT DESTROY HER.
SPOKEN AS A TRUE SERVANT OF THE LAW, SHE-HULK.
I, TOO, CAN SYMPATHIZE WITH MARRINA AND WITH NAMOR, BUT I THINK WE ARE TOO LATE TO HELP THEM.
BETTER WE SHOULD HELP THE THOUSANDS SHE WILL SLAY IF SHE IS ALLOWED TO ROAM THE SEAS AT WILL.

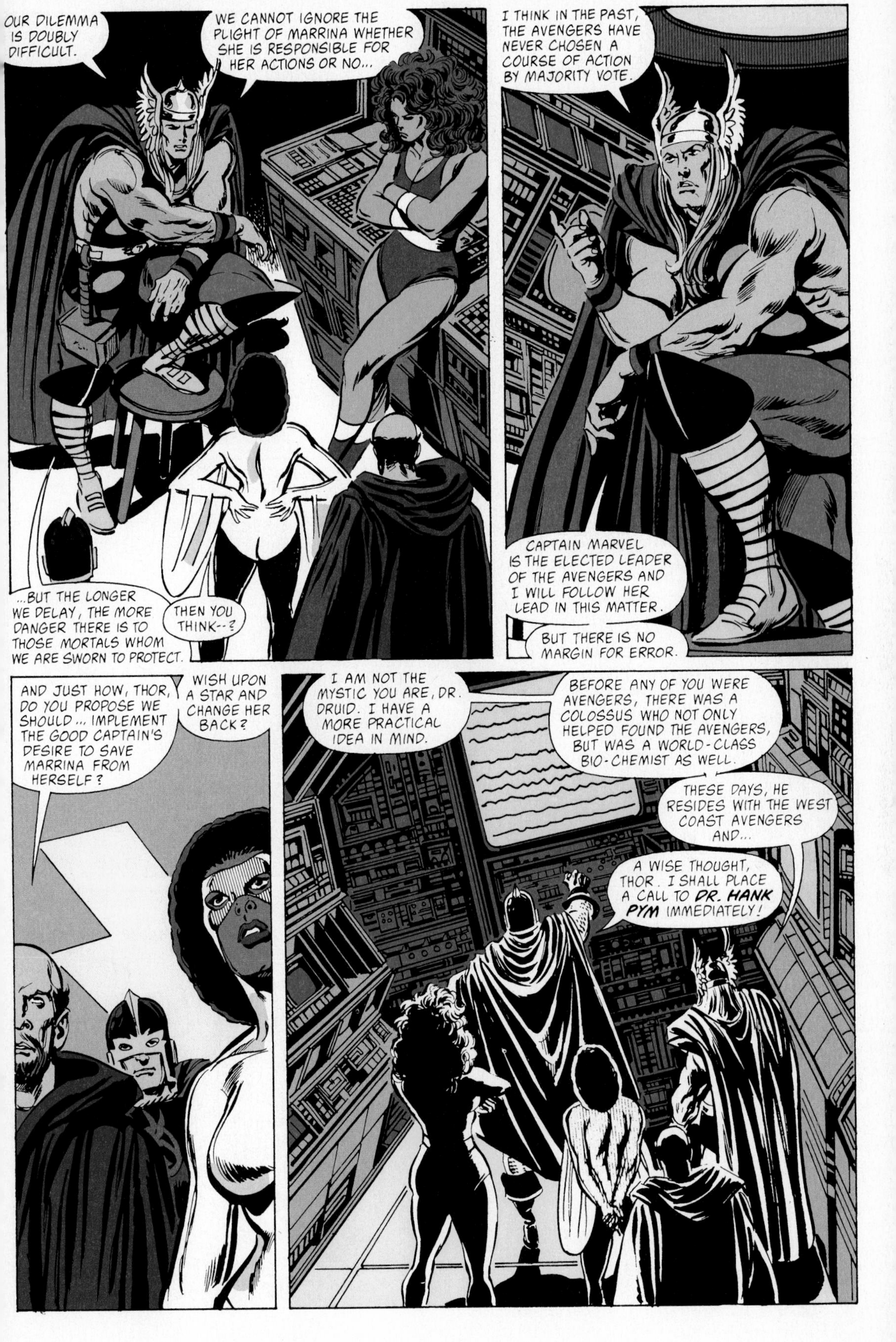
OUR DILEMMA IS DOUBLY DIFFICULT.
WE CANNOT IGNORE THE PLIGHT OF MARRINA WHETHER SHE IS RESPONSIBLE FOR HER ACTIONS OR NO...
...BUT THE LONGER WE DELAY, THE MORE DANGER THERE IS TO THOSE MORTALS WHOM WE ARE SWORN TO PROTECT.
THEN YOU THINK--?
I THINK IN THE PAST, THE AVENGERS HAVE NEVER CHOSEN A COURSE OF ACTION BY MAJORITY VOTE.
CAPTAIN MARVEL IS THE ELECTED LEADER OF THE AVENGERS AND I WILL FOLLOW HER LEAD IN THIS MATTER.
BUT THERE IS NO MARGIN FOR ERROR.
AND JUST HOW, THOR, DO YOU PROPOSE WE SHOULD... IMPLEMENT THE GOOD CAPTAIN'S DESIRE TO SAVE MARRINA FROM HERSELF?
WISH UPON A STAR AND CHANGE HER BACK?
I AM NOT THE MYSTIC YOU ARE, DR. DRUID. I HAVE A MORE PRACTICAL IDEA IN MIND.
BEFORE ANY OF YOU WERE AVENGERS, THERE WAS A COLOSSUS WHO NOT ONLY HELPED FOUND THE AVENGERS, BUT WAS A WORLD-CLASS BIO-CHEMIST AS WELL.
THESE DAYS, HE RESIDES WITH THE WEST COAST AVENGERS AND...
A WISE THOUGHT, THOR. I SHALL PLACE A CALL TO DR. HANK PYM IMMEDIATELY!

AND SHORTLY...

IT IS TRUE THAT I HAVE CONDUCTED DETAILED INVESTIGATIONS OF PHYSIOLOGICAL RADICALISM IN LIVING ORGANISMS, BLACK KNIGHT...

BUT IF WHAT YOU TELL ME IS TRUE, THIS GOES FAR **BEYOND** THE WORK THAT I HAVE DONE IN THE PAST.

THEN YOU THINK THERE'S NO HOPE?

SOMEBODY ONCE SAID WHERE THERE'S LIFE, THERE'S HOPE, DANE. THERE WAS A TIME WHEN I WASN'T SURE IT WAS TRUE.

BUT I'VE SEEN TOO MUCH OF THE WORLD TO EITHER BELIEVE OR DISBELIEVE NOW.

SO I JUST TRY TO SURVIVE. AND I CAN EMPATHIZE WITH ANY OTHER SURVIVOR. I'LL DO WHATEVER I CAN.

WHAT DO YOU NEED?

EVERYTHING YOU'VE GOT. COMPLETE GENETIC RECORDS, PERSONAL HISTORY, DETAILED BACKGROUND OF HER KNOWN CAREER, THE **WORKS**.

AS **FAST** AS POSSIBLE.

BUZZZCT!

THE AUTOMATIC MONITOR'S PICKING SOMETHING UP ON AN EMERGENCY FREQUENCY.

WHAT--?

SHHHHHH!

MAYDAY! MAYDAY! THIS IS **SS GOSNOLD** OUT OF CAPE MAY.

WE ARE UNDER ATTACK BY AN UNIDENTIFIED SEA CREATURE!

ENGINE ROOM FLOODING! TWO LIFEBOATS **SMASHED!**

WE'RE GOING DOWN BY THE **STERN!**

AT LIGHTSPEED, I CAN TRACK THAT SIGNAL IN A FLASH!

MAYBE THERE'S STILL TIME TO HELP THOSE POOR SOULS!

KLAPT!

GET OUT, ALBERT!

IT'S PULLING US **UNDER!** THE BLASTED **THING** IS **PULLING** US **UNDER!**

MAYDAY! MAYDAY!

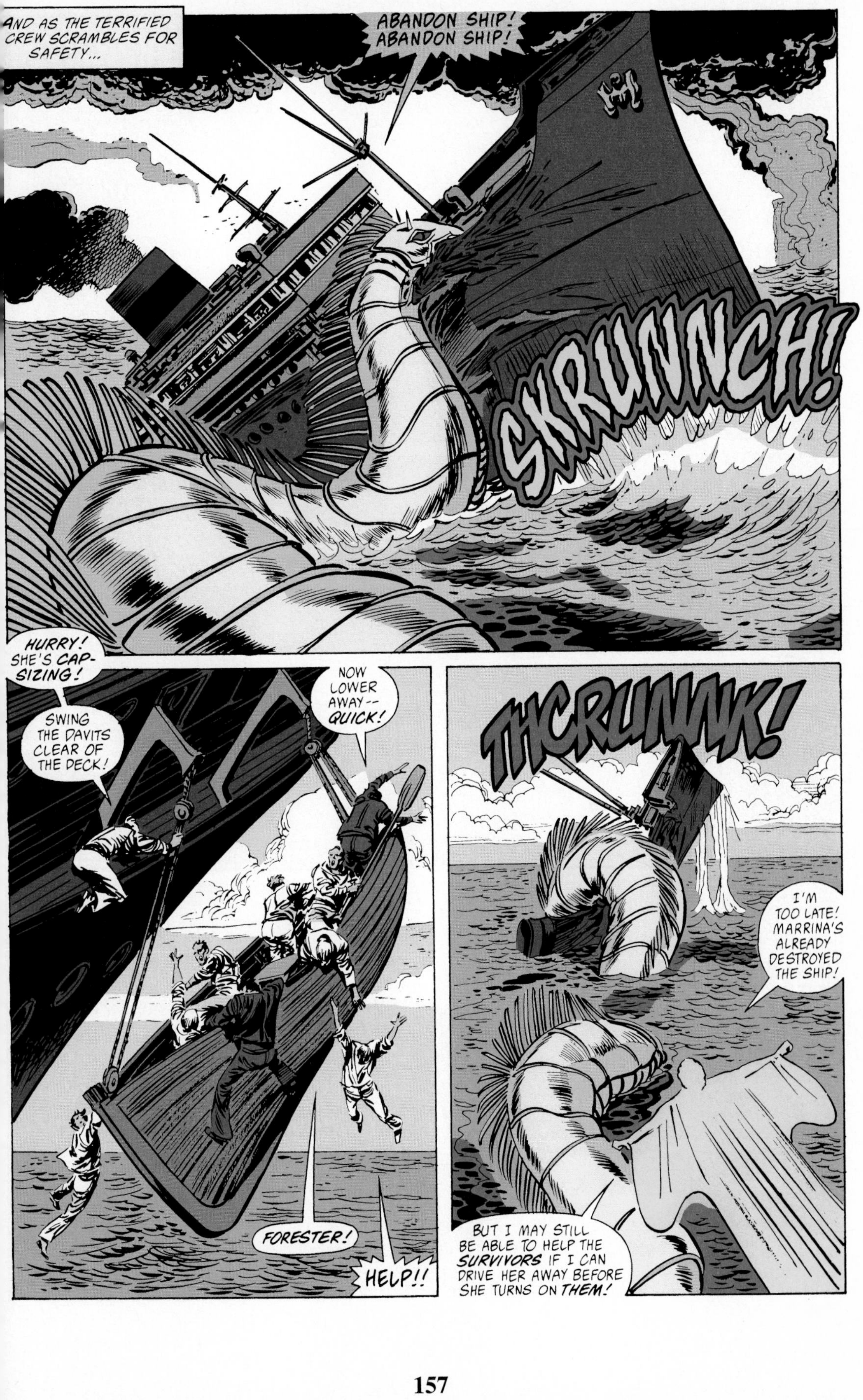
AND AS THE TERRIFIED CREW SCRAMBLES FOR SAFETY...
ABANDON SHIP! ABANDON SHIP!
SKRUNNCH!
HURRY! SHE'S CAPSIZING!
SWING THE DAVITS CLEAR OF THE DECK!
NOW LOWER AWAY-- QUICK!
FORESTER!
HELP!!
THCRUNNK!
I'M TOO LATE! MARRINA'S ALREADY DESTROYED THE SHIP!
BUT I MAY STILL BE ABLE TO HELP THE SURVIVORS IF I CAN DRIVE HER AWAY BEFORE SHE TURNS ON THEM!

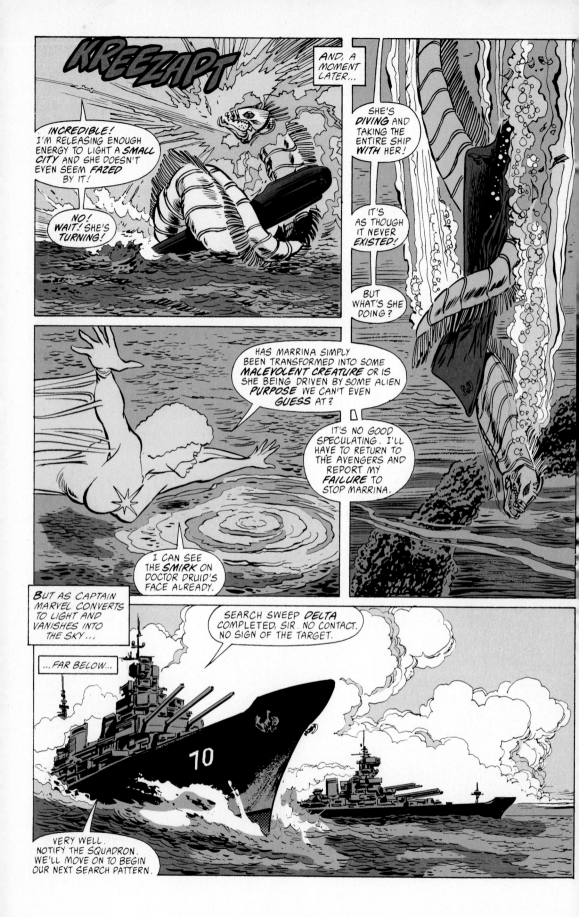

KREEZAPT

AND, A MOMENT LATER...

INCREDIBLE! I'M RELEASING ENOUGH ENERGY TO LIGHT A *SMALL CITY* AND SHE DOESN'T EVEN SEEM *FAZED* BY IT!

NO! WAIT! SHE'S TURNING!

SHE'S *DIVING* AND TAKING THE ENTIRE SHIP *WITH* HER!

IT'S AS THOUGH IT NEVER *EXISTED!*

BUT WHAT'S SHE DOING?

HAS MARRINA SIMPLY BEEN TRANSFORMED INTO SOME *MALEVOLENT CREATURE* OR IS SHE BEING DRIVEN BY SOME ALIEN *PURPOSE* WE CAN'T EVEN *GUESS* AT?

IT'S NO GOOD SPECULATING. I'LL HAVE TO RETURN TO THE AVENGERS AND REPORT MY *FAILURE* TO STOP MARRINA.

I CAN SEE THE *SMIRK* ON DOCTOR DRUID'S FACE ALREADY.

BUT AS CAPTAIN MARVEL CONVERTS TO LIGHT AND VANISHES INTO THE SKY...

...FAR BELOW...

SEARCH SWEEP *DELTA* COMPLETED, SIR. NO CONTACT. NO SIGN OF THE TARGET.

70

VERY WELL. NOTIFY THE SQUADRON. WE'LL MOVE ON TO BEGIN OUR NEXT SEARCH PATTERN.

SIR! SONAR SHOWS AN UNIDENTIFIED *BLIP* MOVING AN *INCREDIBLE SPEED* RIGHT *TOWARDS* US--!

IT'S ALREADY ON *TOP* OF US!

ATTENTION! THIS VESSEL AND ITS COMPANIONS ARE TO REVERSE COURSE IMMEDIATELY!

CONDUCT ME TO YOUR *COMMANDER* AT ONCE!

SO SPEAKS THE *SUB-MARINER!*

CAPTAIN!

AT EASE, FIRST. NOTIFY *SECURITY*. HAVE THEM REPORT TO *THE BRIDGE* ON THE DOUBLE! QUIETLY.

THERE'S NO NEED FOR ANY *CONDUCTING*, PRINCE NAMOR. I'M THE CAPTAIN.

THEN YOU ARE THE ONE I *SEEK!* YOU *MUST* ORDER YOUR SHIPS AWAY FROM THIS AREA!

IT IS *DANGEROUS* FOR YOU TO REMAIN HERE!

WE *KNOW*, THAT, NAMOR.

BUT OUR ORDERS ARE TO SEEK OUT AND *DESTROY* WHATEVER'S BEEN DISRUPTING THE SHIPPING LANES.

THE DANGER IS FAR *GREATER* THAN YOU CAN IMAGINE, CAPTAIN.

SIR, SURFACE RADAR'S PICKING UP A SIZABLE *VESSEL* OF SOME KIND BEARING DOWN ON THE SQUADRON!

WHERE AWAY?

TWO O'CLOCK AND CLOSING *FAST!*

LOOKOUT REPORTS *VISUAL SIGHTING!*

THEN IT IS *TOO* LATE.

IF THAT'S TRUE, NAMOR, THEN YOU CAN BET THAT WE AREN'T GOING TO ACT LIKE *SITTING DUCKS.*

GOOD LORD! LOOK AT THE **SIZE** OF THAT THING!

RANGE 3000 YARDS AND CLOSING.

Schoosh

THERE IS YET ONE **FAINT HOPE** REMAINING!

MR. HOUGH, BRING US TO A COURSE OF ZERO --NINE--ZERO.

MAIN BATTERIES, PREPARE TO **OPEN FIRE.**

AND MR. HOUGH, INFORM NAVAL COMMAND THAT WE ARE ABOUT TO **ENGAGE.**

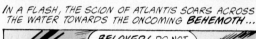

IN A FLASH, THE SCION OF ATLANTIS SOARS ACROSS THE WATER TOWARDS THE ONCOMING **BEHEMOTH**...

...AND NO **MERCY.**

BELOVED! DO NOT DO THIS THING, I **BEG** YOU!

FOR A MOMENT, THE GREAT EYE REGARDS THE NOBLE FIGURE HOVERING BEFORE IT...

...BUT THIS TIME, THERE IS NO **RECOGNITION**...

SIR, RADIO ROOM REPORTS HEAVY **STATIC.** NO RADIO CONTACT WITH ANYONE.

THEY THINK THAT THING MAY BE GENERATING SOME SORT OF **INTER-FERENCE.**

THEN WE'LL DO WHAT WE CAME TO DO, MR HOUGH. **ALONE.**

BRING US AROUND. ALL MAIN BATTERIES TO BEAR ON TARGET.

BAKAKAROOOM

MAIN BATTERIES **OPEN FIRE!**

BUT WHEN THE SMOKE AND CORDITE CLEAR...

IT'S -- IT'S *UNTOUCHED*, SIR! NOT A MARK ON IT!

GUNS TO THE READY! *NOW*, MISTER!

TOO LATE, SIR! SHE'S *DIVING!*

SIR! SONAR REPORTS CONTACT RIGHT *BELOW* US! *COMING UP FAST*, SIR!

STILL *COMING*, SIR!

SKHRAAACKK!

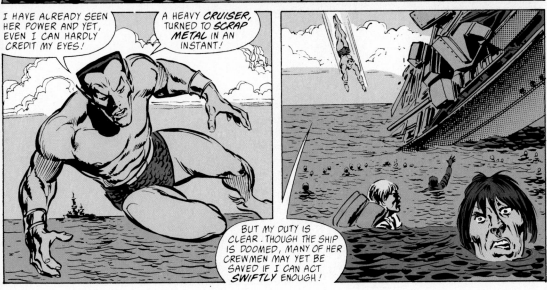

I HAVE ALREADY SEEN HER POWER AND YET, EVEN I CAN HARDLY CREDIT MY EYES!

A HEAVY *CRUISER*, TURNED TO *SCRAP METAL* IN AN INSTANT!

BUT MY DUTY IS CLEAR. THOUGH THE SHIP IS DOOMED, MANY OF HER CREWMEN MAY YET BE SAVED IF I CAN ACT *SWIFTLY* ENOUGH!

AND IN THE AVENGERS' HQ...

I'M MONITORING REPORTS OF **NAVAL ACTIVITY**, CAPTAIN.

THE NAVY HAS A SQUADRON OF SHIPS SOMEWHERE OUT THERE LOOKING FOR MARRINA.

PERHAPS **SHE** FOUND THEM FIRST!

MUCH OF THE MIDDLE ATLANTIC HAS BEEN BLACKED OUT BY SOME KIND OF **STATIC INTERFERENCE.**

WE'RE OUT OF TIME.

GET TO THE **QUINJET.** I'LL FIND MARRINA IF SHE'S ATTACKING THE NAVY AND REPORT BACK.

NO WORD YET FROM **THOR.** HE HASN'T RETURNED FROM DR. PYM'S LABORATORY.

THEN WE'LL DO WITHOUT **EITHER** OF THEM.

BUT MONICA, WHAT CHANCE DO YOU HAVE OF FINDING MARRINA WITHOUT ANY REAL **BEARING?**

AT LIGHTSPEED, JENNIFER, I CAN SEARCH THE ENTIRE ATLANTIC IN ABOUT **THREE SECONDS.**

IF SHE'S ON THE SURFACE, **I'LL FIND HER.**

GET MOVING.

AND IN A MATTER MOMENTS...

...THE AVENGERS ARE AIRBORNE!

SHE WASN'T KIDDING! SHE'S BACK ALREADY!

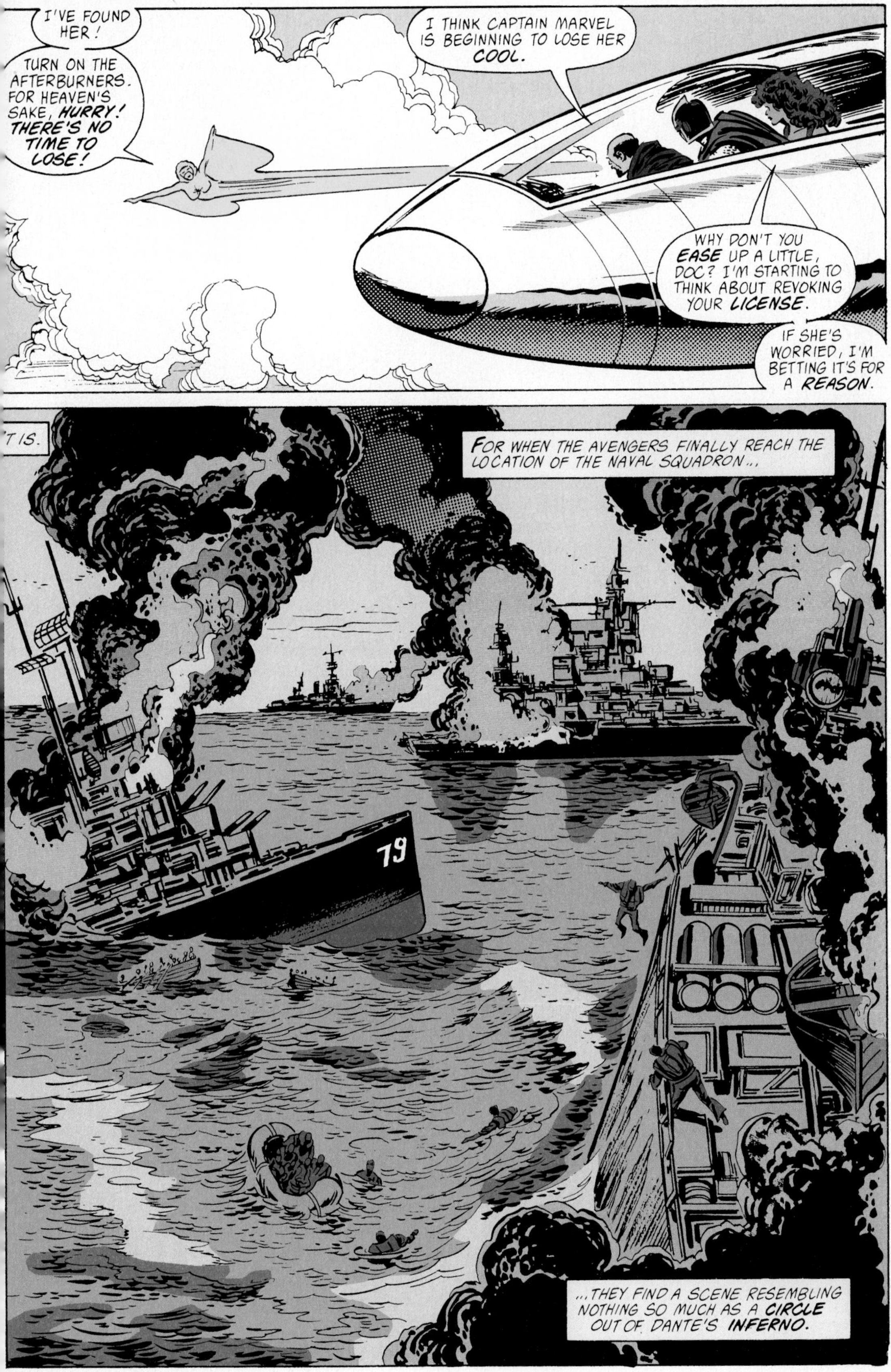
I'VE FOUND HER! TURN ON THE AFTERBURNERS. FOR HEAVEN'S SAKE, HURRY! THERE'S NO TIME TO LOSE!
I THINK CAPTAIN MARVEL IS BEGINNING TO LOSE HER COOL.
WHY DON'T YOU EASE UP A LITTLE, DOC? I'M STARTING TO THINK ABOUT REVOKING YOUR LICENSE.
IF SHE'S WORRIED, I'M BETTING IT'S FOR A REASON.
T IS.
FOR WHEN THE AVENGERS FINALLY REACH THE LOCATION OF THE NAVAL SQUADRON...
79
...THEY FIND A SCENE RESEMBLING NOTHING SO MUCH AS A CIRCLE OUT OF DANTE'S INFERNO.

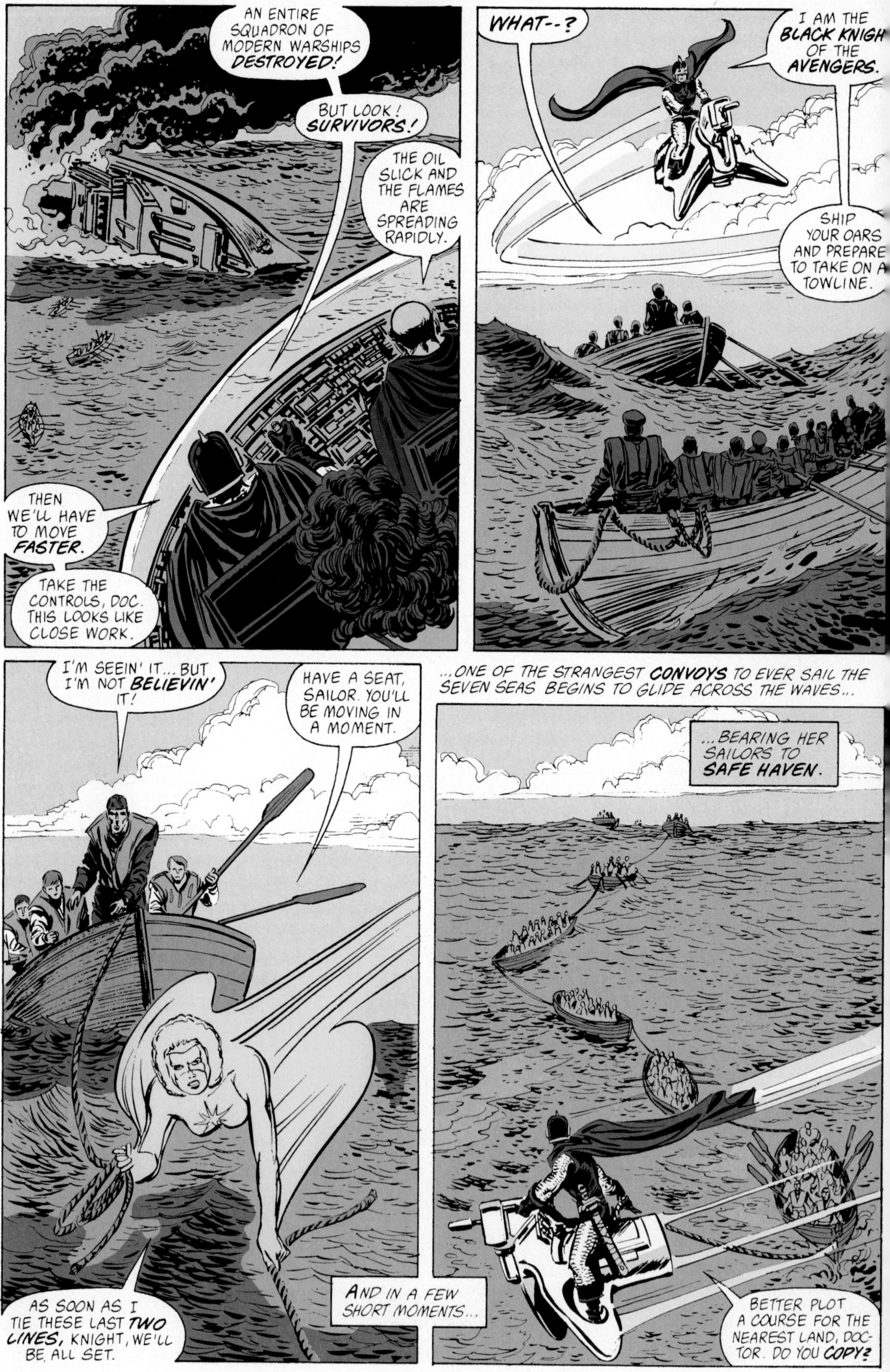
AN ENTIRE SQUADRON OF MODERN WARSHIPS DESTROYED!
BUT LOOK! SURVIVORS!
THE OIL SLICK AND THE FLAMES ARE SPREADING RAPIDLY.
THEN WE'LL HAVE TO MOVE FASTER.
TAKE THE CONTROLS, DOC. THIS LOOKS LIKE CLOSE WORK.
WHAT--?
I AM THE BLACK KNIGH OF THE AVENGERS.
SHIP YOUR OARS AND PREPARE TO TAKE ON A TOWLINE.
I'M SEEIN' IT... BUT I'M NOT BELIEVIN' IT!
HAVE A SEAT, SAILOR. YOU'LL BE MOVING IN A MOMENT.
AS SOON AS I TIE THESE LAST TWO LINES, KNIGHT, WE'LL BE ALL SET.
AND IN A FEW SHORT MOMENTS...
...ONE OF THE STRANGEST CONVOYS TO EVER SAIL THE SEVEN SEAS BEGINS TO GLIDE ACROSS THE WAVES...
...BEARING HER SAILORS TO SAFE HAVEN.
BETTER PLOT A COURSE FOR THE NEAREST LAND, DOC-TOR. DO YOU COPY?

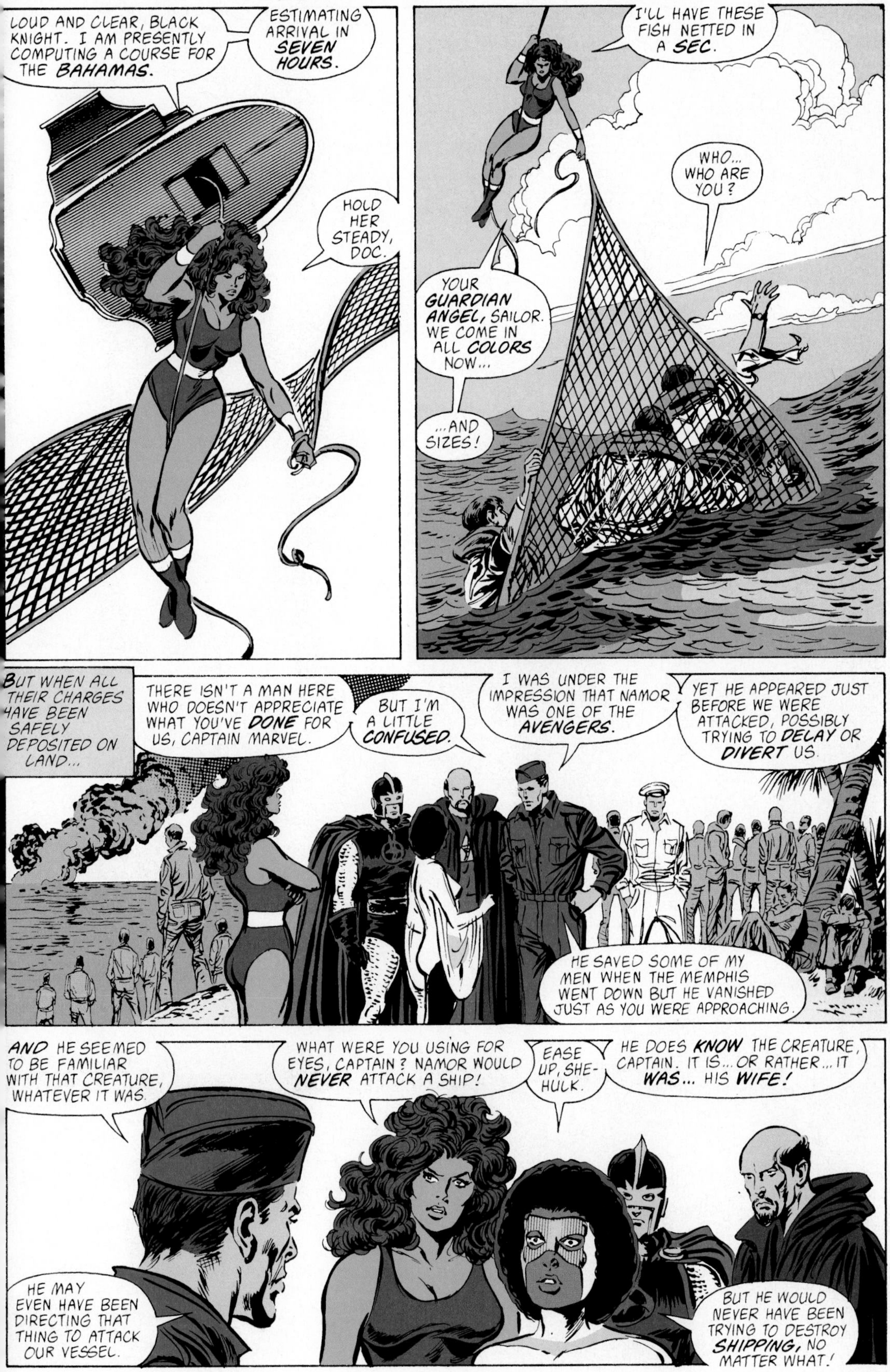
LOUD AND CLEAR, BLACK KNIGHT. I AM PRESENTLY COMPUTING A COURSE FOR THE BAHAMAS.
ESTIMATING ARRIVAL IN SEVEN HOURS.
HOLD HER STEADY, DOC.
I'LL HAVE THESE FISH NETTED IN A SEC.
WHO... WHO ARE YOU?
YOUR GUARDIAN ANGEL, SAILOR. WE COME IN ALL COLORS NOW...
...AND SIZES!
BUT WHEN ALL THEIR CHARGES HAVE BEEN SAFELY DEPOSITED ON LAND...
THERE ISN'T A MAN HERE WHO DOESN'T APPRECIATE WHAT YOU'VE DONE FOR US, CAPTAIN MARVEL.
BUT I'M A LITTLE CONFUSED.
I WAS UNDER THE IMPRESSION THAT NAMOR WAS ONE OF THE AVENGERS.
YET HE APPEARED JUST BEFORE WE WERE ATTACKED, POSSIBLY TRYING TO DELAY OR DIVERT US.
HE SAVED SOME OF MY MEN WHEN THE MEMPHIS WENT DOWN BUT HE VANISHED JUST AS YOU WERE APPROACHING.
AND HE SEEMED TO BE FAMILIAR WITH THAT CREATURE, WHATEVER IT WAS.
WHAT WERE YOU USING FOR EYES, CAPTAIN? NAMOR WOULD NEVER ATTACK A SHIP!
EASE UP, SHE-HULK.
HE DOES KNOW THE CREATURE, CAPTAIN. IT IS... OR RATHER... IT WAS... HIS WIFE!
HE MAY EVEN HAVE BEEN DIRECTING THAT THING TO ATTACK OUR VESSEL.
BUT HE WOULD NEVER HAVE BEEN TRYING TO DESTROY SHIPPING, NO MATTER WHAT!

THAT **CREATURE** IS HIS **WIFE**? AND NAVAL INTELLIGENCE HAS HAD NO **WORD** OF THIS?

AS FOR YOU, MS. GREEN-EYES... MAYBE **YOUR** MEMORY IS TOO SHORT OR TOO FAULTY TO WORK PROPERLY...

...BUT IT WASN'T SO LONG AGO THAT **PRINCE NAMOR** DECLARED **WAR** ON THE **HUMAN RACE**.*

I DON'T KNOW WHAT THAT THING REALLY **IS** OR WHAT PART NAMOR... OR THE **AVENGERS**... HAVE TO PLAY IN ALL THIS...

...BUT I'D SUGGEST YOU BETTER DECIDE WHERE YOUR PRIORITIES LIE CAPTAIN MARVEL.

WE DON'T HAVE ANY DOUBTS IN THE UNITED STATES NAVY.

THANKS FOR **ALL** YOUR HELP!

* TOO FAR BACK FOR OUR MEMORIES TO WORK PROPERLY EITHER!

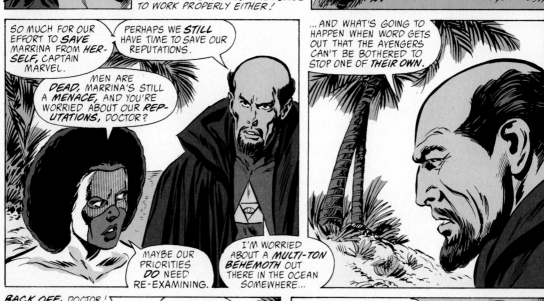

SO MUCH FOR OUR EFFORT TO **SAVE** MARRINA FROM HER-**SELF**, CAPTAIN MARVEL.

PERHAPS WE **STILL** HAVE TIME TO SAVE OUR REPUTATIONS.

MEN ARE **DEAD**, MARRINA'S STILL A **MENACE**, AND YOU'RE WORRIED ABOUT OUR **REP-UTATIONS**, DOCTOR?

MAYBE OUR PRIORITIES **DO** NEED RE-EXAMINING.

I'M WORRIED ABOUT A **MULTI-TON BEHEMOTH** OUT THERE IN THE OCEAN SOMEWHERE...

...AND WHAT'S GOING TO HAPPEN WHEN WORD GETS OUT THAT THE AVENGERS CAN'T BE BOTHERED TO STOP ONE OF **THEIR OWN**.

BACK OFF, DOCTOR! WE'LL DO WHATEVER WE HAVE TO.

WHENEVER WE HAVE TO!

AND SO WILL **I**. WHILE CAPTAIN MARVEL FAILS TO MAKE THE TOUGH DECISIONS, MEN DIE.

THE AVENGERS MUST BE **CONVINCED** THAT THE LEVIATHAN, WHATEVER HER ORIGIN OR FORM, SHOULD BE **KILLED**!

AND I THINK I KNOW **HOW**.

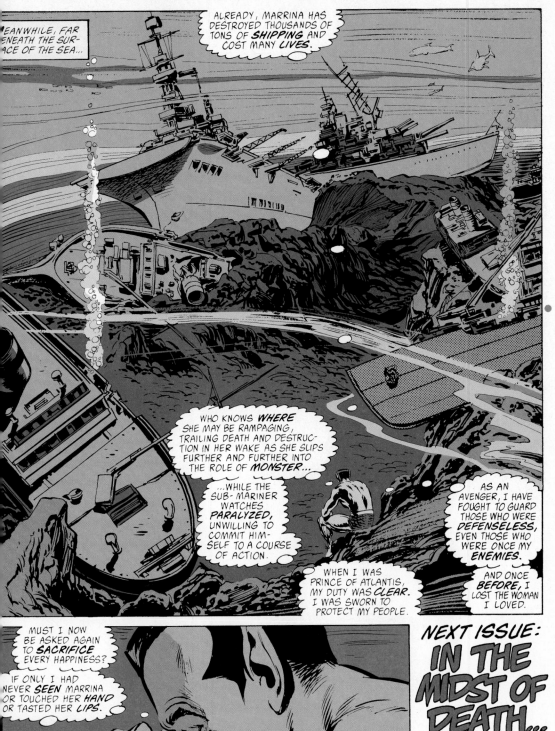

MEANWHILE, FAR BENEATH THE SURFACE OF THE SEA...

ALREADY, MARRINA HAS DESTROYED THOUSANDS OF TONS OF *SHIPPING* AND COST MANY *LIVES*.

WHO KNOWS *WHERE* SHE MAY BE RAMPAGING, TRAILING DEATH AND DESTRUCTION IN HER WAKE AS SHE SLIPS FURTHER AND FURTHER INTO THE ROLE OF *MONSTER*...

...WHILE THE SUB-MARINER WATCHES *PARALYZED*, UNWILLING TO COMMIT HIMSELF TO A COURSE OF ACTION.

WHEN I WAS PRINCE OF ATLANTIS, MY DUTY WAS *CLEAR*. I WAS SWORN TO PROTECT MY PEOPLE.

AS AN AVENGER, I HAVE FOUGHT TO GUARD THOSE WHO WERE *DEFENSELESS*, EVEN THOSE WHO WERE ONCE MY *ENEMIES*.

AND ONCE *BEFORE*, I LOST THE WOMAN I LOVED.

MUST I NOW BE ASKED AGAIN TO *SACRIFICE* EVERY HAPPINESS?

IF ONLY I HAD NEVER *SEEN* MARRINA OR TOUCHED HER *HAND* OR TASTED HER *LIPS*.

WOE TO *LOVE* THAT IT SHOULD DEMAND SUCH A *PRICE*.

FOR SURELY I MUST NOW *CUT OUT* MY LIVING *HEART*!

NEXT ISSUE:

IN THE MIDST OF DEATH...

GASP AT THE *SECRETS* OF *DOCTOR PYM!* THRILL TO THE *DEATH-DEFYING* FEATS OF THE *AVENGERS!* SHUDDER AT THE *CHOICE* OF THE *SUB-MARINER!* AND *WEEP* AT THE ... BUT *THAT*... WOULD BE TELLING!

AVENGERS #293 IN ONE MONTH -- BE *HERE!*

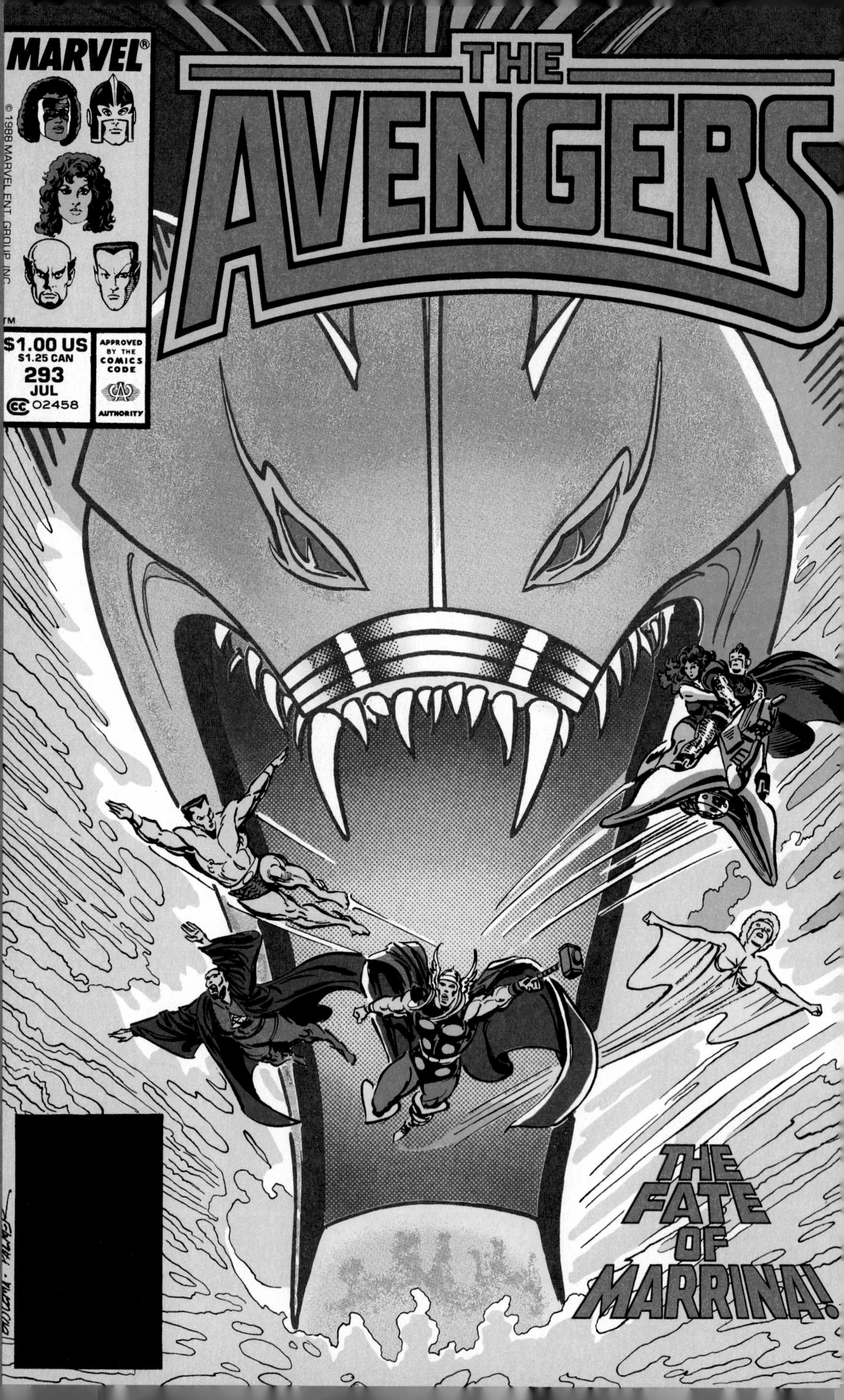

MARVEL®
© 1988 MARVEL ENT. GROUP, INC.
TM
THE AVENGERS
$1.00 US
$1.25 CAN
293
JUL
02458
APPROVED BY THE COMICS CODE AUTHORITY
THE FATE OF MARRINA!

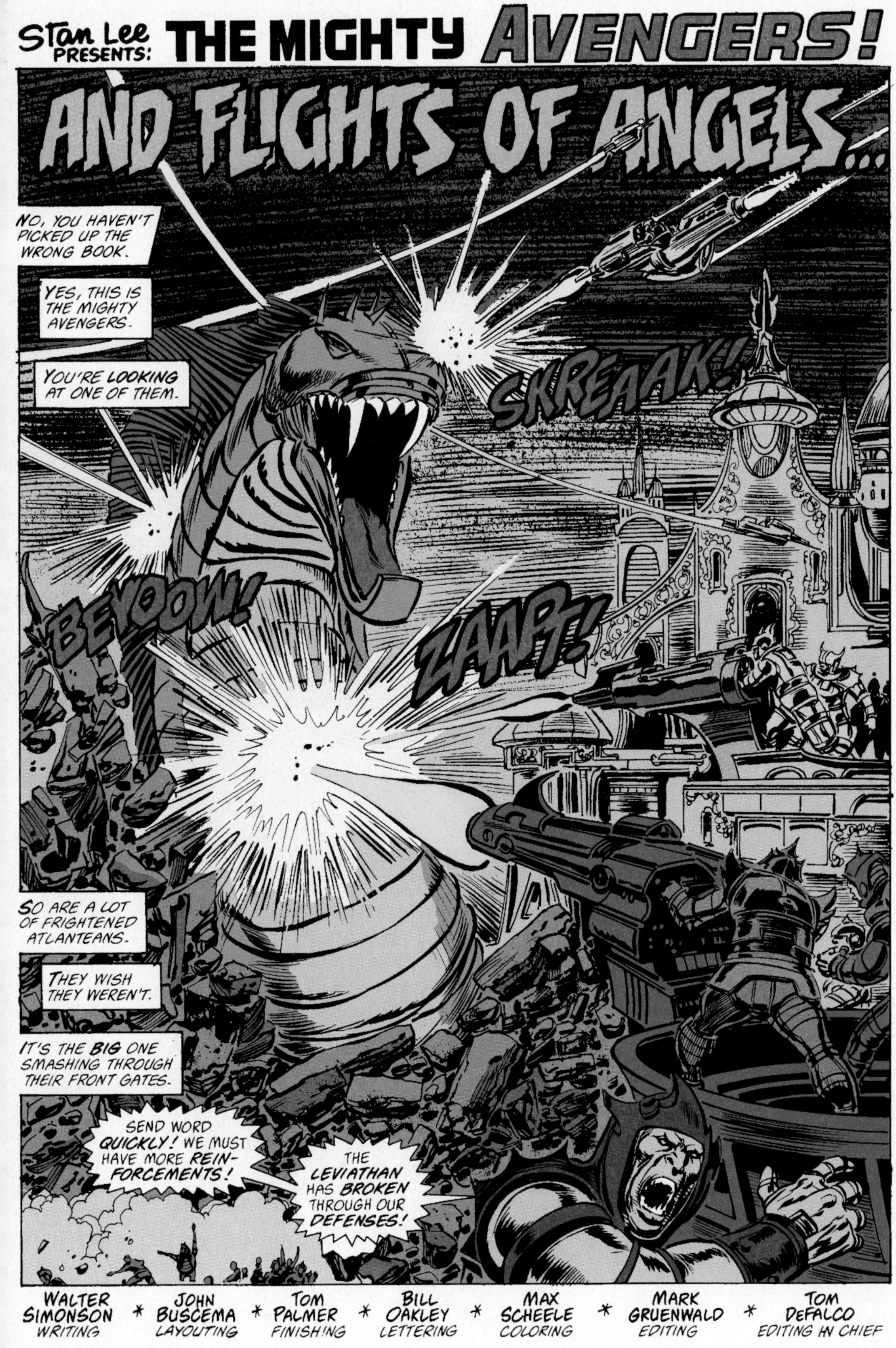
Stan Lee PRESENTS: THE MIGHTY AVENGERS!
AND FLIGHTS OF ANGELS...
NO, YOU HAVEN'T PICKED UP THE WRONG BOOK.
YES, THIS IS THE MIGHTY AVENGERS.
YOU'RE LOOKING AT ONE OF THEM.
SKREAAAK!!
BEYOOW!
ZAAPT!
SO ARE A LOT OF FRIGHTENED ATLANTEANS.
THEY WISH THEY WEREN'T.
IT'S THE BIG ONE SMASHING THROUGH THEIR FRONT GATES.
SEND WORD QUICKLY! WE MUST HAVE MORE REIN-FORCEMENTS!
THE LEVIATHAN HAS BROKEN THROUGH OUR DEFENSES!

WALTER SIMONSON WRITING * JOHN BUSCEMA LAYOUTING * TOM PALMER FINISHING * BILL OAKLEY LETTERING * MAX SCHEELE COLORING * MARK GRUENWALD EDITING * TOM DEFALCO EDITING IN CHIEF

BUT WHAT DEFENSE CAN THERE BE AGAINST...
LEVIATHAN?

FOR IS IT NOT WRITTEN ELSEWHERE...

"THERE LEVIATHAN HUGEST OF LIVING CREATURES, ON THE DEEP STRETCH'D LIKE A PROMONTORY SLEEPS OR SWIMS, AND SEEMS A MOVING LAND, AND AT HIS GILLS DRAWS IN, AND AT HIS TRUNK SPOUTS OUT A SEA."

--MILTON, PARADISE LOST

AIIIIEEEEEEE!

THEN SUDDENLY, AS INEXPLICABLY AS IT APPEARED...

...THE LEVIATHAN TURNS AND GLIDES AWAY.

AND WE ARE LEFT TO WONDER...

...AT SUCH PRODIGIES AS WE HAVE WITNESSED...

...BUT ONLY FOR A MOMENT.

I HAVE TRACKED THE CREATURE TOO LATE!

SHE HAS VANISHED AGAIN LEAVING ONLY DE-STRUCTION AS THE TANGIBLE EVIDENCE OF HER PASSING!

THE LEVIATHAN HAS RAVAGED THE COASTAL HABITATS OF THE SURFACE HUMANS AND DESTROYED TONS OF SHIPPING AS WELL!

NOW, SHE HAS TURNED ON THE KINGDOMS BENEATH THE SEA AND NEARLY DESTROYED MY OWN HOME-LAND!

170

MY EYES HAVE SEEN WHAT I NEVER THOUGHT TO BEHOLD...

...JUST AS MY THOUGHTS CONTEMPLATE WHAT I NEVER THOUGHT POSSIBLE!

THERE CAN NO LONGER BE ANY DOUBT.

MARRINA, THE WIFE OF THE SUB-MARINER, MUST *DIE* THAT ALL OTHERS MAY *LIVE!*

AND ONLY THE *AVENGERS* CAN ACCOMPLISH IT. SO TO THEM I MUST RETURN!

SUCCESS!

I'VE DONE IT! I'VE-- *UH!*

THE *STRAIN*-- TOO GREAT!

I'M--UHHHHHH...

AND FOR AN INSTANT...

...AS THE BARRIERS OF THE MIND ARE SUBMERGED IN THE WAVE OF UNCONSCIOUSNESS...

...A VISION OF THE RECENT PAST FLASHES BEFORE OUR STARTLED EYES...

APPARENTLY ONLY *I* HAVE THE *WILL* TO SAVE *ALL* WHO CAN BE SAVED. I PRAY THIS WILL GIVE ME THE STRENGTH TO DO WHAT MUST BE DONE!

CONTROLLED CLAIRVOYANCE HAS ENABLED ME TO LOCATE THE CREATURE...

"NOW AN ILLUSION. A TEMPTING VESSEL OF THE SEA SKIMMING ACROSS THE SEA SHOULD DO NICELY.

"SO, MY TERRIBLE FRIEND, LET US SEE WHAT WE CAN DO TO CONVINCE THE *OTHERS* THAT YOU ARE INDEED A *MENACE* THAT MUST BE DEALT WITH *PROMPTLY!*

"AS I *HOPED.* WHATEVER *INTELLIGENCE* MARRINA HAD BEFORE SHE TRANSMOGRIFIED INTO THE LEVIATHAN HAS DEPARTED.

"SHE IS A SIMPLE *BEAST...*

"...AND FOLLOWS HER PREY NO MATTER *WHERE* IT MAY LEAD, WHETHER THE CHASE IS LOGICAL OR NOT!

"AND THERE IS THE REALM THAT I SEEK!"

A GREAT *SHADOW* BEARS DOWN UPON US! *SOUND THE ALARM!*

TURN OUT THE *GUARD!* *TO ARMS! TO ARMS!*

THE KINGDOM OF ATLANTIS IS UNDER ATTACK!

SKREAK!

REEATHKK!

BWREAM

172

FERAHAMM! DRAKOUM! THREEACK!

FOR THE BATTLE IS ALREADY OVER.

AND THOUGH I MAY HAVE PLACED MY IMMORTAL SOUL IN JEOPARDY FOR THIS DAY'S WORK...

THE SOUNDS OF BATTLE FILL MY MIND STILL. A FINAL VISION OF POSTCOGNITION.

...HOW MANY COUNTLESS SOULS WILL I HAVE SAVED IF THE SUB-MARINER RETURNS TO US TO HELP ME CONVINCE THE OTHERS THAT MARRINA'S DEATH IS OUR ONLY POSSIBLE RECOURSE?

SHE IS TOO DANGEROUS TO BE ALLOWED TO ROAM THE SEAS AT WILL...

...WHILE CAPTAIN MARVEL WASTES TIME AND LIVES SEEKING VAINLY FOR SOME ILLUSORY CURE FOR MARRINA'S CONDITION.

BUT THERE IS NO TIME TO WASTE IN THAT DIRECTION. FOR I HAVE HAD SUCH DREAMS THAT FORETELL OF GRAVE DANGER IN THE NEAR FUTURE...

...AND MARRINA COULD BE JUST THE BEGINNING.

YET HOW COULD I CONVINCE MY FELLOW AVENGERS OF A THREAT HERALDED BY DREAMS?

BEST TO KEEP MY OWN COUNSEL...

...AND DEFLECT THE AVENGERS FROM CAPTAIN MARVEL'S USELESS ENDEAVORS...

...SUCH AS THIS ONE!

THEN MARRINA'S GOT A CHANCE, DR. PYM?

MAYBE NOT EVEN THAT, SHE-HULK.

WHAT I'M PROPOSING IS DANGEROUS BEYOND BELIEF.

BUT THE CASES I GAVE THOR TO FLY BACK TO YOU CONTAIN THE ONLY SOLUTION I COULD FIND.

BUT MARRINA DOES HAVE A CHANCE, DR. PYM?

I'M NOT OPTIMISTIC, CAPTAIN MARVEL. BUT I'VE DONE ALL THAT I CAN.

I HAVE EXAMINED THE RECORDS YOU PROVIDED ME OF MARRINA'S GENETIC STRUCTURE. BUT THE MATERIAL IS SO FRAGMENTARY.

WE KNOW MARRINA IS A HYBRID OF HUMAN AND ALIEN GENOTYPES. AND WE KNOW A LITTLE ABOUT HER *PAST* TRANSFORMATIONS.

BUT THERE'S NOTHING THAT WE CAN EXTRAPOLATE FROM CLEARLY TO ASSESS HER *PRESENT* CONDITION.

ANYTHING WE TRY IS ESSENTIALLY GOING TO BE A SHOT IN THE DARK.

AND THESE... *HARPOONS* ARE GOING TO DO THE SHOOTING, HANK?

HARPOONS? WELL, SHIVER ME TIMBERS. LOOKS LIKE THE AVENGERS ARE ABOUT TO GO WHALING.

I HAD HOPED WE WEREN'T GOING TO TRY TO *KILL* HER, DR. PYM.

AND YOU'RE *NOT.*

WHAT THE BLACK KNIGHT HOLDS IN HIS HANDS IS RATHER MORE LIKE A HYPODERMIC *NEEDLE* THAN A HARPOON. AT LEAST IN FUNCTION.

THE DARTS ARE MADE WITH A HOLLOW CORE NEEDLE DESIGNED TO INJECT ITS CONTENTS INTO THE LEVIATHAN AFTER PENETRATION.

INSIDE EACH NEEDLE IS A CHARGE OF VIRAL RECOMBINANT DNA *SUPPRESSOR,* DESIGNED AROUND MARRINA'S OWN GENETIC STRUCTURE AS BEST I COULD DETERMINE IT.

HANDLE THE DARTS WITH EXTREME CARE! THERE'S NO TELLING WHAT MIGHT HAPPEN IF ANYONE ELSE SHOULD ACCIDENTALLY RECEIVE THE CHARGE.

I THINK I CAN CONSTRUCT A PAIR OF MODIFIED BAZOOKAS THAT WILL FIRE THESE DARTS IN A COUPLE OF HOURS.

WHAT DO *YOU* THINK, DANE?

ONCE MARRINA RECEIVES THE CHARGE, THE RECOMBINANT DNA WILL COMBINE WITH HER OWN DNA, PRODUCING A REGRESSION THAT WILL REDUCE HER PHYSIOLOGICAL RADICALISM TO HER ORIGINAL FORM.

AND THEN...

...WE'LL HAVE TO GO *WHALING.*

HERE IS ONE **ADDITIONAL** PROBLEM. WHEREVER WE FIND MARRINA, WE'RE LIKELY TO FIND **NAMOR** AS WELL.

I DON'T KNOW THAT HE'S GOING TO TAKE KINDLY TO THE THOUGHT OF HARPOONING HIS WIFE, NO MATTER **HOW** NOBLE THE CAUSE.

A **TRUE** MONARCH, DANE, WILL SACRIFICE **ANYTHING**, EVEN HIS OWN HAPPINESS, FOR THE GOOD OF THE SUBJECTS HE RULES.

THAT IS HIS **SACRED TRUST.**

NAMOR!

AND THOUGH I AM NO LONGER A MONARCH, AM I NOT A GUARDIAN OF **EARTH** AND ITS MORTAL INHABITANTS?

IS MY TRUST NOT AS **SACRED?**

WELL SPOKEN, PRINCE NAMOR.

I DO NOT BID THEE **WELCOME,** FOR WHAT GLAD GREETING CAN CLOAK THE **GRIM TASK** THAT CONFRONTS US -- A **KINSLAYING.**

BUT I SPEAK AS ONE AVENGER TO ANOTHER ...THY SACRED TRUST IN THIS HOUR OF TRIAL IS GRATEFULLY RECEIVED.

NO OTHER WARRIOR WOULD I AS **LIEF** HAVE AT MY SIDE.

MY THANKS ON THAT, THOR.

I MAY BE OF MORE HELP THAN SIMPLY AS A **WARRIOR.** I KNOW WHERE MARRINA HAS HIDDEN HER **PRIZES.**

THOUGH I DO NOT NOW KNOW WHERE IN THE SEVEN SEAS SHE ROAMS PRESENTLY, SURELY HER TREASURE WOULD BE A GOOD PLACE TO **BEGIN** OUR SEARCH.

NOT A BAD PLAN, BUT REALLY, CAN NAMOR BE TRUSTED? I MEAN...WE ARE TALKING ABOUT HIS **WIFE,** FOR PITY'S SAKE!

WHEN ALL'S SAID AND DONE, NAMOR IS A **PRINCE** OF THE **BLOOD.** HIS WORD IS HIS BOND.

YEAH? SO WAS THE WORD OF **KING HEROD** TO THE WISE MEN.

"I'M GETTING A BAD FEELING ABOUT THIS."

NAVIGATION COMPUTER INDICATES THAT WE'RE CRUISING ABOVE MARRINA'S BASE OF OPERATIONS, NAMOR.

NO INDICATIONS OF ANY MAJOR LIFE FORMS BELOW.

MAYBE SHE'S OUT SHOPPING.

MARRINA COULD WELL BE HUNTING. SHE NEVER STAYS LONG WITH HER PRIZES.

THEN WE MUST BEGIN OUR OWN HUNT.

A CLAIRVOYANT TRANCE MAY ENABLE ME TO LOCATE HER, THOR.

ANY METHOD THAT WORKS IS ACCEPTABLE TO ME, DR. DRUID...

...BUT, PERSONALLY, I HAVE MORE FAITH IN THE LATEST SONAR POD WE CARRY.

TO EACH HIS OWN, DANE. I SHALL COVER THE WORLD'S OCEANS IN A FEW MINUTES.

IF MARRINA IS ANYWHERE ON THE SURFACE, I'LL FIND HER.

BUT AS THE HOURS DRAG BY...

...THERE IS NO SIGN OF LEVIATHAN...

...UNTIL...

WHAT IS IT, DANE?

LOOK, SHE-HULK. AN AREA OF STATIC. LIKE THE CHAFF MARRINA BROADCAST BEFORE TO JAM SHIPS' DISTRESS CALLS!

I'VE GOT A FIX! FEED IT TO THE COMPUTER! AND KICK IN THE AFTERBURNERS!

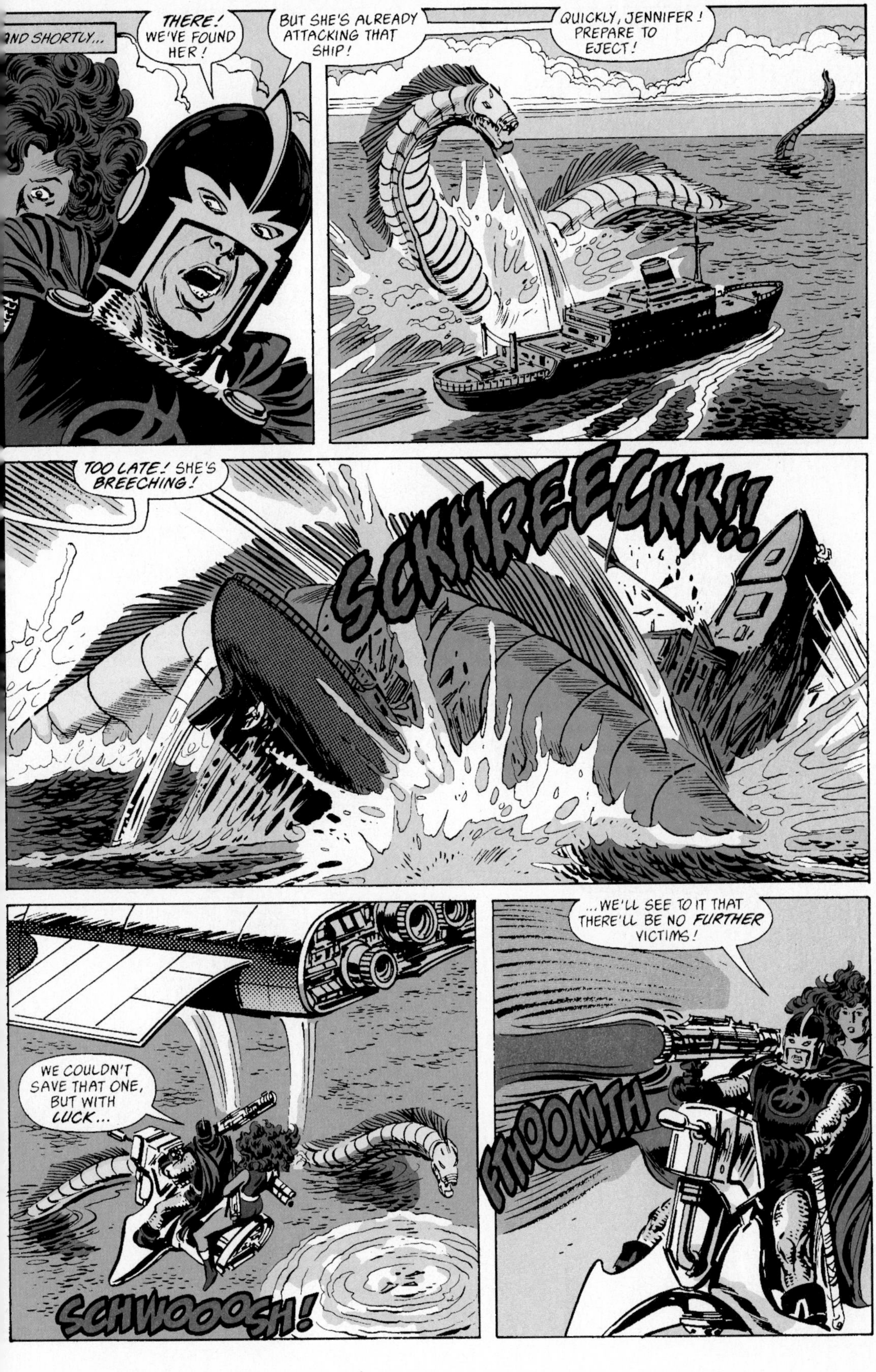
AND SHORTLY...
THERE! WE'VE FOUND HER!
BUT SHE'S ALREADY ATTACKING THAT SHIP!
QUICKLY, JENNIFER! PREPARE TO EJECT!
TOO LATE! SHE'S BREECHING!
SCHHREECKK!!
WE COULDN'T SAVE THAT ONE, BUT WITH LUCK...
SCHWOOOSH!
...WE'LL SEE TO IT THAT THERE'LL BE NO FURTHER VICTIMS!
FHOOMTH

PTHWAAANNG!

NO GOOD! THE DART SHATTERED AGAINST HER ARMOR PLATE!

TRY AGAIN! YOU'RE LOADED!

PERHAPS SHE IS LESS WELL ARMORED BENEATH!

PTHWAANNG!

BY THE VEIL OF THE VIRGIN! THE LEVIATHAN'S TWISTED AROUND AND TAKEN THE DART AGAINST HER ARMORED HEAD!

READY ANOTHER SHOT, BLACK KNIGHT!

THOR SHALL SEE TO IT THAT THOU HAST A TARGET!

HAVE AT THEE, CREATURE OF THE DEPTHS!

THE AVENGERS SHALL ENDEAVOR TO SAVE THEE IN SPITE OF THYSELF!

CHRARAAANNG!

WELL DONE, THOR! SHE'S STUNNED FOR A MOMENT AND I HAVE A CLEAR SHOT AT THE UNDERBELLY!

FTHOOMTH!

PTHWRANNGK

BLAST THE DEMON! HER BELLY ARMOR IS NO LESS FORMIDABLE THAN HER BACK!

AND WE HAVE BUT A SINGLE DART LEFT!

THAT'S IT! HER MOUTH! AIM FOR HER MOUTH, DANE! NO ARMOR!

SHE RISES TO TRY TO SWALLOW US! LOOK AT THE SIZE OF HER MAW!

HURRY! FIRE! SHE'S ALMOST GOT US!

I'LL FIRE WHEN I CAN SEE HER TONSILS! THIS SHOT AT LEAST SHALL NOT GO ASTRAY!

FTHOOUMTH!

A DIRECT HIT!

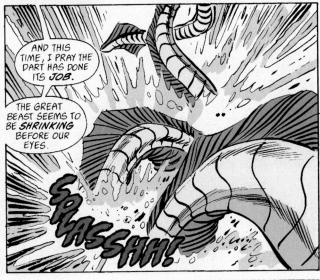

AND THIS TIME, I PRAY THE DART HAS DONE ITS JOB.

THE GREAT BEAST SEEMS TO BE SHRINKING BEFORE OUR EYES.

SPLASSHH!

AND A FEW MINUTES LATER...

IT... IT WORKED!

MY HEART! MY HEART! MAY YOU NOT BE SLAIN!

FOR HOW SHALL NAMOR SURVIVE IF HIS SPIRIT IS TORN FROM HIS BODY?

IF YOU YET LIVE, I SWEAR BY THE THRONE OF FATHER NEPTUNE, I WILL SET MYSELF TO SAFEGUARD YOUR SOUL FOREVER.

OH, MY LOVE. IS THIS ANOTHER FEVERED *ILLUSION...*

...OR HAVE MY FONDEST DREAMS COME *TRUE?*

FEAR NOT, MY HEART. YOU'RE *SAFE* NOW, I PROMISE. AND HERE IS MY KISS UPON IT.

AND AS NAMOR MAKES GOOD HIS WORD... ELSEWHEN...

IT'S *RARE* FOR A KANG TO SURVIVE A COUNCIL WAR...

...AND THOSE THAT DO, WE *MONITOR.* IF THEY MERIT IT, WE *EXAMINE* THEM.

AND IF THEY *PASS* THE EXAMINATION, WE OFFER THEM...

...*MEMBERSHIP.* MEMBERSHIP IN THE MOST UNIQUE, POWERFUL, AND... *AMBITIOUS* SECRET COUNCIL IN THE OMNIVERSE!

THE *COUNCIL* OF *CROSS-TIME KANGS!*

YOU... ARE A SURVIVOR. YOUR PRESENCE HERE IS THE *PROOF.*

NOT ONLY HAVE YOU SURVIVED YOUR LOCAL COUNCIL WAR* BUT YOU SUCCESSFULLY COUNTERED AN ASSASSINATION ATTEMPT BY A *RENEGADE* OF OUR OWN COUNCIL.**

MOST UNUSUAL.

CONSIDER THAT YOU HAVE ALREADY *PASSED* THE ENTRANCE EXAMINATION.

WE OFFER YOU PROVISIONAL MEMBERSHIP PENDING MORE THOROUGH CONSIDERATION, KANG OF EARTH 123486.23497.

* AVENGERS #267-269.

** AVENGERS #291

AND SHOULD I *REFUSE?*

THEN YOU WOULD NATURALLY *CEASE* TO BE A SURVIVOR.

THEN *NATURALLY,* I ACCEPT.

EXCELLENT.

NEBULA WILL ESCORT YOU TO YOUR QUARTERS AND EXPLAIN A LITTLE ABOUT US.

NEBULA?

TO AVOID CONFUSION, WE HAVE EACH CHOSEN AN INDIVIDUAL NAME.

CHOOSE ANY NAME YOU WISH. PERHAPS ONE THAT REPRESENTS YOUR HEART'S DESIRE.

FRED.

FRED?

AS IN FLINTSTONE.

AN APPROPRIATELY STONE-AGE NAME FOR A BACKWARD NOVITIATE IN SUCH A UNIQUE, POWERFUL, AND... AMBITIOUS SECRET COUNCIL.

INTERESTING. ALMOST NONE OF THE KANGS HAS A SENSE OF HUMOR.

I DOUBT IF THEY'LL KNOW HOW TO LOG THAT INTO YOUR FILE.

THESE ARE YOUR QUARTERS.

MINE ARE JUST DOWN THE HALL.

COME VISIT ME SOMETIME.

PERHAPS I'LL TELL YOU A BEDTIME STORY... ALL ABOUT KINGS AND KANGS AND THE HUNT FOR THE DEADLIEST WEAPON IN THE OMNIVERSE.

IT'S WHAT THE COUNCIL IS ALL ABOUT.

YOU'LL ENJOY IT.

181

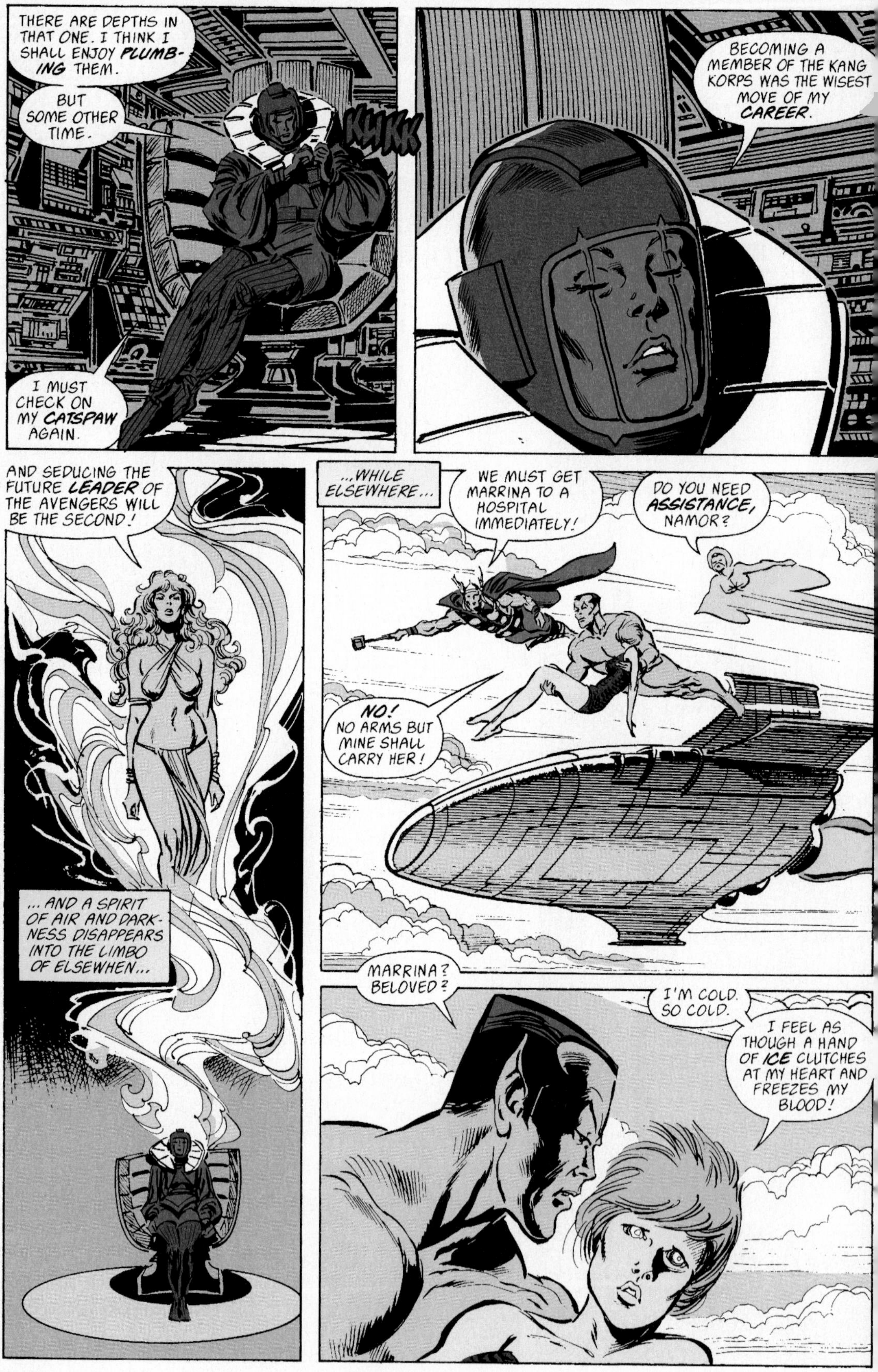
THERE ARE DEPTHS IN THAT ONE. I THINK I SHALL ENJOY PLUMBING THEM.
BUT SOME OTHER TIME.
KLIKK
I MUST CHECK ON MY CATSPAW AGAIN.
BECOMING A MEMBER OF THE KANG KORPS WAS THE WISEST MOVE OF MY CAREER.
AND SEDUCING THE FUTURE LEADER OF THE AVENGERS WILL BE THE SECOND!
...AND A SPIRIT OF AIR AND DARKNESS DISAPPEARS INTO THE LIMBO OF ELSEWHEN...
...WHILE ELSEWHERE...
WE MUST GET MARRINA TO A HOSPITAL IMMEDIATELY!
DO YOU NEED ASSISTANCE, NAMOR?
NO! NO ARMS BUT MINE SHALL CARRY HER!
MARRINA? BELOVED?
I'M COLD. SO COLD.
I FEEL AS THOUGH A HAND OF ICE CLUTCHES AT MY HEART AND FREEZES MY BLOOD!

THEN LET NAMOR'S *KISS* KINDLE A FIRE WITHIN YOU THAT WOULD MELT THE POLAR ICE CAP!

YOUR LIPS! THEY *ARE* LIKE ICE!

MARRINA!

NAMOR! OH, MY PRINCE! HELP ME! HELP ME! HELLLPPMMRRR!

RROAARRR

THE LIGHT IN HER EYE HAS *FAILED!*

THE MARRINA I HOLD DEARER THAN LIFE ITSELF IS *SLIPPING AWAY!*

I FEAR THAT DR. PYM'S BEST EFFORTS HAVE *FAILED!*

STRIKE NOW, NAMOR! *BEFORE* SHE REGAINS HER PRODIGIOUS *STRENGTH* AND *SIZE!*

SHE STRUGGLES SO I CAN NO LONGER REMAIN *ALOFT!*

SKPLASSH!

ALREADY HER FORM BE-GINS TO *SHIFT* AND *GROW.*

I MUST SLAY HER *NOW* WHILE I STILL CAN *BUT--*

OH, *FATHER NEPTUNE!* WHAT DREAD *DEED* YOU ASK OF YOUR AVENGING SON!

TOO LATE! I'M LOSING MY GRIP! THE WAVES SHE GENERATES ARE TEARING US APART!

I'VE LOST HER!

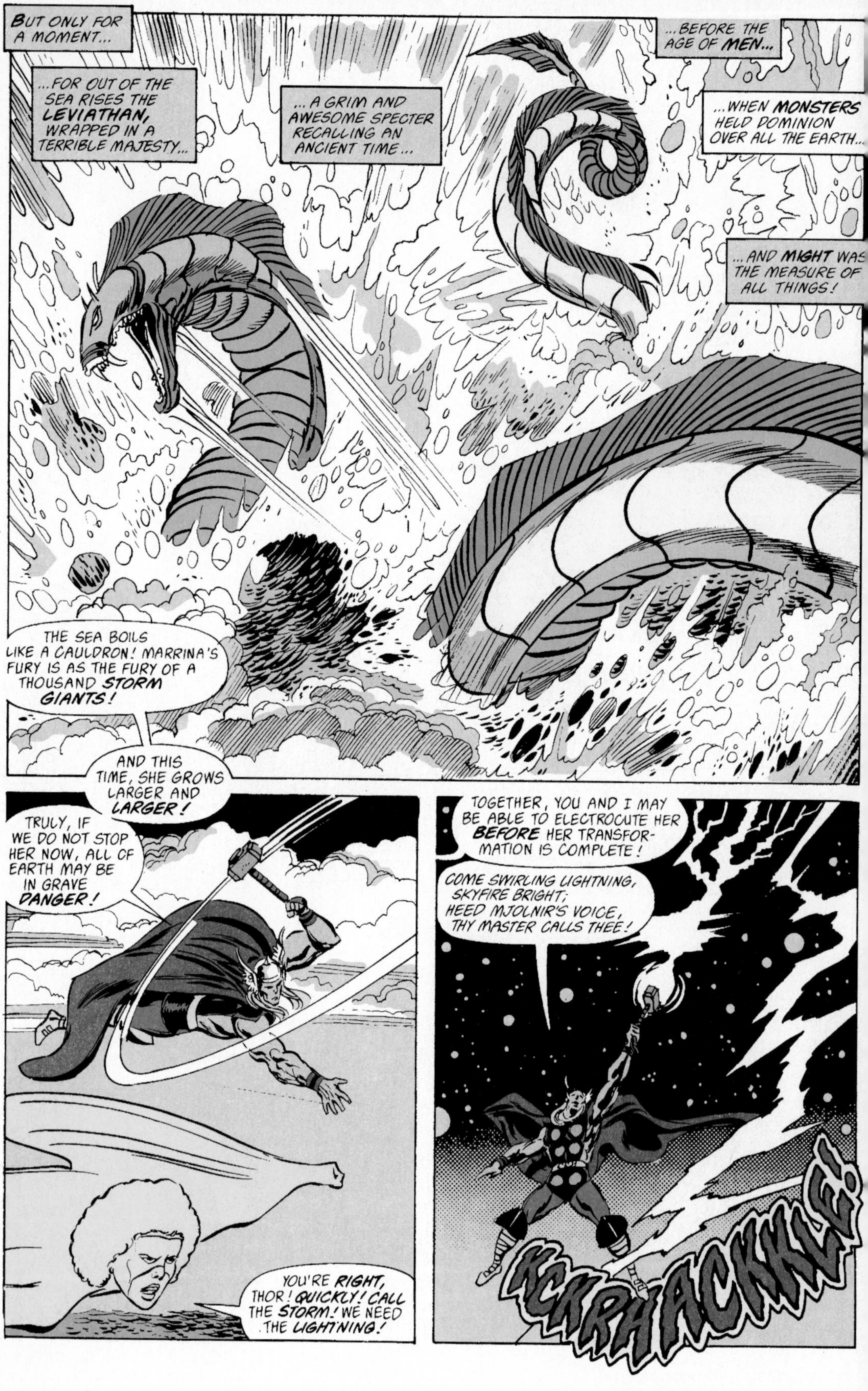

BUT ONLY FOR A MOMENT...
...FOR OUT OF THE SEA RISES THE LEVIATHAN, WRAPPED IN A TERRIBLE MAJESTY...
...A GRIM AND AWESOME SPECTER RECALLING AN ANCIENT TIME...
...BEFORE THE AGE OF MEN...
...WHEN MONSTERS HELD DOMINION OVER ALL THE EARTH...
...AND MIGHT WAS THE MEASURE OF ALL THINGS!
THE SEA BOILS LIKE A CAULDRON! MARRINA'S FURY IS AS THE FURY OF A THOUSAND STORM GIANTS!
AND THIS TIME, SHE GROWS LARGER AND LARGER!
TRULY, IF WE DO NOT STOP HER NOW, ALL OF EARTH MAY BE IN GRAVE DANGER!
YOU'RE RIGHT, THOR! QUICKLY! CALL THE STORM! WE NEED THE LIGHTNING!
TOGETHER, YOU AND I MAY BE ABLE TO ELECTROCUTE HER BEFORE HER TRANSFORMATION IS COMPLETE!
COME SWIRLING LIGHTNING, SKYFIRE BRIGHT; HEED MJOLNIR'S VOICE, THY MASTER CALLS THEE!
KKRHACKKLE!

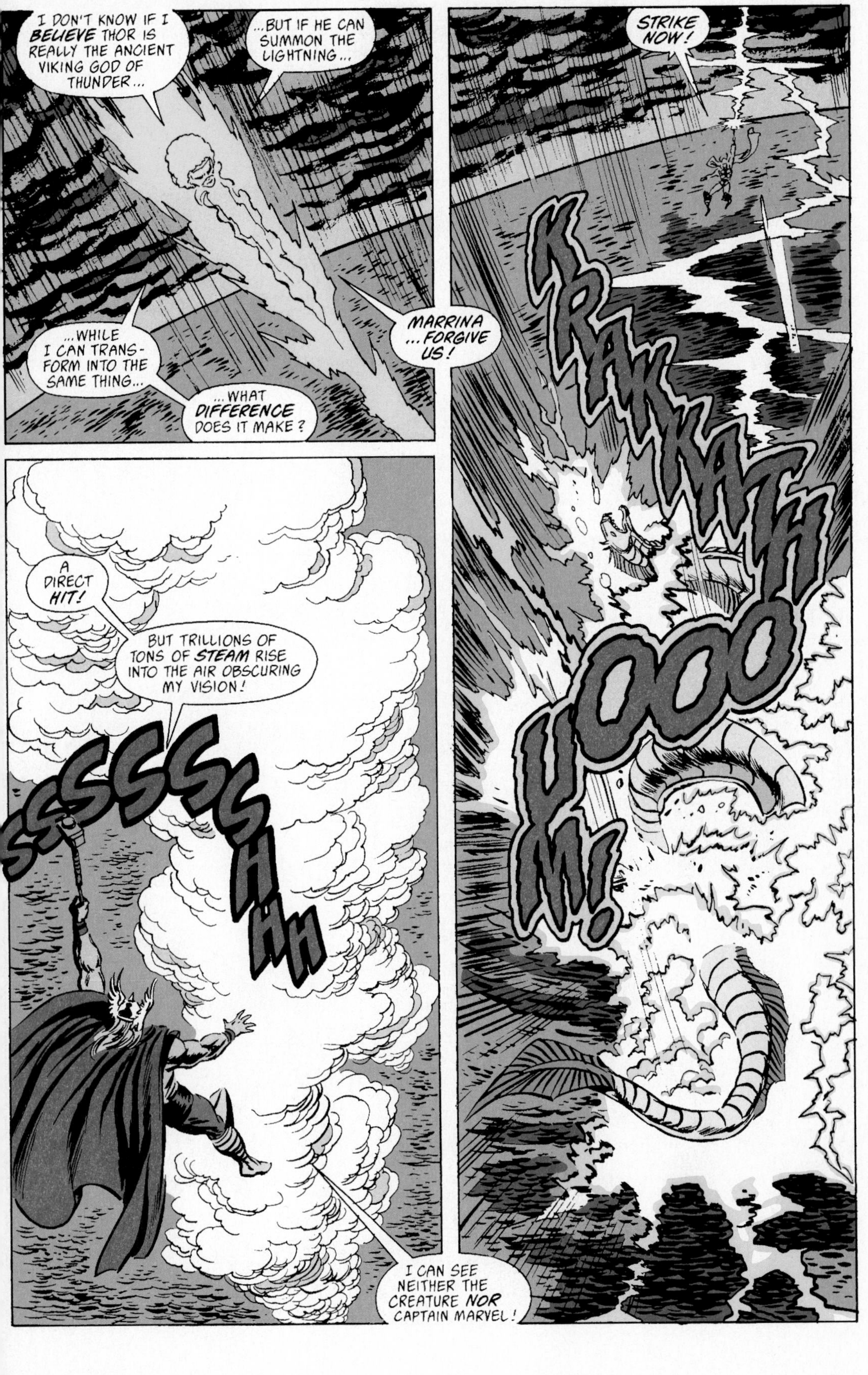

I DON'T KNOW IF I BELIEVE THOR IS REALLY THE ANCIENT VIKING GOD OF THUNDER...
...BUT IF HE CAN SUMMON THE LIGHTNING...
...WHILE I CAN TRANS-FORM INTO THE SAME THING...
...WHAT DIFFERENCE DOES IT MAKE?
MARRINA ...FORGIVE US!
A DIRECT HIT!
BUT TRILLIONS OF TONS OF STEAM RISE INTO THE AIR OBSCURING MY VISION!
SSSSSSSHHH
I CAN SEE NEITHER THE CREATURE NOR CAPTAIN MARVEL!
STRIKE NOW!
KRAKATHOOOM!

MY INSTRUMENTS INDICATE A LIFE-FORM, JENNIFER!

THE LEVIATHAN STILL *LIVES!* THERE *IS* NO OTHER CHOICE!

THE *BLACK BLADE* AGAINST WHICH *ALL* ARMOR IS IN VAIN MUST ONCE AGAIN DRAW BLOOD!

DANE! *NO.* REMEMBER THE SWORD'S *CURSE!*

DOES A SINGLE *LIFE* MATTER AGAINST WHAT WILL HAPPEN IF THE LEVIATHAN *SURVIVES* TO BECOME EVEN GREATER THAN SHE IS ALREADY?

NAMOR SPOKE OF A SACRED TRUST.

SUCH IS *ALSO* THE TRUST OF AN *AVENGER!*

THE STEAM CLEARS! AND MY DESTINY IS *CLEAR* AS WELL!

FAREWELL, JENNIFER.

HOLD.

THE BLACK KNIGHT SHALL *NOT* DRAW BLOOD THIS DAY.

NAMOR!

DID I NOT *SWEAR* TO SAFEGUARD THE VERY SOUL OF MY BELOVED?

AM I NOT A PRINCE OF MY *WORD?*

BUT YOUR *TRUST?*

...IS AS SACRED TO ME AS MY OATH.

MARRINA, MY BELOVED. HEAR ME, WHEREVER YOU MAY BE.

THAT WHICH I SWORE TO GUARD HAS BEEN TAKEN FROM US BOTH...

...AND ONLY DEATH NOW CAN FREE YOUR SOUL FROM WITHIN THIS LIVING PRISON!

RISE, LEVIATHAN! RISE UP, AND MEET YOUR NEMESIS!

KREEEGAUGGHH!

FOR MY BELOVED! FOR MARRINA!

SLAASSHH!

THE BLOOD! THE BLOOD!

ARRRGGHH!

187

DANE WHITMAN PLUNGES INTO THE WAITING ARMS OF THE SEA!

BUT IS HE *DEAD* OR--

NAY. ALIVE BUT UNCONSCIOUS.

YET IF THE CURSE OF BLOOD UPON HIS SWORD HATH TRULY BEEN INVOKED, MAYHAP HE WOULD BE BETTER OFF *DEAD.*

I MUST RETURN HIM TO THE QUINJET QUICKLY!

EEEYYYOOOWWW

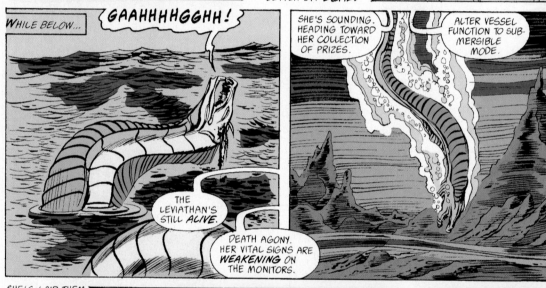

WHILE BELOW...

GAAHHHHGGHH!

THE LEVIATHAN'S STILL *ALIVE.*

DEATH AGONY. HER VITAL SIGNS ARE *WEAKENING* ON THE MONITORS.

SHE'S SOUNDING. HEADING TOWARD HER COLLECTION OF PRIZES.

ALTER VESSEL FUNCTION TO SUBMERSIBLE MODE.

SHE'S LAID THEM OUT IN A GREAT CIRCLE.

LOOK YONDER! IN THE FURTHEST SHADOWS OF THE DERELICTS!

MARRINA!

UP AHEAD! IT'S THE GRAVEYARD OF SHIPS SHE SANK!

UNBELIEVABLE!

"OH, *NO*, THOR! *IT CAN'T BE!* THAT *CAN'T* HAVE BEEN WHAT THIS WAS ALL ABOUT!"

"*EGGS!* THE LEVIATHAN LAID A CLUTCH OF *EGGS*..."

"...AND *THIS* WAS HER *NEST!*"

KRAKKK!

"EVEN NOW, THE *HATCHLINGS* EMERGE!"

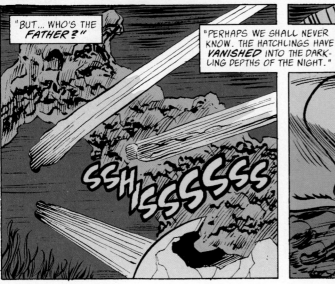

"BUT... WHO'S THE *FATHER?*"

"PERHAPS WE SHALL NEVER KNOW. THE HATCHLINGS HAVE *VANISHED* INTO THE DARK-LING DEPTHS OF THE NIGHT."

SSHISSSSSS

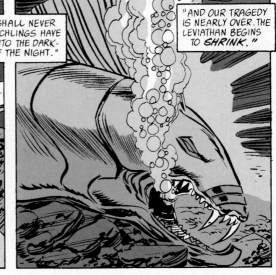

"AND OUR TRAGEDY IS NEARLY OVER. THE LEVIATHAN BEGINS TO *SHRINK*."

"HER ORIGINAL FORM DOTH *RETURN*."

IT IS FINISHED.

WE DARED TO LOVE THOUGH WE WERE OF TWO WORLDS, AND *THIS* IS OUR FATE.

LET IT BE OUR GLORY... AND OUR *EPITAPH*.

I WILL SEEK OUT YOUR *SONS,* BELOVED, AND TEACH THEM OF THEIR MOTHER'S SPIRIT.

BUT FIRST, I SHALL BUILD FOR YOU A BIER FIT FOR A *QUEEN*...

...WHERE YOU WILL REST FOREVER AMIDST THE CORAL, THE SEA JADE, AND MOTHER-OF-PEARL...

...THE MOST PRECIOUS *JEWEL* IN ALL THE SEA.

AND WITHOUT A BACKWARD GLANCE, NAMOR, THE SUB-MARINER, THE AVENGING SON, GLIDES INTO THE DARKNESS AND IS LOST FROM *SIGHT.*

LONG MOMENTS LATER, AN AVENGERS' QUINJET SURFACES IN SILENCE.

DANE WHITMAN REMAINS UNCONSCIOUS. WE HAD BEST RETURN AS QUICKLY AS POSSIBLE TO THE MAINLAND AND MEDICAL FACILITIES.

THOR, *WAIT!*

LOOK AROUND. WHAT'S *MISSING?*

HUH?

IN ALL THE EXCITEMENT, WE'VE OVER-LOOKED SOMETHING.

WHERE'S CAPTAIN MARVEL?

NEXT: *IF WISHES WERE HORSES... (OR WHAT IF DREAMS REALLY DID COME TRUE -- AND OTHER FABLES!)*

AVENGERS ASSEMBLE!

℅ MARVEL COMICS GROUP-387 Park Avenue South-New York, New York-10016

Attention correspondents: if you don't want your full address printed, please be sure to tell us so!

MARK'S REMARKS

With this issue, this magazine undergoes a Changing of the Guard as Roger Stern steps down as resident AVENGERS writer, a post he has ably occupied for over five years. Roger, once the editor of this book for two years in the late 70s, has had a meritorious run as scripter on this title, racking up an impressive run of sixty tales of the mighty Assemblers.

It is customary in making a pronouncement like this to avoid the subject of why a given creative person is leaving the book or to make a vague pseudo-explanation like "So and So has decided it was time to move on to other projects. . ." Generally, the reasons why people leave assignments are personal or political and not really anyone's business but the creative person's own. But with Roger's kind indulgence, I'd like to talk about this particular leave-taking in greater detail, in order to help illuminate the writer/editor working relationship.

First, let me say that I like Rog and probably owe my job at Marvel Comics to a recommendation from him. We've had a long and pleasurable working relationship for almost a decade, him as my editor and later me as his. He was always dependable, enthusiastic, and meticulous, and for my money, one of the best wordsmiths in the business today. So then, what happened?

Sometime mid-April, I had Roger fly in to New York for a conference to map out the next year's AVENGERS story line and coordinate them with our two component books CAPTAIN AMERICA and THOR. In an afternoon long session attended by the various concerned writers and editors (two of whom are both writers and editors but not of the same title), we worked out what I thought to be an interesting, innovative direction. It seemed like all participants agreed. However, when Roger got back home and began to work out the specific details to the scenario, he reported that he couldn't come up with any way to make the scenario work without doing injustices to some of the characters involved. The bottom line was that he didn't want to proceed with the story line we all discussed.

I was not interested in doing any injustices to any characters either, but I also believed that the story line could be done without hurting any characters. I was also not interested in forcing a writer to write something he didn't want to. So, despite our five years' plus of amicable working relations, we had developed what seemed to be irreconcilable differences. Something had to give. I informed Roger that I wanted to proceed with the agreed-upon story line and thus, I would hire another writer who could get behind the scenario enough to do it justice.

So that's the straight poop. I hope to work with Rog again on a regular basis in the future (I have managed to get him to write some SOLO AVENGERS stories), but right now I imagine that we're both a bit gun-shy. (I know what it feels like to leave a series not fully of one's volition — it happened to me twice.) Anyway, I'd like to thank Roger for five years of good hard avenging, and give him a chance to say good-bye.

—Mark Gruenwald

> In the past five years, I have had the privilege of working with a number of very, very talented people. They know who they are (and so do you, if you've been reading the credits), so I really don't think we need to go into a long Academy Awards-type listing here. It's never easy working on as complex a book as this, but despite all the headaches, I liked writing the AVENGERS. I'm going to miss it.
> —Roger Stern

Dear Roger and the Gang,

I thought for sure there was no way you could top the Masters of Evil story line (which, I might add, beat the Mutant Massacre and many of the "Versus" titles that have recently come out), but you are proving me wrong with the Greek Gods battle currently in progress. I've loved every minute of it so far. I am really glad to see the Sub-Mariner back again, whether he is here to stay or not. I am also pleased with the She-Hulk's return. I have mixed feelings about Doctor Druid, so let's give him time to prove himself. But I'm concerned about Thor.

I generally disapprove of a character who has his own book joining a team, and Thor has helped to convince me. As all of Marveldom must know by now, Thor has donned new (and awesome, I might add) armor to protect himself from a curse placed on him by Hela. Keeping up with current events like a good team book should, Thor has appeared with this armor in his Avengers appearances, and has mentioned the curse (in AVENGERS #282, for instance). But a close reading of Thor's own book shows that there is really no time for Thor to appear with the Avengers while he has the curse. At only one point does he appear on Midgard with both the armor and the curse, while the Midgard Serpent (in the guise of Fin Fang Foom) is searching for him. Yet Thor must spend about a week with the Avengers while the curse is upon him. The only explanation I can come up with is that several days passed while the Serpent was searching for Thor, and in that time, Thor and the other Avengers took off to fight the Greek Gods. After they return from this epic battle, Thor goes to that park in Bay Ridge to gather his thoughts (as shown in THOR #379) when he encounters the Serpent. (From that point on, Thor was too busy to appear with the Avengers until after the curse was removed.)

I want to make sure that when the battle with the Olympians is over, Thor will stop making reference to the curse, and that you guys never do anything like this again.

Anyway, thanks for issue after issue of great stories. Until the relatives of Jarvis come seeking revenge on the Avengers for allowing ol' Jarv to be injured, make mine Marvel.

Jeff Miller
3304 Lindberg Road
Anderson, IN 46011

Congratulations, Jeff! You figured out exactly where our Olympian War saga fit into the continuity with Thor's own book. (So what's the problem?)

Dear Mr. Stern and company,

Thank you, thank you, thank you! Thank you for the return of the Sub-Mariner, my second favorite Marvel character. Thank you for having him come in and actually rescue the other Avengers! Never have I been so ecstatic to see anyone. Too many times I've seen Namor portrayed as a piece of muscle with an enormous mouth

---

attached. Thank you for demonstrating that he does have a brain!

I would like you to get rid of Doctor Druid, however. Maybe he could be an active consultant or something, because he doesn't seem to be much good in a free-for-all. And that's what the Avengers do best. And get rid of Marrina. No, no, no, I don't mean kill her off! That would be disastrous! Namor might lose his memory again and go wandering off! What I mean is, keep her out of the picture. Or else, buy some more black ink and fill in her eyes, so they'll look the way they're supposed to look. I mean, I know each artist has his own style, but Marrina's looked downright hideous lately, and that's been without her alien condition.

The rest of the Avengers have been their usual exemplary selves. I miss Hercules though. His fights with the Sub-Mariner were a welcome bit of comic relief. By the way, how's Namor going to take care of that two billion dollar lawsuit? That should keep him on the surface for a while!

(By the way, my favorite character is Doctor Doom. Any chance of seeing him in these pages?)

Cynthia Scott
(No address given)

Anything is possible, Cynthia. Let's see, that's two happy Sub-Mariner fans. Any more?

Dear Mark,

Regarding issue #282 of the AVENGERS, rack up another great job. Roger Stern's story line remains interesting, and working in the mythology of the Olympian gods made for great reading. Best of all, we now have the Sub-Mariner back in the Avenger ranks. What was good to see in the handling of Namor was the showing that he doesn't keep charging headlong into everything. His use of a disguise to gain further entrance into the Hadean dungeons is a good sign of thinking. Now, if we could just have him say "Avengers Assemble!"

Keeping things cooking were the team of John Buscema and Tom Palmer, who are still Marvel's best in the art department. Also, kudos to Christie Scheele for coloring in anything but an every day style.

The tribute to Gardner Fox in this issue's edition of "Mark's Remarks" took me quite by surprise. It was very well done.

AVENGERS #300 is just about a year away. Are there any special plans?

Hurricane Heeran
15908 Sherman Way #5
Van Nuys, CA 91406

Special plans? Mmmm, could be.

Dear Roger, Tom, and John,

AVENGERS #282 was like a snack before the main meal. If the team could rip apart Hades, I can't wait to see what they do with Zeus and his pompous children. It's good to see Subby back again. How about bringing his wife along, too? Marrina would make for one mean Avenger, or Avenger-in-training.

Brian Daly
50 Rhode Island Drive
Jackson, NJ 08527

Marrina has been hanging out with the Avengers lately, Brian, but whether anything official comes of it remains to be seen!

MARK GRUENWALD, editor . . . . GREGORY WRIGHT, assistant editor

AVENGERS ASSEMBLE!

℅ MARVEL COMICS GROUP-387 Park Avenue South-New York, New York-10016
Attention correspondents: if you don't want your full address printed, please be sure to tell us so!

MARKS REMARKS

Thanks to our annual Statement of Ownership, space is at a premieum this month, and rather than skimp on your righteous responses, I'll keep my bit short and sweet.

This month a new era of Avengers excitement begins as wild and wooly *Walt Simomson* picks up the scripting reins of Marvel's heaviest hero-group. I trust no one needs reminding of the heights "Uncle" Walt propelled THE MIGHTY THOR to for four years. (Hands up, those of you who recall that I was the editor who coaxed W.S. onto that book back when I edited the title.) Anyway, Walt's determined to make his AVENGERS saga even more cosmic and cataclysmic than his THOR sagas — after all, as big a menace as Thor can handle on his own, he can handle even *bigger* menaces with a handful of Avengers at his side! The unparalleled art team of *John Buscema* and *Tom Palmer* will continue.

Finally, a tip of the hat to Riotous *Ralph Macchio* who stepped into the breach these past few issues, scribbling the wrap-up to the Adaptoid Epic, and giving Walt time to hit the ground running. Thanks, Ralfy, feel free to call out "Avengers Assemble" any time you get the urge!

—Mark Gruenwald

To the creative Staff of the AVENGERS:

I really must strongly disagree with John C. Hartley's letter in AVENGERS #285. I have been reading comics for almost twenty years, and throughout that time I have always enjoyed well-written female characters the most. Dynamic strong-willed women are in the majority at Marvel, and I'm thrilled to see you utilizing them. I, for one, would never call She-Hulk, Captain Marvel, or the Wasp weak! (After all, who took out the Absorbing Man and Titania almost all by herself?)

It shouldn't really matter what sex characters are, as long as they are believable and well-written. What *does* matter is the fact that for years women in comics were in the backround, suitable only for being kidnaped. (How many times was the *old* Sue Richards kidnaped?) Today, men and women should stand side by side in every medium, especially comics.

As to the Avengers in particular, Captain Marvel is the perfect choice to replace the already sorely missed Wasp. (Anyone who thinks the Avengers were meek during the Wasp's office, remember this . . . it was during her term that the Avengers faced some of their greatest challenges, including two Secret Wars.) Captain Marvel was a police officer, and she possesses great power in additon to a fierce sense of duty. As stated many times, Captain America has other commitments (and numerous problems, now that Steve Rogers has been forced out of costume by the government). Namor, if he could control his temper, he would actually be a good leader. Hercules is out, thank God, and Thor is too overbearing and self-important. She-Hulk would probably handle the chair nicely, but she probably wouldn't want the responsibility. Doc Druid is much too new to the team, and the Black Knight was out of touch for too long. Captain Marvel is the perfect choice!!

Keep up the good work. The Zeus storyline was great, and thanks for remembering Marrina. Please have her become an official member of the team. Thanks for listening.

Michael R. Colford
Reading, MA

Dear Roger, John, and Tom:

The AVENGERS is now my favorite series, replacing the X-MEN and John Byrne's SUPERMAN. I loved the Masters of Evil storyline, and wondered how you'd top it. Man, this is much better.

Roger, you wrote the story perfectly. It had all the elements that make for a good comic story: suspense, action, and characterization. Seeing Thor in action alongside the Sub-Mariner was exceptional. A lot of unexpected events took place — such as the Black Knight confronting Zeus, and Prometheus aiding the heroes behind the scenes — but the whole plotline made sense. Since I know a great deal about Grecian mythology, I was watching for slips. I was impressed by your superior knowledge of the myths, including the mention of Hercules' rescue of Prometheus, the fact of Hephaestus being lame, and the personal natures of the various gods (from the fun-loving Dionysus to the craven Ares). There were even little bits of information of which I was unaware, such as the flaming River Phlegeton. That more than made up for depicting Cerberus as a giant, when everybody knows he's a hellhound.

John and Tom, what can I say? Your art is part of the reason why I love the series so much. I consider your art better even than that of Byrne or Art Adams. I only hope you two remain with the AVENGERS for a long time to come.

Finally, I'd like to address John C. Hartley. I disagree very strongly with his remarks. First of all, I doubt that one sex is weaker than the other. Secondly, the Wasp was not responsible for Hercules' misfortunes. His injuries were his own fault, something which he recently admitted. The Wasp proved herself as a capable (if not exceptional) leader in AVENGERS #275-278. Few people, men included, could possibly have pulled themselves up from defeat as she did.

While Hartley is entitled to his opinions, I find them rather old-fashioned and sexist. He seems to think that men and women should follow only traditional roles. I feel that the world has changed, becoming more egalitarian. Further, I feel that with the exception of Captain America, no one is better qualified to lead the Avengers than Captain Marvel.

Good luck in future adventures. I'd like to see Nebula return, and to find out what Starfox has been doing. Also, the Avengers should encounter foes — such as Hybrid, Dormammu, Ymir, or Graviton — who are worthy of their power and skill. But I'll leave that in your more than capable hands.

Derrick Matthew Wildestar
1700 North Pelham Road NE
Atlanta, GA 30324

Thanks for your vote of confidence, Derrick.

(By the way, Marvel's Cerberus *is* a giant warrior . . . but he is able to *transform* himself into a huge three-headed hellhound. He first appeared way back in THOR #130.)

Dear Assemblers,

A lot of Hercules' fans may have been upset over the events of AVENGERS #285. "Will we ever see old Herc again?" they might ask. Prometheus assured the Avengers that "despite the edict of Zeus, you may not have seen the last of Hercules!", but some readers may have doubts. Well, they needn't have any worries if they'll just read closely.

You see, when the Sub-Mariner said that Zeus had barred all Olympians from Earth, he wasn't correct. A careful reading of Zeus' edict on Page 18 reveals the vow, " . . . no one born of Olympus shall ever again set foot upon the Earth!" Whether by design or accident on Zeus' part, that vow excludes Hercules, who was born on Earth!

As for Zeus, he should count himself lucky that Thor was so impaired by Hela's curse. The other time the two of them went at each other (as recorded in THOR ANNUAL #8), Zeus was obliged to talk Thor into a truce! Had Thor been at his peak, Zeus would have been defeated by the Avengers! As that would have probably caused Olympus to declare war upon the Earth, things all worked out for the best.

Robert Mallory
P.O. Box 0133
Baldwin, NY 11510

U.S. POSTAL SERVICE STATEMENT OF OWNERSHIP, MANAGEMENT AND CIRCULATION (REQUIRED BY 39 U.S.C. 3685)

1. Title of Publication: AVENGERS
2. Date of Filing: 02745240
3. Frequency of Issue: MONTHLY.
3A. No. of issues published annually: 12.
3B. Annual subscription price: $9.00 U.S., $11.00 Canada.
4. Complete mailing address of known office of publication: Marvel Entertainment Group, 387 Park Avenue South, New York, N.Y. 10016.
5. Complete address of the headquarters of general business offices of the publisher: Marvel Entertainment Group, 387 Park Avenue South, New York, N.Y. 10016.
6. Full names and complete mailing address of publisher, editor, and managing editor: Stan Lee, Marvel Entertainment Group, 387 Park Avenue South, New York, N.Y. 10016; Editor: Tom DeFalco, Marvel Entertainment Group, 387 Park Avenue South, New York, N.Y. 10016; Managing Editor: Tom DeFalco, Marvel Entertainment Group, 387 Park Avenue South, New York, N.Y. 10016.
7. Owner (if owned by a corporation, its name and address must be stated and also immediately thereunder the names and addresses of stockholders owning or holding 1 percent or more of total amount of stock. If not owned by a corporation, the names and addresses of the individual owners must be given. If owned by a partnership or other unincorporated firm, its name and address, as well as that of each individual must be given. If the publication is published by a nonprofit organization, its name and address must be stated.): NEW WORLD PICTURES, INC., 1440 South Sepulveda Blvd., Los Angeles, CA 90025.
8. Known bondholders, mortgagees, and other security holders owning or holding 1 percent or more of total amount of bonds, mortgages or other securities: None.
9. For completion by nonprofit organizations authorized to mail at special rates (Section 411.3, DMM only). The purpose, function, and nonprofit status of this organization and the exempt status for Federal income tax purposes. (Check one.) ☐ Have not changed during preceding 12 months. ☐ Have changed during preceding 12 months. (If changed, publisher must submit explanation with this statement.)
10. EXTENT AND NATURE OF CIRCULATION.
A. Total No. Copies Printed (net press run): Average no. of copies each issue during preceding 12 months: 386,809. Single issue nearest to filing date: 385,033.
B. Paid Circulation: 1) Sales through dealers and carriers, street vendors and counter sales: Average no. of copies each issue during preceding 12 months: 207,483. Single issue nearest to filing date: 210,663. 2) Mail subscriptions: Average no. of copies each issue during preceding 12 months: 9,358. Single issue nearest to filing date: 8,330.
C. Total Paid Circulation: (Sum of 10B1 and 10B2): Average no. of copies each issue during preceding 12 months: 216,841. Single issue nearest to filing date: 218,993.
D. Free Distribution by mail, carrier, or other means, samples, complimentary, and other free copies: Average no. of copies each issue during preceding 12 months: 132. Single issue nearest to filing date: 126.
E. Total Distribution: (Sum of C and D): Average no. of copies each issue during preceding 12 months: 216,973. Single issue nearest to filing date: 219,119.
F. Copies Not Distributed: 1) Office use, left-over, unaccounted, spoiled after printing: Average no. of copies each issue during preceding 12 months: 902. Single issue nearest to filing date: 739. 2) Returns from News Agents: Average no. of copies each issue during preceding 12 months: 168,934. Single issue nearest to filing date: 165,175.
G. Total (Sum of E, F1 and 2 should equal net press run shown in A): Average no. of copies each issue during preceding 12 months: 386,809. Single issue nearest to filing date: 385,033.
11. I certify that the statements made by me above are correct and complete.
(signed) Janet Pezzuto — Business Manager

MARK GRUENWALD, editor . . . . GREGORY WRIGHT, assistant editor

THEY WERE EARTH'S MIGHTIEST HEROES. NOTHING LASTS FOREVER.

THE END BEGINS. ISSUE #291, BY
WALT SIMONSON, JOHN BUSCEMA AND TOM PALMER.
MONTHLY FROM MARVEL®.

WALT SIMONSON

The **Avengers** are in for quite a few changes when **Walt Simonson** takes the helm chronicling their adventures as of issue #291. Any fan who remembers Walt's stint on the MIGHTY THOR will attest to that statement. MARVEL AGE MAGAZINE tracked Walt down for this exclusive interview:

*Walt, you once turned **Thor** into a frog! What, pray tell, have you in store for the Avengers?*

Well, my first thought was an opening cover with the existing Avengers lined up like bowling pins in their super hero outfits all as frogs. I was talked out of it by people with more sense, so I'm not going to do that—at least not in my first issue.

I begin on issue #291. Number 300 is coming up. It's a big number and big numbers traditionally become big issues. I'd like to do a big issue—something of relevant importance. So, I'm starting a storyline in which we're going to see the downfall of the Avengers. Essentially, the Avengers are going to be reduced in number over the next several issues until by issue #297 there will be no Avengers. The Avengers will fold in issue #296, and in the following issue we will see what it's

like when there are no Avengers. I'll start putting the team back together again in the subsequent three issues. Of course, there will be a revised lineup. A former member will return in issue #298 as the *only* Avenger, and will recruit another former member. Together they will start trying to pick up the pieces.

The storyline for those three issues will tie into the "Hell on Earth" saga in the mutant books at that time.

Anyway, **'Weezie [Louise Simonson**, Walt's wife and writer of X-FACTOR] and **Chris [Claremont]** have some big stuff planned, which I'm not at liberty to reveal. But I intend to tie into that storyline, wrapping it up in AVENGERS #300.

Before that, I intend to reduce the current lineup. Once I'm through, there will be some new members as well as old.

Will you be doing the cover artwork on the AVENGERS?

Just cover sketches. I belong to the school of thought where I like seeing the artwork on the inside match the art on the outside of a comic book. But the actual artwork, interior and exterior, is being done by **John Buscema** and

Tom Palmer.

When did you first start writing comics?

The first thing I wrote was BATTLESTAR GALACTICA, which I also drew. I was the writer/artist on four of the last five issues. Now I've graduated to writing one title and drawing another.

That would be X-FACTOR. What are the advantages of working so close to the writer of that series?

Well, it saves a lot of Federal Express bills. But more so, I can get much more immediate and personal feedback if I have any questions about Weezie's plots. I think that makes the stories tighter. We can work back and forth, constantly giving each other constructive criticism, which is very convenient.

Are you happy drawing one book and writing another, or would you rather write and draw the same book, as you did on THOR?

It's hard to say yet. I enjoyed writing THOR for **Sal Buscema** to draw because I liked the work he was doing. I had a good relationship with Sal and I got to know him better by working with him. Sal was one of the guys whose comics I read before getting into the business. It was a gas to work with him.

POSSIBLY THE MOST UNUSUAL *THOR* STORY EVER PUBLISHED!

In the same sense, I'm getting to know John Buscema better through the AVENGERS. He's also a treat to work with and I enjoy it tremendously. Of course, it is different when you're writing your own stuff. The main difference is that I don't write as complex for myself as I do for others. I tend to do more crosscutting from plot to subplot when I write for myself. I know what I can handle. I've never actually written and drawn a team book, but on THOR I was able to juggle more stuff since it primarily dealt with a single character.

Being an artist, how does that affect your writing?

The biggest advantage is that I've been able to provide artists a certain amount of visual material, whereas some writers without artistic training are not able to set up a scene visually. I try to provide artists stuff to draw that they will find fun to do. I look at my artists and gauge what they can do and what they like to do, and I try to work that into the storyline.

I'm doing a **Doctor Strange** story for MARVEL FANFARE that **Dave Gibbons** is drawing. I called Dave and talked to him, and I discovered that Doc is a character that he's always wanted to draw. So we talked about the character and we talked about what Dave liked to draw. He wanted to draw Doc's house in Greenwich Village; he wanted to

draw some of those weird **Ditko** dimensions; he wanted to draw some moody atmosphere shots filled with weather—you know, rain, mist, fog. I think coming off the WATCHMEN he didn't feel like drawing a lot of perspective and buildings. He'd like to get away from that work for a while.

Naturally, I construed a story that is built around these parameters. I mean, Dave didn't come out and say, "I want this specifically." He just told me what he likes to draw. So I tried to write a story that captured all that stuff. I'm not so sure that by the end of it he found that he's gotten away from drawing buildings and such, but it's a compromise. He was delighted with it. He had the layouts back to me within a week and they're absolutely gorgeous!

But that's a case where I specifically tailored a story to try and take advantage of what the artist wanted to draw. That way I can be pretty sure that the artist will be enthusiastic about the project.

What led you to the pages of the AVENGERS?

That's a hard question to answer. I think probably the mystique as much as anything else. Truth to say, I haven't been following the AVENGERS much recently. For me, the AVENGERS was at its peak when **Roy Thomas** was writing it, with John Buscema's pencils

and Tom Palmer's inks. **George Klein** also inked nicely over John's artwork. In any case, John was doing some nice stuff, with large figures and panels. But the **Surtur/Ymir** "Fire and Ice" story, and the introduction of the **Vision** in "Death be Not Proud"—that was some great stuff. I thought it would be fun to get back and recapture that feeling for me. I'm not going to rehash Roy's stories, but they were powerful tales about powerful characters. I also thought, "Hey, I get to write a bit of Thor again, too!"

Thor will remain an Avenger?

Yes, Thor will remain in the lineup for, shall we say, "Post-Crisis"?

Will you be incorporating some of the things you introduced in THOR into the AVENGERS?

As a matter of fact, **Roger Stern** introduced the idea of a Council of **Kangs**. When I first heard about it, I envisioned an amphitheater filled with thousands and thousands of Kangs. But that's not quite how it worked out. So I figured, since they haven't done that yet, why not do it now? I'll be introducing the Council of Cross-Time Kangs. I got the idea when I was a kid reading **Keith Laumer** and other science-fiction writers.

It's like this: our Marvel Universe is point-zero on the temporal graph. As you move left or right of this point, things change only slightly from point to point. Therefore, the Kangs from areas close to point-zero will be very similar to the one we know. But as you get further from this point, they will get increasingly bizarre, until eventually you get female Kangs, child Kangs, alien Kangs, that kind of stuff. And there's a council of a zillion of these Kangs. I will introduce this council as the dark side of a much bigger organization which I first introduced briefly in the "Justice Peace" issues of THOR. This organization is known as the T.V.A.—the Time Variance Authority.

The Avengers will be finding out more about the cosmic function of the T.V.A. as opposed to the Council of Kangs. The Council discovers the possibility for a major weapon not too far in the future of the Marvel Universe. This is all a continuity pickup from the "Justice Peace" stories I did in THOR. I'm just turning it into a much bigger storyline. The first issue I take over builds up this Kang stuff, so the major storyline will be ready by issue #301.

The Avengers are a bunch of very powerful heroes and I feel that they should face a bunch of very powerful adversaries. So I want to invent a plot that will be worth the Avengers' time.

How many of the current lineup will you be maintaining in the Avengers?

Right now I plan on three. Actually, I was going to write out one of them from the strip, but I had so much fun with the character that I changed my mind.

In THOR you added a lot of nice comic relief. Will we be seeing this in the AVENGERS?

Ideally, that's the way I always like to write. My feelings about super hero comics date back to the early Marvels that I read: **Stan Lee, Jack Kirby**, Steve Ditko, **Don Heck**, Roy Thomas…etc. The lesson all those guys taught me is that you can get away with anything as long as you keep a straight face. The minute you start to nudge or wink at your audience, as if saying, "Hey, aren't we clever?" you lose them because you push them outside the limits of the material. But if you keep a straight face, you can get away with murder using a lot of outrageous storylines. The frog stuff I did in THOR was pretty much a parody of the work I had done on the book up to that point. The Frog-Rat Wars of Central Park was a parody of the Surtur War. So, while I had a lot of fun with it, I kept a straight face. The mixed reactions to it made it all the more fun.

Do you consider yourself a writer or an artist?

Oh, just a guy who's trying to make an honest living. No, really what I consider myself, even before I started writing, is a storyteller. I didn't get into comics to write them; I didn't have enough confidence in my abilities to come in as a writer. But I did have enough confidence to become an artist since I've been drawing since I was three or four. I didn't start writing until college or so.

Where did you attend college?

I went to Amherst College and then to Rhode Island School of Design in Providence. I liked college, so I stayed there a long time. I graduated from Amherst in '68 with a degree in geology. I graduated from R.I.S.D. in '72 with a major in illustration. At first, I wanted to go into paleontology to study dinosaurs and all that, but I got away from it after a while.

Is that where the origin of your distinctive signature lies?

Sure. That actually pre-dates my art career. I was in the 11th grade, in the Spring of '63, and I was doing a lot of drawings. Every kid who draws knows that artists have classy signatures: **Frank Frazetta, Norman Rockwell**, and so on down the line. Some people put a dagger through their names, while others put it in a scroll. In my case I was just printing my name, and it just wasn't classy enough—no style. So I decided to try and place it within the silhouette of an animal. My mother suggested a dinosaur because I was such a dinosaur fanatic. So I did a bunch of simple outlines of various dinosaurs and tried fitting my name inside each one. And the sauropods, such as the

brontosaurus, diplodocus, and other long-necked heavyweights, worked the best. In the old days my signature was much more proportioned to a real dinosaur. Now the O has gotten a lot bigger, I've put a head at the front, and it's become much more stylized. Actually, one of the more humorous things about all this is that now that they're recontructing dinosaurs and reviewing what they looked like, my signature is an obsolete vision of the sauropods' appearance. But I don't plan to change it, even if it is out of date.

What comic books would you like to work on in the future?

I wouldn't mind doing THOR again some time. Maybe the FANTASTIC FOUR. I also like the SILVER SURFER. Beyond that, I have several graphic novels planned including another STARSLAMMERS story that I'd like to tell. Maybe if I had 72 hours in a day, I'd

be able to accomplish all this stuff. I wouldn't mind doing DOCTOR STRANGE; I'm delighted for the opportunity to do this Doctor Strange story for FANFARE with Dave.

Now that you're working on the AVENGERS, do you see yourself writing a lot of your favorite characters into your stories?

I didn't take on the assignment with that in mind. When I took over THOR, one of the things that I wanted to do at that time was to reestablish the identity of the character in connection with the Norse myth. I was a big fan of Norse mythology and I wanted to use a lot of that stuff as raw material for the comic. I didn't want to retell the myths, but I wanted to use the myths as springboards for other stories—make the comic more mythic. For me, it's what made Thor different from, say, **Superman**. So, I didn't do much guest-

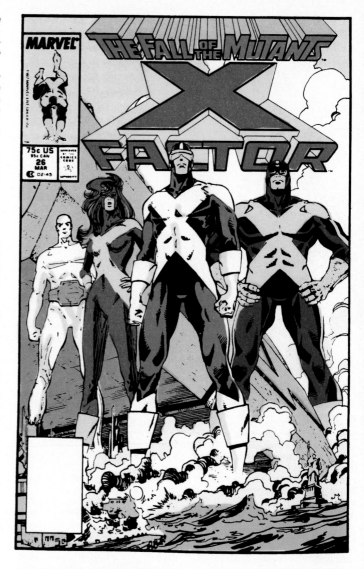

WHO--?

starring in the course of the three and a half years I was doing the book. Here and there I did some crossover stuff, but not a whole lot. I wanted to re-acquaint Thor with his supporting cast.

The AVENGERS, by virtue of being a more mainstream title involving a number of regular Marvel characters, some in their own books, of course presents the opportunity to bring in many other characters. In fact, what I would like to do ideally is have a core lineup of four characters in the Avengers, refreshing it from time to time with one or two new members using mostly pre-existing Marvel characters. But I am creating a new character, but he's still in the developing stages. A new character gives you the chance to explore the old characters in new ways. I'd like also to give the other Marvel characters a chance to become Avengers—ones that have never been Avengers before.

Will any of the ever-popular mutants be given their chance?

Possibly. It depends on who's loose out there and who I'd be permitted to get my hands on. There's a bunch of tremendous characters in the mutant subculture of the Marvel Universe. So I'd be real happy to use one or two. I have no one in mind specifically yet.

Will you be writing this year's AVENGERS ANNUAL?

Yes. It's the last Annual in the **High Evolutionary** series, so I have to tie up the storylines. I have to figure out how the Earth's heroes actually win—if they win. But I haven't figured it out yet, although I have some ideas. It should be a lot of fun.

Will you be tying many of your stories into the WEST COAST AVENGERS storyline, as has been done in the past?

I don't think a whole lot. I know **Steve Englehart** has his own ideas of what he wants to do with his characters. So I don't think there's going to be a great deal of crossing over unless the circumstances call for it.

Any words of wisdom for your fans?

My final words of wisdom are, "Buy this book!"

As far as advice to people who want to break into the comics field, there's no real secret. I originally went to school to study geology and paleontology. One of the things I often see in art submissions is work from young artists that is obviously heavily influenced by the visual idioms of comic books, and not familiar with much else. Well, that can become a real ingrown toenail. If all you know is comics, then your work will probably end up being some strange admixture of second-rate **John Byrne, Frank Miller, Howard Chaykin**, Walt Simonson, whatever. But we already have *first-rate* guys by those names working in the business. You'd be much better off to learn to see with your own eyes and draw with your own hands. That doesn't mean you should stop looking at other artists—almost every artist in the industry starts off by emulating an artist they like. I did it. I remember doing a drawing of Thor where I tried to be as close to Jack Kirby and **Vinnie Colletta** as possible. I also did a picture of **Bill Everett's Hulk, Gene Colan's Iron Man**, and so on. It isn't really necessary to flog yourself to develop an artistic style just because Byrne, Miller and Simonson have distinctive styles.

But, unlike yourself, most people do not enter the industry with a unique "style"…

Well, the trick is, if you practice drawing and practice seeing, letting the drawing reflect your vision, you will develop a style whether you want to or not. You can't prevent yourself from developing a style, so it's the last thing you should worry about. At first, you look at an artist's work to analyze how they see you can learn a lot from it. Ultimately, you set that aside and begin to develop your own eyes. Every young artist goes through that. Art school taught me that there were a great many ways to look at the world that I was unaware of. I discovered that there were a lot more options than I even thought existed, and that was extremely beneficial. If you're clever, you can bring some of those options into comics and bring a fresh look to it.

I did something similar with typographical sound effects. Now I see them everywhere. I'd like to think that I had something to do with bringing that into the cosmic consciousness of comic books, and I hope the comic history books will say the same. **Bill Sienkiewicz** has brought in a whole different style—the use of illustration and the knowledge of illustration. He was very innovative. So anyone who's any good has taken stuff from a lot of different sources and melded it all together into a style of some kind. Art school can help, but it's not necessary. Most guys in comics haven't gone to art school, at least the older guys. But art school was very valuable to me. Two of my most important courses, in terms of the style I draw today, were silkscreening and lithography. I mean, I don't silkscreen my comics, I don't lithograph them, I don't use silkscreen tools or lithographic tools, but silkscreening taught me patience and lithography taught me texture. If I had just learned from comics, I never would have tried those techniques. So the more you experience, the more possibilities are open to you. I've experienced a great deal in my life, but I'm experiencing more and more every day. And that's what I recommend to everyone: experience all that you can in life.

—*Glenn Herdling*

THE AVENGERS® Vol. 1, No. 286, December, 1987 issue. (ISSN 0274-5240) Published by MARVEL COMICS, A NEW WORLD COMPANY. James E. Galton, President. Stan Lee, Publisher. Michael Hobson, Group Vice-President. Milton Schiffman, Vice-President, Production. OFFICE OF PUBLICATION: 387 PARK AVENUE SOUTH, NEW YORK, N.Y. 10016. Published monthly. Copyright © 1987 by Marvel Entertainment Group, Inc. All rights reserved. Price 75¢ per copy in the U.S. and 95¢ in Canada. Subscription rate $9.00 for 12 issues. Canada and Foreign, $11.00. Printed in the U.S.A. No similarity between any of the names, characters, persons, and/or institutions in this magazine with those of any living or dead person or institution is intended, and any such similarity which may exist is purely coincidental. This periodical may not be sold except by authorized dealers and is sold subject to the conditions that it shall not be sold or distributed with any part of its cover or markings removed, nor in a mutilated condition. THE AVENGERS (including all prominent characters featured in the issue), and the distinctive likenesses thereof, are trademarks of the MARVEL ENTERTAINMENT GROUP, INC. POSTMASTER: SEND ADDRESS CHANGES TO AVENGERS, 387 PARK AVENUE SOUTH, 9TH FLOOR, NEW YORK, N.Y. 10016. SECOND CLASS POSTAGE PAID AT NEW YORK, N.Y. AND AT ADDITIONAL MAILING OFFICES.

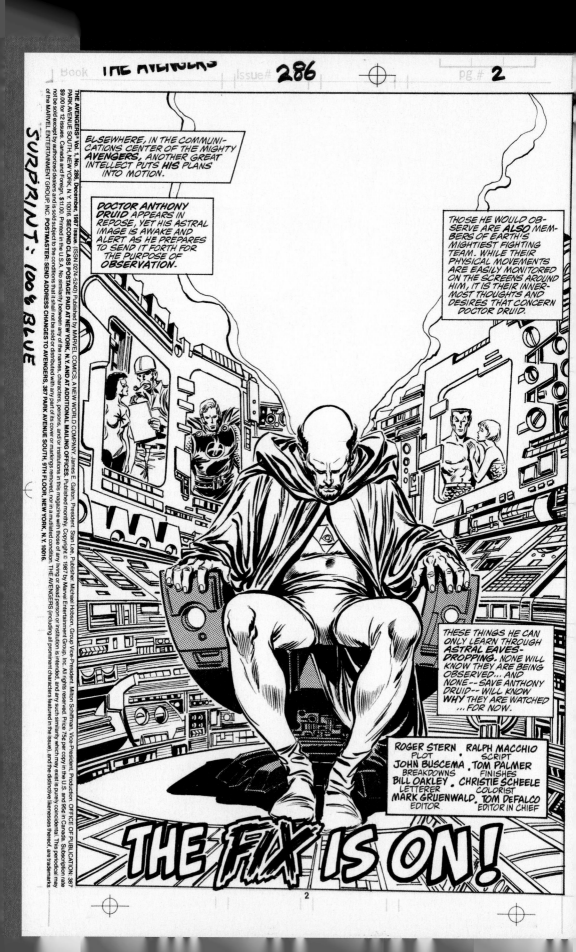

ELSEWHERE, IN THE COMMUNI-CATIONS CENTER OF THE MIGHTY AVENGERS, ANOTHER GREAT INTELLECT PUTS *HIS* PLANS INTO MOTION.

DOCTOR ANTHONY DRUID APPEARS IN REPOSE, YET HIS ASTRAL IMAGE IS AWAKE AND ALERT AS HE PREPARES TO SEND IT FORTH FOR THE PURPOSE OF OBSERVATION.

THOSE HE WOULD OB-SERVE ARE *ALSO* MEM-BERS OF EARTH'S MIGHTIEST FIGHTING TEAM. WHILE THEIR PHYSICAL MOVEMENTS ARE EASILY MONITORED ON THE SCREENS AROUND HIM, IT IS THEIR INNER-MOST THOUGHTS AND DESIRES THAT CONCERN DOCTOR DRUID.

THESE THINGS HE CAN ONLY LEARN THROUGH *ASTRAL EAVES-DROPPING.* NONE WILL KNOW THEY ARE BEING OBSERVED... AND NONE-- SAVE ANTHONY DRUID-- WILL KNOW *WHY* THEY ARE WATCHED ...FOR NOW.

ROGER STERN — RALPH MACCHIO
PLOT — SCRIPT
JOHN BUSCEMA — TOM PALMER
BREAKDOWNS — FINISHES
BILL OAKLEY — CHRISTIE SCHEELE
LETTERER — COLORIST
MARK GRUENWALD — TOM DeFALCO
EDITOR — EDITOR IN CHIEF

THE FIX IS ON!

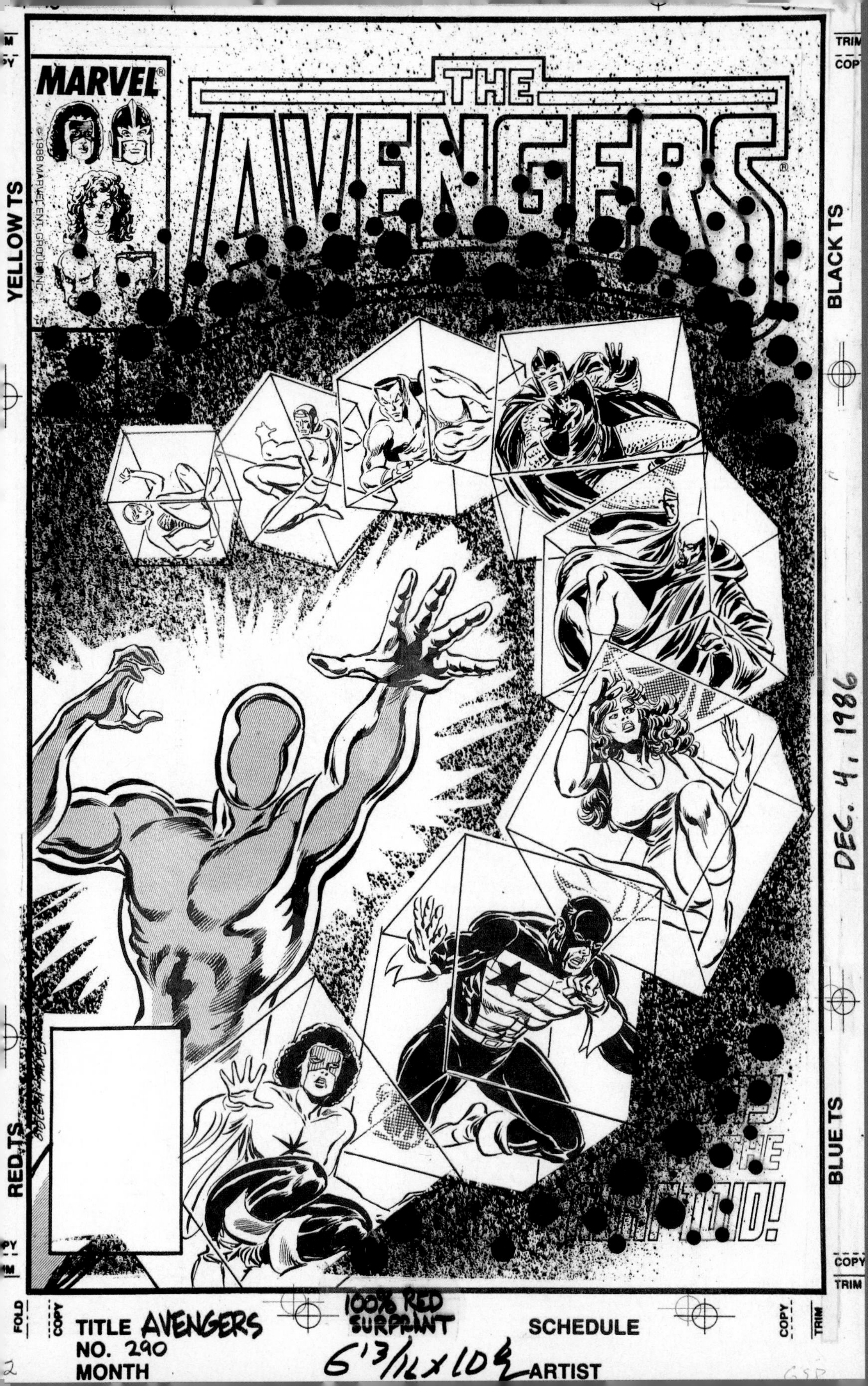
MARVEL
© 1988 MARVEL ENT. GROUP, INC.
THE AVENGERS
DEC. 4, 1986
TRIM
COPY
YELLOW TS
BLACK TS
RED TS
BLUE TS
FOLD
TITLE AVENGERS
NO. 290
MONTH
100% RED SURPRINT
6 13/16 x 10 1/2
SCHEDULE
ARTIST

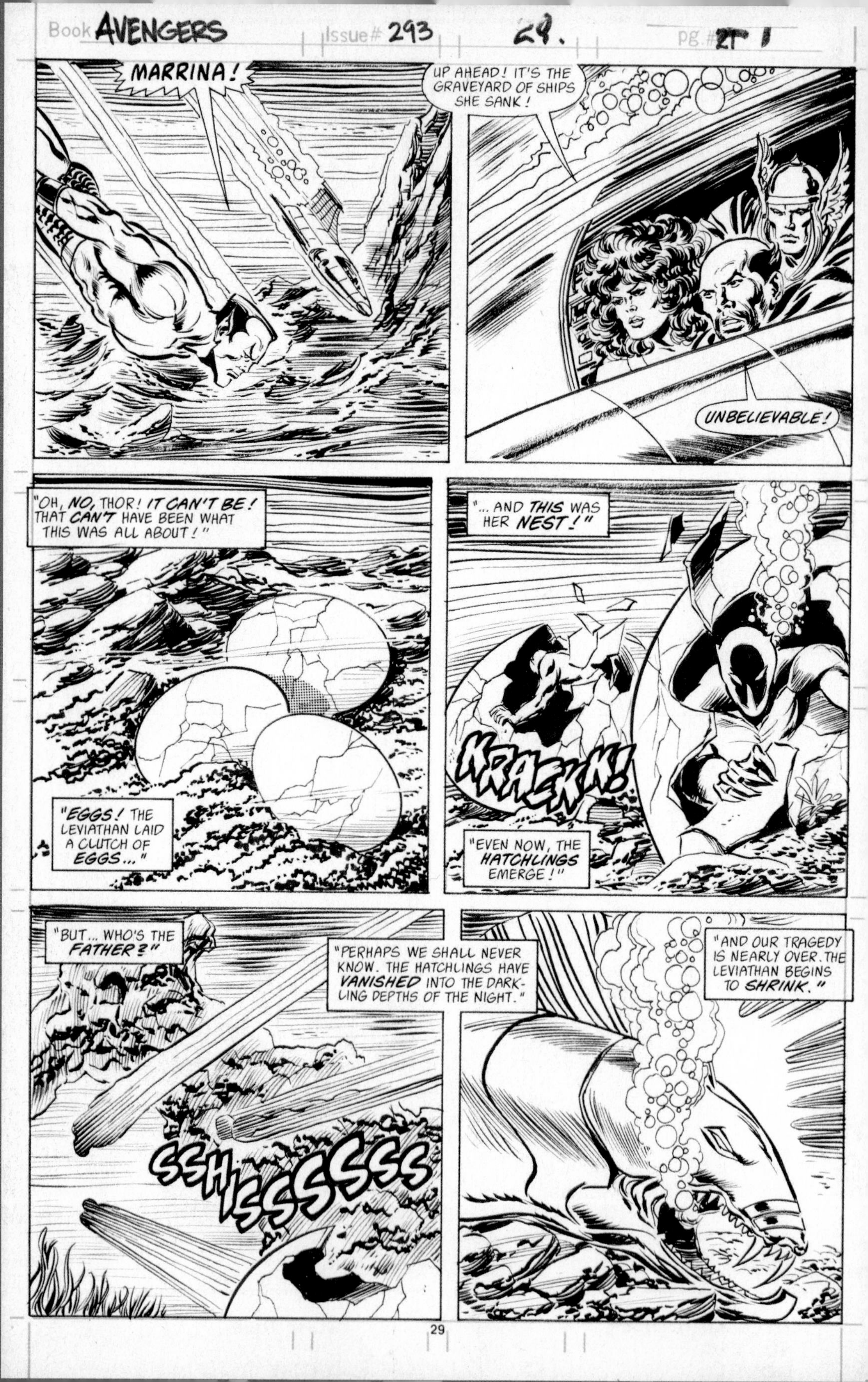
Book AVENGERS
Issue # 293
29.
MARRINA!
UP AHEAD! IT'S THE GRAVEYARD OF SHIPS SHE SANK!
UNBELIEVABLE!
"OH, NO, THOR! IT CAN'T BE! THAT CAN'T HAVE BEEN WHAT THIS WAS ALL ABOUT!"
"EGGS! THE LEVIATHAN LAID A CLUTCH OF EGGS..."
"...AND THIS WAS HER NEST!"
KRACKK!
"EVEN NOW, THE HATCHLINGS EMERGE!"
"BUT... WHO'S THE FATHER?"
"PERHAPS WE SHALL NEVER KNOW. THE HATCHLINGS HAVE VANISHED INTO THE DARKLING DEPTHS OF THE NIGHT."
SSHISSSSSS
"AND OUR TRAGEDY IS NEARLY OVER. THE LEVIATHAN BEGINS TO SHRINK."
29